주한미군지위협정(SOFA)

한·미
합동위원회 2

주한미군지위협정(SOFA)

한 · 미 합동위원회 2

한국학술정보

머리말

미국은 오래전부터 우리나라 외교에 있어서 가장 긴밀하고 실질적인 우호 · 협력관계를 맺어 온 나라다. 6 · 25전쟁 정전 협정이 체결된 후 북한의 재침을 막기 위한 대책으로서 1953년 11월 한미 상호방위조약이 체결되었다. 이는 미군이 한국에 주둔하는 법적 근거였고, 그렇게 주둔하게 된 미군의 시설, 구역, 사업, 용역, 출입국, 통관과 관세, 재판권 등 포괄적인 법적 지위를 규정하는 것이 바로 주한미군지위협정(SOFA)이다. 그러나 이와 관련한 협상은 계속된 난항을 겪으며 한미 상호방위조약이 체결로부터 10년이 훌쩍 넘은 1967년이 돼서야 정식 발효에 이를 수 있었다. 그럼에도 당시 미군 범죄에 대한 한국의 재판권은 심한 제약을 받았으며, 1980년대 후반 민주화 운동과 함께 미군 범죄 문제가 사회적 이슈로 떠오르자 협정을 개정해야 한다는 목소리가 커지게 되었다. 이에 1991년 2월 주한미군지위협정 1차 개정이 진행되었고, 이후에도 여러 사건이 발생하며 2001년 4월 2차 개정이 진행되어 현재에 이르고 있다.

본 총서는 외교부에서 작성하여 최근 공개한 주한미군지위협정(SOFA) 관련 자료를 담고 있다. 1953년 한미 상호방위조약 체결 이후부터 1967년 발효가 이뤄지기까지의 자료와 더불어, 이후 한미 합동위원회을 비롯해 민 · 형사재판권, 시설, 노무, 교통 등 각 분과위원회의 회의록과 운영 자료, 한국인 고용인 문제와 관련한 자료, 기타 관련 분쟁 자료 등을 포함해 총 42권으로 구성되었다. 전체 분량은 약 2만 2천여 쪽에 이른다.

2024년 3월

한국학술정보(주)

| 일러두기

· 본 총서에 실린 자료는 2022년 4월과 2023년 4월에 각각 공개한 외교문서 4,827권, 76만 여 쪽 가운데 일부를 발췌한 것이다.

· 각 권의 제목과 순서는 공개된 원본을 최대한 반영하였으나, 주제에 따라 일부는 적절히 변경하였다.

· 원본 자료는 A4 판형에 맞게 축소하거나 원본 비율을 유지한 채 A4 페이지 안에 삽입하였다. 또한 현재 시점에선 공개되지 않아 '공란'이란 표기만 있는 페이지 역시 그대로 실었다.

· 외교부가 공개한 문서 각 권의 첫 페이지에는 '정리 보존 문서 목록'이란 이름으로 기록물 종류, 일자, 명칭, 간단한 내용 등의 정보가 수록되어 있으며, 이를 기준으로 0001번부터 번호가 매겨져 있다. 이는 삭제하지 않고 총서에 그대로 수록하였다.

· 보고서 내용에 관한 더 자세한 정보가 필요하다면, 외교부가 온라인상에 제공하는 『대한민국 외교사료요약집』 1991년과 1992년 자료를 참조할 수 있다.

| 차례

분류번호	729.41 1968 28-29차	등록번호	246	보존기간	영구
기능명칭	SOFA-한미합동위원회 회의록, 제28-29차. 1968				
생 산 과	안보담당관실		생산년도	1968	

주;

1. 제28차. 1968. 7. 3
2. 제29차. 1968. 8. 14

촬영불요

M/F편집완료	M/F No.	6

1

결번

넘버링 오류

결 번

넘버링 오류

MINISTRY OF FOREIGN AFFAIRS
REPUBLIC OF KOREA

1. 제 28 차. 1968. 7. 3

4

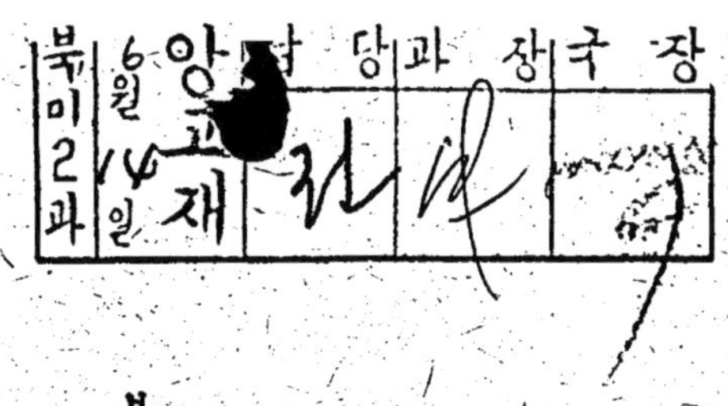

외 무 부

미이 1968. 6. 14.

수 신 : 총무처장관

참 조 : 총무국장

제 목 : 회의실 사용 신청

당부에서는 다음과 같이 회의를 개최코자 하오니 제1회의실 사용을 허락하여 주시기 바랍니다.

다 음

1. 일 시 : 1968. 7. 3. (수)
2. 장 소 : 중앙청 제1회의실
3. 회의명 : 한.미 합동위원회 제28차 회의
4. 참석자수 : 약 40명. 끝

발송
1968. 6 14
외무부

외 무 부 장 관

5

총 무 처

관 리 152-1195 (72-9167) 68.6.18

수 신 외무부 장관

제 목 회의실 사용신청

1. 미이 20282 (68.6.14)에 대한 응신임.

2. 귀부에서 요청한 중앙청 제1회의실 사용 신청에 대하여는 당처 사정에 의하여 사용 불가능 하니, 528호 회의실을 사용도록 하시기 바랍니다. 끝.

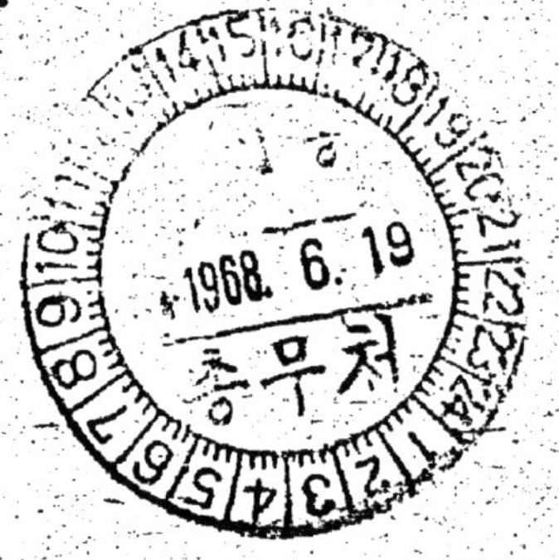

총 무 처 장

문서처리인
접수일시 1968 6 19
21148
분류자

6
북미2과

외 무 부

외미이 723-　　　　　　　　　　1968. 6. 21.

수 신 : 배부처 참조

참 조 :

제 목 : 한미합동위원회 회의 개최 통지

1. 오는 1968년 7월 3일(수요일) 15.00시에 중앙청 제528호 ~~제1회의실, 주한미군사령부~~ 회의실에서 한미합동위원회 제 28 차 회의가 개최될 예정이오니 각 위원의 참석을 바랍니다.

2. 한편, 동 회의에 대비한 한국 대표단의 대책회의를 오는 7월 2일(화요일) 10.00시에 외무부 회의실에서 개최하오니 참석하시기바랍니다. 끝.

외 무 부 장 관

배부처 : 법무부 장관(법무실장, 검찰국장), 국방부장관(기획국장, 시설국장), 재무부장관(세관국장), 상공부장관(상역국장), 교통부장관(항공국장), 노동청장(노정국장). 경제기획원장관(경제기획국장).

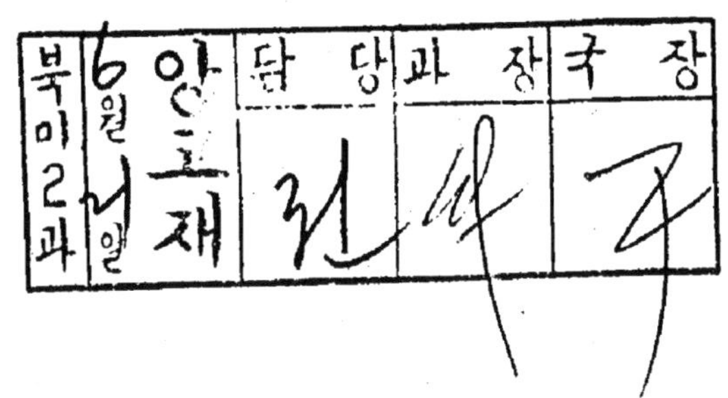

북미2과	6월 21일	안 재	담 당	과 장	국 장

7

한.미 군대지위협정 합동위원회

제 28 차 회의

1968. 7. 3.

한국 대표

발언취지 (안)

8

공 란

(의 제 2 - 형사재판권 분과위원회 과제부여 - 미측 설명)

감사합니다.

다음 의제는 형사재판권 분과위원회에 대한 과제부여 건입니다.

미국대표께서 형사재판권 분과위원회에 부여할 과제 1건을 설명해 주시기 바랍니다.

(미측 설명과 제의)

감사합니다.

대한민국 대표는 미국 대표가 제의한 형사재판권 분과위원회에 대한 과제부여를 동의하는 바입니다.

10

공 란

(의 제 4 - 교통분과위원회 건의)

다음 의제4번은 교통분과위원회의 건의입니다.

한.미 양국 대표는 1967년 1월 19일 제2차 예비 실무자 회의에서 군대지위협정 제24조 3항에 의거한 사유차량의 면허 및 등록을 규제하는 절차 제정을 지시하였는바 교통 분과위원회는 마침내 동 건에 관한 건의를 제출하였읍니다. 이와같은 지연은 여러 요인이 있은 가운데 주로 해당 차량의 부보에 관한 절충에 기인하는 것이였읍니다.

이와 관련하여 한국 대표는 등록 [illegible]용 접수 후의 한국측 통보에 관하여 동 건의 절차 제5항 마지막 절에서 사용한 "가능한 한 신속히" 라는 어구는 통상적으로 집무일 1일 또는 2일 이내를 의미한다고 양해 합니다.

한국 대표는 승인 일자후 세번째 월초부터 시행하게될 동 교통분과위원회 건의의 합동위원회 승인을 제안하는 바입니다.

(미측 동의 표시)

감사합니다.

(의 제 5 - 교통분과위원회에 대한 과제부여)

군대지위협정 제24조 1항은 "대한민국은 합중국이나 그 하부 행정기관이 합중국 군대의 구성원, 군속 및 그들의 가족에 대하여 발급한 운전 허가증이나 운전면허증 또는 군의 운전 허가증을 운전 시험 또는 수수료를 과하지 아니하고 유효한 것으로 승인한다" 고 규정하고 있읍니다.

현실적으로 이러한 허가증 또는 면허증을 대한민국 공무원이 인정할 수 있고 해독할 수 있는 형태로 변형하여야 함이 자명한 것으로 생각됩니다. 따라서 한국 대표는 이러한 필요성을 충족하는 방식을 건의하는 과제를 교통분과위원회에 부여할 것을 제의하고저 합니다.

또한 본 건 과제와 지위협정 대상 인원의 사유차량 면허 및 등록 사이의 밀접한 관계를 참작하여 사유차량 면허등록 절차와 본 건 절차가 동시에 발효할 수 있도록 차량 관계 절차 발효 일자전에 본 건과제를 완결하도록 교통 분과위원회에 지시할 것을 제의 하는 바입니다.

(미측 동의 표시)

감사합니다.

13

(의 제6 - 합동수사반 압수물자 처리에 관한 건의)

다음 의제는 합동 수사반 압수물자 처리에 관한 건의입니다. 미국 대표께서 설명하시기 바랍니다.

(미측 설명)

감사합니다.

한국 대표는 ~~양측 감사 기타 관계관의 노고와 상식의 결정이라 할 수 있는~~ 동 건의의 합동위원회 승인에 동의하는 바입니다.

그러나 정의, 구분, 석명을 그것이 아무리 정확하고 구체적이라할지라도 ~~하더라도~~ 그것만으로는 ~~이러한 종류의 일의~~ 합동수사반운영의 성공을 기할 수 없다는 점을 강조하고저 합니다. 미국 대표께서 말씀 ~~언급~~하신 바와 같이 우애와 협조정신, 특히 상호 존경이 원활한 운영의 필수 불가결한 요소입니다. 이와 더불어 마찬가지로 강조하여야 할 또 하나의 측면이 있읍니다. 관세법 또는 세관 통제에는 관세지역 개념에 고유하는 배타성이 있는 것으로 군대지위협정은 이러한 배타성, 독자성을 명백히 인정하고 있읍니다. 즉, 제7조는 "현지 법률의 존준 의무"를 말하고 있는데 반하여 특히 통관과 관세를 취급하고 있는 제9조는 1항에서 "합중국 군대의 구성원, 군속 및 그들의 가족은 본 협정에서 규정된 경우를 제외하고는 대한민국 세관 당국이 집행하고 있는 법령의 적용을 받는다"고 규정하고 있읍니다. 군대지위협정 시행에 있어 관세법령이 지니는 이와같은 특수성을 항상 명기할 것을 희망하는 바입니다.

(미측 견해 표시)

14

(의 제 7 - 제16조 1항 해석에 관한 미측 각서에 대한 한국측 회답)

한국 대표는 한.미 군대지위협정 제16조 1항 해석에 관하여 공식 각서를 제출하는바, 본 각서는 미국 대표가 1968년 6월 7일 합동위원회 제27차 회의에 각서를 제출하여 한국 법률 제979호에 내포된 제반 제한 조항이 군대지위협정 제16조 1항의 자구나 정신에 위배된다는 견해를 표시한데 대한 공식 회답입니다.

한국 대표는 동 법률 979 호에 관하여 다음 제 점을 지적하고저 합니다.

가. 동 법은 미군 또는 국련군과의 군납업 종사에 대하여 특별 면허를 규정하는 것이 아니고 이들 업자의 단순한 등록을 규정하고 있읍니다. 동 등록 소요 문서는 군납 계약 이행상 최소한의 책임 기준과 최소한의 재정 책임 보장에 필요한 것들입니다. 실적이 없는 신규업자에 대하여는 가등록 제도가 마련되어 있읍니다. 각서에서 상세히 분석한바와 같이 본 등록 제도는 제한 목적이 전혀 없으며 또 제한적 성격도 없읍니다.

나. 동 법의 목적은 미군 또는 국련군에 대한 군납업의 촉진 및 확장에 있으며, 이러한 목표 달성을 위하여 다음과 같은 조항을 설정하고 있읍니다.

즉, (1) 장관의 자문에 응할 군납 촉진위원회의 설치

(2) 상호 협조와 체계적 대변을 위한 업종별 조합 형성

(3) 각종 계획의 발간, 이로서 개개업자의 사업계획에 합리적 기초를 제공하고 불안 요소를 제거할 수 있읍니다.

(4) 필요시 품질 검사의 실시

(5) 특별 보조금 또는 보상금의 지급

(6) 수입제한의 특별 해제

다. 계약의 순조롭고 효율적인 이행을 위하여는 전력 및 용수배정, 수송기관, 노동력 배정상 우선 순위 배정등 법률 979호에 명기되지 않은 다른

15

여러가지 행정지원이 필요하며 동 등록 제도는 이러한 행정적 원조의 기초가 된다는 점에 유의하여야 할 것입니다.

라. 동 법은 등록 업자에게 다음과 같은 의무를 부과하고 있읍니다.

(1) 계약 완료후 30일 이내에 계약 대금을 소정 절차에 따라 외환 은행을 통하여 회수하여야 하며, 30일까지 미회수된 분에 대하여는 그 처리에 관하여 상공부장관의 승인을 얻어야 합니다.

본 규정은 현행 외환 관리제도 하에서는 불가피한 것이고 또한 대한민국 정부의 정당한 관심사인 것으로 사료됩니다.

(2) 장관이 요구하는 각종 보고를 제출하여야 합니다. 이들 보고서는 합리적 정책 수립의 기초가 되는 것이며, 주한 미군의 조달 업무에 지장을 초래하는 것으로는 간주되지 않읍니다.

마. 일견하여 제한적 성질의 것이라고 보일수도 있는 유일한 조항인 제8조는 특정 물품 납품 계약에 있어서는 장관의 사전 승인을 얻을 것을 규정하고 있는바 본 규정은 한국의 안전이나 경제에 불리한 계약을 사전 방지할 것을 목적으로 하고 있는 것으로서 이는 군대지위협정 제16조 2항 규정에 부합하는 것입니다. 그러나 본 규정은 실지로는 불필요함이 판명되어 상금 적용된바 없으며 동조에서 언급된 각령 조차 제정되지 않았읍니다.

법률 979호는 그 목적이나 성격에 있어 제한적 요소가 없으며 따라서 동 법과 군대지위협정 제16조 간에는 저촉이 없다는 것이 한국 정부의 견해이며, 한국 정부는 동 법이 한.미 양국의 이익에 부합하는 것으로 믿읍니다.

(미측 견해 표시)

16

공 란

(의 제 9 - 주한 미군 초청계약자 지명에 관한 미측 각서 - 미측 설명)

다음 의제는 초청계약자 지명에 관한 미측 각서입니다. 미국 대표께서 설명하시기 바랍니다.

(미측 설명)

한국 대표는 주한 미군 초청계약자로서 Daniel, Mann, Johnson & Mendenhall; Lyon Associates Inc., 및 Trans-Asia Engineering Associates, Inc. 등 3개 미국 상사를 지명하였다는 미측 통고 접수를 확인하는 바이며 또한 이들 지명에 있어 합의된 협의 절차를 거쳤음을 확인하고자 합니다.

18

(의제 10 - 상무분과위원회 건의 - **Trans-Asia Engineering Associates, Inc.**

다음 의제 10번은 상무분과위원회 건의입니다. 인천시는 상수도 시설 확장 공사에 있어 주한 미군 초청계약자인 **Trans-Asia Engineering Associates, Inc.**를 이용할 것을 계획하고 본격적인 교섭을 진행중에 있읍니다. 동 계획에 따라 지위협정 제16조 2 (나)항의 제한 조항이 문제로서 제기됩니다.

상무분과위원회는 본 건에 있어 1967년 8월 14일자 합동위원회 제12차 회의에서 **Collins Radio Company** 에 관하여 이미 선례가 수립되었으며 초청계약자 지위와 여타 상업 활동과의 상충을 배제하는 전기 규정 해석을 **Trans-Asia Engineering Associates, Inc.** 에도 적용할 것을 건의하고 있읍니다.

한국 대표는 동 분과위원회 건의의 합동위원회 승인을 제의하는 바입니다.

(미측 동의 표시)

감사합니다.

19

(의 제 11 - 제13조 시행에 관한 한국측 각서)

의제 다음 항목은 지위협정 제13조 시행에 관한 것으로서 한국 대표는 동 건에 관하여 공식 각서를 제출합니다.

1. 제13조 1 (가) 항은 합중국 당국이 공인하고 규제하는 군 판매점, 식당, 사교클럽, 극장, 신문 및 기타 비세출 자금기관은 합중국 군대의 구성원, 군속 및 그들의 가족의 이용을 위하여 합중국 군대가 설치할 수 있다고 규정하고 있읍니다.

2. 제13조에 대한 합의의사록은 합중국 군대는 다음 각 호의 자에게 제13조 제1항에 규정된 제 기관의 사용을 허용할 수 있다고 규정하고 있읍니다.

(가) 통상적으로 이와같은 특권이 부여되는 합중국 정부의 기타 공무원 및 직원;

(나) 합중국 군대로 부터 군수지원을 받는 통합사령부 산하 주한 외국 군대 및 그 구성원 ;

(다) 대한민국 국민이 아닌자로서 그의 대한민국 체류 목적이 합중국 정부에 의하여 재정적 지원을 받는 계약 용역의 이행만을 위한 자 ;

(라) 미 적십자사, "유.에세.오" 와 같은, 주로 합중국 군대의 이익이나 용역을 위하여 대한민국에 체류하는 기관 및 대한민국 국민이 아닌 직원 ;

(마) 전 각호에 규정된자의 가족, 및

(바) 대한민국 정부의 명시적인 동의를 얻은 기타 개인과 기관

3. 한국 대표는 피.엑스 특권 남용통제를 위한 미국 당국의 최선의 노력의 표시인 1968년 2월 22일자 미8군 규정 60-1 (EA Reg. 60-1) 에 언급하고저 합니다.

20

4. 동 규정 첨부 1, "피.엑스 배급표 배부 해당자 명단 및 발급 기관"은 다음과 같은 부류의 인원을 포함하고 있읍니다.

(11항) 퇴역 미군인

(14항) 다음 사람의 미망인 (미국 시민)으로서 재혼하지 않은자 및 그 부양가족; 연장 현역 복무기간중 전사한 군인, 훈련목적으로 예비 소집되거나 예비소집 훈련중의 예비역 군인, 군표사용이 허용됨 퇴역 군인.

(15 d 항) 본인이 한국에 주둔하지 않는 군인 가족 (조건부, 16, 17 및 18 항)

(15 j 항) 퇴역군인의 가족

(15 k 항) 한국에 임시 체류하는 군표사용이 허용됨 가족, 특권은 90일을 초과하지 않는 기간에 한 한다.

5. 한국 정부는 이러한 부류의 인원에게 피.엑스 특권을 허여함에 있어서 인정상의 고려 요소가 개재되고 있음을 인정하기는 하나 지위협정 제13조에 이들에게 적용될 수 있는 관계 규정을 발견하지 못합니다.

6. 따라서 미국 당국은 이들 인원의 종류별 구구에 대하여 다음과 같은 조치중 그 하나를 취할 것을 요청하는 바입니다.

(가) 군대지위협정 제 조항의 적용이 가능하다는데 대한 만족할 수 있는 설명을 제시하는것.

(나) 제13조 합의의사록 (바) 항에 의거하여 한국 정부의 명시적인 동의를 요청하는 것.

(미측 견해 표시)

21

(의 제 12 - 협정시행상의 제 각서 - 미측 설명)

다음 의제로 넘어가서, 미국 대표께서 군대지위협정 시행상 한국 정부측에 제출하는 제문서를 열거해 주시기 바랍니다.

(미측 열거)

대한민국 대표는 대한민국 간사가 미국측 간사로 부터 열거한 제 문서를 정히 접수했음을 확인하는 바입니다.

22

(의 제 13 - 차기회의)

다음 의제는 차기회의에 관한 건 입니다.

대한민국 대표는 차기회의를 8월 14일 (수) 용산에 있는 미국 SOFA 회의실에서 개최토록 제의하는 바입니다.

(미측 수락)

23

(의 제 14 - 신문 발표문)

최종 의제인 공동 신문발표문에 관해서, 대한민국 대표는 합동위원회 양측 간사가 준비하여 배부한바 있는 공동 신문 발표문을 그대로 채택 하도록 제의하는 바입니다.

(미측 수락)

이제 의제 전부를 토의한것 같읍니다.

프리드만 장군, 기타 토의안건이 없으면 폐회 하겠읍니다.

24

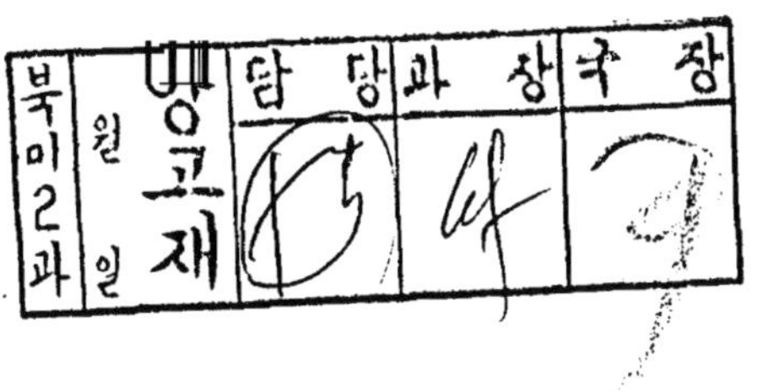

JOINT COMMITTEE
UNDER
THE REPUBLIC OF KOREA AND THE UNITED STATES
THE TWENTY-EIGHTH MEETING

(3 July 1968)

NOTES
FOR
THE REPUBLIC KOREA REPRESENTATIVE

25

General Friedman, if you are ready, I will call the meeting to order.

(Agenda I - Assignment of Additional Tasks to Facilities and Areas Subcommittee)

U.S. Presentation

The first item of the Agenda is about the assignment of additional tasks to the Facilities and Areas Subcommittee.

I understand that the U.S. Representative has seven tasks to be assigned and eight tasks assigned already as ~~based on~~ exigency action to the Facilities and Areas Subcommittee to present.

(U.S. Presentation)

Thank you.

The Republic of Korea Representative is pleased to concur in the assignment of 7 tasks and at the same time, to confirm formally the assignment of 8 tasks acted on exigency basis to the Facilities and Areas Subcommittee.

ROK Presentation

The Republic of Korea Representative ~~has~~ one task [illegible] noted for which has been already assigned to the Facilities and Areas Subcommittee as exigency action.

26

공 란

(Agenda II - Assignment of Task to Criminal Jurisdiction Subcommittee - U.S. Presentation)

Thank you.

The next item of the Agenda is about the assignment of task to the Criminal Jurisdiction Subcommittee.

I believe the U.S. Representative will present ~~the~~ one task to be assigned to the Criminal Jurisdiction Subcommittee.

(U.S. Presentation and proposal)

Thank you.

The Republic of Korea Representative is happy to concur in the assignment of the task proposed by the U.S. Representative to the Criminal Jurisdiction Subcommittee.

28

공 란

US Presentation - 8

Now, the U.S. Representative will please present the remaining 8 recommendations of the Facilities and Areas Subcommittee.

(U.S. presentation and proposal)

Thank you.

The Republic of Korea Representative is pleased to concur in the Joint Committee's approval of 8 recommendations of the Facilities and Areas Subcommittee.

70

(Agenda IV - Recommendations of the Transportation Subcommittee)

Next on the Agenda, item IV, is the Recommendations of the Transportation Subcommittee.

The Republic of Korea and the United States Representatives directed at the Second Preliminary Meeting of Working Group on 19 January 1967 development of procedures governing licensing and registration of privately owned vehicles pursuant to Article XXIV, paragraph 3, of the Status of Forces Agreement. And now the Transportation Subcommittee is finally presenting its recommendations. The considerable delay was due mainly, among other things, to arrangements relative to insurance coverage of such vehicles.

At this juncture, The Republic of Korea Representative understands ~~wishes to note for the record the understanding~~ that the expression "as exditiously as possible," used in the last sentence of paragraph 5 of the recommended procedures in connection with the ROK notification after receipt of registration information, normally means within one or two working days.

~~With this understanding~~, The Republic of Korea Representative is pleased to propose Joint Committee approval of the recommendation of the Transportation Subcommittee which is to take effect from the first day of third month following the date of approval.

(US Concurrence)

31 Thank you very much.

(Agenda V - Assignment of Task to Transportation Subcommittee)

Paragraph 1, Article XXIV of the Status of Forces Agreement provides that the Republic of Korea shall accept as valid, without a driving test or fee, the driving permit or license or military driving permit issued by the United States, or political subdivision thereof, to a member of the United States armed forces, the civilian component, and their dependents.

It is obvious for practical reasons that such licenses or permits should be converted into a form recognizable and readable by officials of the Republic of Korea. Therefore the Republic of Korea Representative wishes to propose assignment of a task to Transportation Subcommittee to recommend ways and means to insure ~~the satisfaction of~~ aforementioned requirements.

It is further proposed that in view of the close co-relation between the licensing and registration of privately owned vehicles of the SOFA covered personnel and the proposed task, the Transportation Subcommittee be instructed to complete this task before the effective date of the licensing and registration procedures for privately owned vehicles so that two procedures will take effect at the same time.

(US Concurrence)

Thank you very much.

(Agenda VI - Recommendations to Joint Committee on Disposition of Goods confiscated by Joint Investigative Teams - US Presentation)

Next on the agenda are "Recommendations to Joint Committee on Disposition of Goods Confiscated by Joint Investigative Teams. Would the United States Representative please present these recommendations.

(US Presentation)

Thank you.

The Republic of Korea Representative is pleased to concur in Joint Committee approval of the recommendations, ~~which embodies the diligence and balanced judgement of two Secretaries and other officials concerned.~~ However, ~~he~~ I would like to emphasize that ~~no amount of~~ mere definitions, demarcations or clarifications, however they might be, and concrete, cannot by themselves insure success in ~~this kind of~~ the Joint Investigation Teams operation. Friendship, spirit of cooperation, and above all mutual respect are essential elements for smooth working, (as the United States Representative has already ~~recognized~~ mentioned.) There is another aspect which calls for equal emphasis. Customs laws or controls have an exclusiveness inherent to the concept of customs zones. This exclusiveness of customs matters is clearly recognized by the SOFA. It is to be noted that while Article VII
33 refers to "the duty to respect local law," Article IX,

which deals specifically with customs duties, provides in paragraph 1 that save as provided in the Agreement, members of the United States armed forces, the civilian component, and their dependents shall be subject to the laws and regulations administered by the customs authorities of the Republic of Korea. It is hoped that in the implementation of the SOFA, the special nature of customs laws and regulations be always kept in mind.

(US comment.)

74

(Agenda VII - ROK Reply to US Memorandum to Joint Committee on Interpretation of Paragraph 1, Article XVI)

The Republic of Korea Representative is presenting a written Memorandum on the subject of Interpretation of Article XVI, paragraph 1, of the ROK-US SOFA. This Memorandum is a formal reply to US memorandum presented at the Twenty-Seventh meeting of the Joint Committee on 7 June 1968 in which the United States Representative expressed the view that restrictions supposedly contained in ROK Law 979 are inconsistent with the purpose and language of paragraph 1, Article XVI of the SOFA.

The Republic of Korea Representative wishes to make these points with regard to Law 979:

a. The Law does not provide for special licensing for performance of contracts with the US/UN armed forces. What the law provides for is simple registration for such contractors.

Documents required for the registration are those needed to ensure minimum standard of responsibility for performance of contracts and also minimum financial responsibility. For prospective contractors without past record, a provisional registration status is provided for. As detailed analysis is given in the written memorandum, the registration is not designed for any

35

restrictive purpose, and is not restrictive in its nature.

b. The purpose of the Law is to promote and encourage expansion of performance of contracts with the US/UN armed forces, and in order to achieve this objective the Law envisages:

(1) Establishment of a Special Committee to advise the Minister;

(2) Formation of Associations of contractors by field of activity, in order to allow mutual cooperation and canalized representation;

(3) Publication of plans, which will give rational basis for individual planning and help eliminating uncertainties;

(4) Inspection of supplies for quality control when necessary;

(5) Award of special subsidies or compensations; and,

(6) Special exemptions from import restrictions.

c. It is to be noted that other administrative supports, not specifically mentioned in Law 979, such as assignment of special priorities in electricity and water supply, transportation, for labor, etc., are needed for orderly and efficient performance of procurement contracts, and the registration provides framework for such administrative assistance.

36

d. The Law imposes on the registered contractors these obligations:

(1) Collecting contract payments within 30 days after completion of contracts through exchange banks in accordance with prescribed procedures, and to receive approval of the Minister of Commerce and Industry for disposition of sums remaining due at this date.

This provision is inevitable under current system of exchange controls, and is considered a legitimate concern of the Government of the Republic of Korea.

(2) Submitting reports as may be required by the Minister.

These reports would serve as a basis for rational formulation of policy and are considered not to constitute interference with the procurement activities of the USFK.

e. The only clause of the Law which may seem restrictive in appearance, Article VIII provides for prior approval of the Minister on supply contracts of certain goods. This provision was conceived to preclude contracts detrimental to the economy or security of the Republic of Korea, and this concern is in conformity with the provisions of paragraph 2, Article XVI of the SOFA. However, the provision proved unnecessary and remain unapplied. The Cabinet Ordinance referred to in the Law has not been formulated.

37

It is the view of the Government of the Republic of Korea that Law 979 is not restrictive in its purpose or nature, and therefore there is no inconsistency between the Law and Article XVI of the SOFA. The Government of the Republic of Korea believes that the said Law is in conformity with best interests of both the Republic of Korea and the United States.

(US Comment)

38

공 란

공 란

(Agenda IX - US Memoranda on Designation of Three USFK
Invited Contractors - US presentation)

Next on agenda is US Memoranda on designation of invited contractors. Would the United States Representative please present these memoranda.

(US Presentation)

The Repgblic of Korea Representative is pleased to acknowledge US notification on designation as USFK Invited Contractors these three US firms: namely, Daniel, Mann, Johnson & Mendenhall;

Lyon Associates, inc., and Trans-Asia Engineering Associates, Inc. and is happy to confirm that agreed procedures on consultation have been observed in these designations.

41

(Agenda X - Recommendations of Commerce Subcommittee - Trans-Asia Engineering Associates, Inc.)

Next on the agenda, Item X, are Recommendations of Commerce Subcommittee. The city of Inchon is planning to have the services of Trans-Asia Engineering Associates, Inc., a USFK Invited Contractor in connection with expansion of water supply system and active negotiations are under way. The plan raises the question of restriction contained in paragraph 2(b), Article XVI, SOFA.

The Commerce Subcommittee recommends that in this instance the interpretation of the said clause on which precedent was established with regard to Collins Radio Company at the twelfth meeting of the Joint Committee on 14 Aug. 1967, and which removes incompatibility between the Invited Contractor status and other business activities be adopted for Trans-Asia Engineering Associates, Inc.

The Republic of Korea Representative wishes to propose Joint Committee approval of the Subcommittee recommendations.

(US Concurrence)

Thank you very much.

42

(Agenda XI - ROK Memorandum on Implementation of Article XIII)

Next item on the agenda concerns implementation of Article XIII, SOFA, on which subject the Republic of Korea Representative is presenting a formal memorandum.

1. Paragraph 1(a), Article XIII provides that military exchanges, messes, social clubs, theatres, newspapers and other non-appropriated fund organizations authorized and regulated by the United States military authorities may be established by the United States armed forces for the use of members of such forces, the civilian component and their dependents.

2. Agreed Minutes to Article XIII provides that the United States armed forces may grant the use of the organizations referred to in paragraph 1 of Article XIII to:

(a) other officers or personnel of the Government of the United States ordinarily accorded such privileges;

(b) those other non-Korean armed forces in the Republic of Korea under the Unified Command which receive logistical support from the United States armed forces, and their members;

(c) those non-Korean persons whose presence in the Republic of Korea is solely for the purpose of providing contract services financed by the Government of the United States;

41

43

(d) those organizations which are present in the Republic of Korea primarily for the benefit and service of the United States armed forces, such as the American Red Cross and the United Service Organizations, and their non-Korean personnel;

(e) dependents if the foregoing; and

(f) other persons and organizations with the express consent of the Government of the Republic of Korea.

3. The Republic of Korea Representative wishes to refer to the Eighth United States Army Regulation Number 60-1 (EA Reg. 60-1) of 22 February 1968 which embodies best efforts of the US authorities to control abuse of PX privileges.

4. Inclosure 1 to the regulation, "Post Exchange Ration Card Eligibility List and Issuing Agencies of Ration Cards," includes the following categories of persons:

(11) Retired US military personnel

(14) Widows (US citizens) who have not remarried and their dependents of the following: Members of the uniformed services, who die on extended active duty; members of Reserve components, inactive duty for training, or inactive duty training; and retired personnel, provided

they are authorized the use of MPC.

(15 d) Dependents of US military personnel whose sponsor is not stationed in Korea. (with limitations, 16, 17 and 18)

(15 j) Dependents of retired military personnel.

(15 k) Dependents otherwise authorized exchange and MPC privileges who are transient in Korea. Privileges will be limited to a period not exceeding 90 days.

5. While recognizing human or humanitarian considerations involved in granting PX privileges to these categories of persons, the Government of the Republic of Korea hardly finds relevant provisions in Article XIII, SOFA, which may be applicable for each of the categories.

6. It is requested that the United States will take one of the following alternative actions for each of the categories;

(a) to give satisfactory explanations for applicability of the SOFA provisions; or

~~(b) to withdraw PX privileges; or~~

(b) to request express consents of the ROK Government in accordance with paragraph (f) of the Agreed Minutes to Article XIII.

(US Response)

45

(Agenda XIII - Memoranda Presented to the ROK Government by the US in the Implementation of the SOFA - US Presentation)

Turning to the next item of the agenda,

I understand that the United States Representative will enumerate the documents presented to the Korean Government in the implementation of the SOFA.

(US enumeration)

The Republic of Korea Representative is pleased to confirm that the Republic of Korea Secretariat has duly received the documents enumerated, ~~by~~ from the United States Secretariat.

46

(Agenda XIII - Next Meeting)

The next item of the agenda is about the next meeting.

The Republic of Korea Representative would like to propose that the next meeting be held on 14th August (Wednesday) at the U.S. SOFA Conference Room, Yongsan.

(US Response)

47

(Agenda XIV - Press Release)

Coming to the final item of agenda, agreement on Joint Press Release, the Republic of Korea Representative would like to propose that the text of Joint press release prepared and distributed by the both secretaries of Joint Committee be adopted as it is.

(U.S. Response)

I think we have covered all agendas.

General Friedman, is there any other to discuss? There is none, I will call the meeting to adjourn.

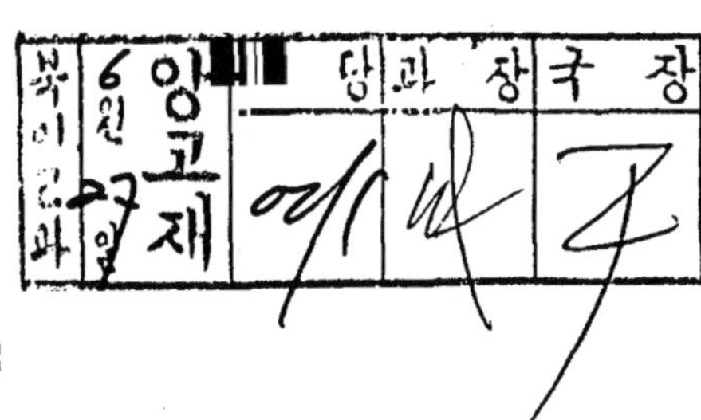

JOINT COMMITTEE
UNDER
THE REPUBLIC OF KOREA AND THE UNITED STATES
STATUS OF FORCES AGREEMENT

3 July 1968

MEMORANDUM FOR: The Joint Committee

SUBJECT : Interpretation of Article XVI, paragraph 1, of the ROK-US SOFA

1. Reference is made to paragraphs 12 to 15 inclusive, minutes of the Twenty-Seventh Joint Committee meeting on 7 June 1968, and inclosure 8 thereto, in which the United States Representative expressed the view that "restrictions contained" in ROK Law 979 are inconsistent with the purpose and language of paragraph 1, Article XVI of the ROK-US Status of Forces Agreement.

2. The following points are made with regard to Law 979:

a. The Law does not provide for special licensing for performance of contracts with the US/UN forces. What the Law provides for is simple registrations for such contractors. (ref. : Article VI of the Law, Article VIII of Cabinet Ordinance No 450, dated 12 February 1962 as amended by Cabinet Ordinance No 1731 dated 16 Dec. 1963)

49

The requirements of the registration ~~is~~ are to submit the following documents (Art. VIII, the said Ordinance):

(1) Curriculum vitae, in case of an incorporated legal person that of the representative;

(2) Certificate of identity, in case of a incorporated legal person that of the representative, issued by the head of local administrative division or in case of a foreign nationals issued by the head of pertinent diplomatic or consular mission.

(3) Certificate of deposit for notless than ₩500,000.00 (approx. US $1,700.00); for persons operating ~~demonstration~~ sales ~~outlet~~ store(s) within Far East/Jakor Exchanges that for not less than ₩100,000.00 (approx. US $350.00); in case of incorporated legal person, official registration copy for paid-in capital of not less than ₩ 1,000,000.00 (approx. US $3,600.00)

(4) Business plans (prospectus)

(5) In case of an incorporated legal person, its statute.

(6) Balance sheet; in case of an incorporated legal person, balance sheet and profit and loss statement authenticated by a certified accountant.

50

(7) In accordance with the following classification, certification of contract performance with the UN command agencies or other foreign agencies covering one year preceding the date of application to register:

(a) For businesses selling materials and supplies, a total of not less than US $ 5,000.00; for suppliers of handicraft products or those operating ~~demonstration selling outlets~~ sales store(s) within facilities of the Far East Exchanges establishments a total of not less than US $2,000.00.

(b) For businesses contracting for construction or repairing works, a total of not less than US $30,000.00; for those providing services a total not less than US $ 20,000.00; however those providing services within facilities of Far East Exchanges or comparable businesses, a total of not less than US $ 2,000.00.

Note: For a new-comer, this requirement is exempted and a provisional registration status is recognized for the initial year, if the business attains the above performance during the first year it ~~was~~ is then recognized the status of permanent registration; if the business attains half of the stipulated performance record during the first year, the provisional status is further extended for another year. (Art. IX, Cabinet Ordinance)

49

51

(8) Documents required by ministerial decree of the Ministry of Commerce and Industry regarding the capacity to perform contracts.

It should be apparent that the registration is not designed for any restrictive purpose, but to ensure minimum standard of responsibility for contract performance and minimum financial responsibility.

b. The purpose of the Law is defined as "to contr-i-bute to improving the balance of external payments and development of the national economy by endeaveting to expand performance of contracts with the (US) armed forces." (Art. I)

In order to achieve the objective the Law envisages:

(1) Establishment of a Military Supplies Promotion Committee, which will advise the Minister of Commerce and Industry on the relevant subject; (Art. III)

(2) Formation of Associations of contractors by field of activity (Art. VI), which will allow canalized representation.

(3) Publication of plans pertaining to (US/UN) armed forces procurement contracts (Art. VII), which will give rational basis for incividual planning and help eliminating uncertainties;

(4) Inspection of supplies when necessary (Art. X);

57

(5) Award of special subsidies or compensations (Art. XI); and,

(6) Special exemptions from import controls when necessary (Art. XII).

c. It is to be noted that other administrative supports, not specifically mentioned in the said Law, such as assignment of special priorities in electricity and water supply, transportation, for labor, etc., are needed for orderly and efficient performance of procurement contracts, and the registration provides framework for such administrative assistance.

d. The Law imposes on the registered contractors the following obligations:

(1) Collection of contract payments within 30 days after completion of contracts through exchange banks in accordance with prescribed procedures; in case of failure to collect the payment within the stipulated period, to receive approval of the Minister of Commerce and Industry for disposition of amounts due, (Art. IX)

This provision is inevitable under current system of exchange controls, and is considered a legitimate concern of the Government of the Republic of Korea.

53

(2) Contractors may be required to submit reports as deemed necessary by the Minister of Commerce and Industry. (Art. XIII)

The reports envisaged by the Law would serve as a basis for rational formulation of policy and should not constitute interference with procurement activities of the USFK.

e. Penalties - Article XIV provides for penalties ranging from suspension for six-month period to cancellation of registration. The provision is designed to ensure responsible behavior of contractors, and the Government of the Republic of Korea would certainly not apply the provision in ways detrimental to interests of either the ROK or the US.

f. The only clause of the Law which may seem restrictive in appearance, Article VIII, is couched in the following language:

"Persons desiring to enter procurement contracts for supply of certain goods shall obtain approval of the Minister of Commerce and Industry as may be stipulated by Cabinet Ordinance."

The provision is designed to preclude contracts detrimental to the economy or security of the Republic of Korea, and this concern is in conformity with the provisions of paragraph 2, Article XVI of the SOFA.

54

However, the provision proved not needed and remain unapplied. The Cabinet Ordinance ~~envaged~~ envisaged referred to in the law has not been formulated.

3. It is the view of the Government of the Republic of Korea that Law 979 is not restrictive in purpose or nature, and therefore there is no inconsistency between the Law and Article XVI of the SOFA. The Government of the Republic of Korea believes that the said law is in conformity with best interests of both the Republic of Korea and the United States.

Yoon Ha Jong
Republic of Korea
Representative

55

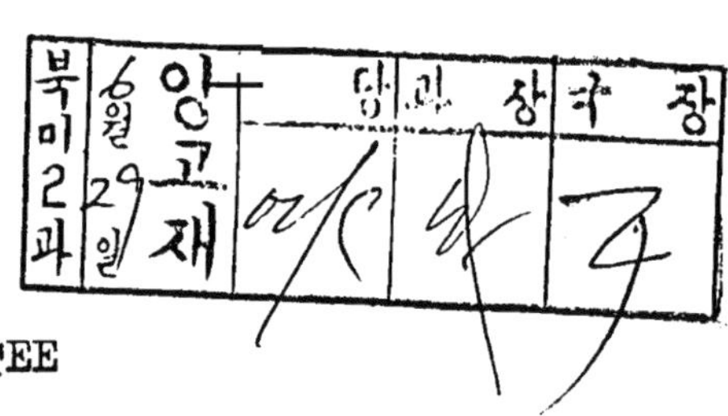

JOINT COMMITTEE
UNDER
THE REPUBLIC OF KOREA AND THE UNITED STATES
STATUS OF FORCES AGREEMENT

3 July 1968

MEMORANDUM TO: The Joint Committee

SUBJECT : Interpretation of Article XIII, Status of Forces Agreement.

1. a. Paragraph 1(a), Article XIII provides that military exchanges, messes, social clubs, theatres, newspapers and other non-appropriated fund organizations authorized and regulated by the United States military authorities may be established by the United States armed forces for the use of members of such forces, the civilian component and their dependents.

b. Agreed Minutes to Article XIII provides that the United States armed forces may grant the use of the organizations referred to in paragraph 1 of Article XIII to:

(a) other officers or personnel of the Government of the United States ordinarily accorded such privileges;

(b) those other non-Korean armed forces in the Republic of Korea under the Unified Command which receive logistical support from the United States armed forces, and

66

their members;

(c) those non-Korean persons whose presence in the Republic of Korea is solely for the purpose of providing contract services financed by the Government of the United States;

(d) those organizations which are present in the Republic of Korea primarily for the benefit and service of the United States armed forces, such as the American Red Cross and the United Service Organizations, and their non-Korean personnel;

(e) dependents of the foregoing; and

(f) other persons and organizations with the express consent of the Government of the Republic of Korea.

2. Reference is made to the Eighth United States Army Regulation Number 60-1 (EA Reg. 60-1) of 22 February 1968 which embodies best efforts of the US authorities to control abuse of PX privileges. ~~The Republic of Korea appreciates the efforts of the US authorities in view of the enormous administrative burden involved.~~

3. ~~Attention is called~~ According to Inclosure 1 to the regulation referred to in the preceding paragraph, "Post Exchange Ration Card Eligibility List and Issuing Agencies

of Ration Cards," ~~which~~ includes the following categories of persons:

(11) Retired US military personnel

(14) Widows (US citizens) who have not remarried and their dependents of the following: Members of the uniformed services, who die on extended active duty; members of Reserve components, inactive duty for training, or inactive duty training; and retired personnel, provided they are authorized the use of MPC.

(15 d.) Dependents of US military personnel whose sponsor is not stationed in Korea. (with limitations, 16, 17 and 18)

(15 j.) Dependents of retired military personnel.

(15 k.) Dependents otherwise authorized exchange and MPC privileges who are transient in Korea. Privileges will be limited to a period not exceeding 90 days.

4. While recognizing human or humanitarian considerations involved in granting PX privileges to the categories of persons enumerated in paragraph 3 above, the Government of the Republic of Korea hardly finds ~~does not see which of the~~ relevant provisions in Article XIII, SOFA which ~~are applied for~~ may be applicable to each of the (above enumerated) categories.

5. It is therefore requested that the United States authorities will take one of the following alternative actions for each of the categories:

(a) to give satisfactory explanations for applicability of the SOFA provisions; or

-3 - ~~to each of these categories of persons~~

58

~~(b) to withdraw PX privileges; or~~

(b) to request express consents of the ROK Government in accordance with paragraph (f) of the Agreed Minutes to Article XIII.

YOON HA JONG
Republic of Korea
Representative
~~SOFA Joint Committee~~

59

These minutes are considered as official documents pertaining to both Governments and will not be released without mutual agreement.

JOINT COMMITTEE
UNDER
THE REPUBLIC OF KOREA AND THE UNITED STATES
STATUS OF FORCES AGREEMENT

MINUTES OF THE TWENTY-~~THIRD~~ Eighth MEETING

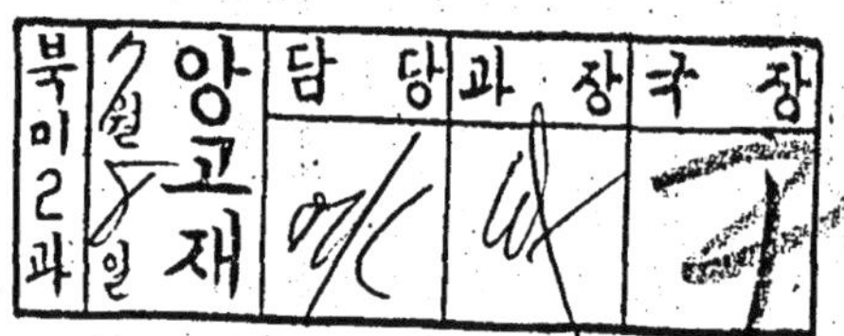

3 July 1968
Capitol Building
Republic of Korea
Seoul, Korea

1. The meeting was convened at 1500 hours by Mr. YOON Ha Jong, the ROK Representative, who presided at the meeting. A copy of the agenda is attached as Inclosure 1.

2. The following were in attendance:

ROK	US
Mr. YOON Ha Jong	CAPT M. R. Massie, USN
Mr. KIM Sung Jae	COL Gerald W. Davis, USA
Mr. CHO Choong Hoon	Mr. P. Wesley Kriebel, US Embassy
Mr. SHIN Chung Sup	Mr. Robert A. Kinney, USFK
Mr. PARK Noh Soo	MAJ Edmund P. Murphy, USAF
Mr. OH Myong Too	

3. The ROK Representative convened the meeting and invited the US Alternate Representative to present seven new tasks for assignment to the Facilities and Areas Subcommittee, as well as eight tasks already assigned as exigency actions. Captain Massie stated that first it was a pleasure for him to introduce a new member of the US SOFA Secretariat, Major Edmund P. Murphy, who succeeded Lieutenant Colonel Paul E. Jones. The ROK Representative welcomed Major Murphy to the Joint Committee.

60

공 란

공　　　란

공 란

공　　란

공 란

17. The ROK Representative stated that the Joint Committee, at the Second Preliminary Meeting of the Working Group on 19 January 1967, directed development of procedures governing licensing and registration of privately owned vehicles pursuant to Article XXIV, paragraph 3, of the SOFA. The Transportation Subcommittee has finally presented its recommendations (Inclosure 12). The considerable delay was due mainly, among other things, to arrangements relative to insurance coverage of such vehicles. The ROK Representative noted that it is mutually understood that the expression "as expeditiously as possible," used in the last sentence of paragraph 5 of the recommended procedures in connection with the ROK notification after receipt of registration information, normally means within one or two working days. The ROK Representative proposed Joint Committee approval of the recommendation of the Transportation Subcommittee which was to take effect from the first day of the third

66

month following the date of approval.

18. The US Representative stated he was happy to approve the recommendations of the Transportation Subcommittee with regard to procedures for licensing and registration of privately owned vehicles under Article XXIV. The US Representative is also pleased to note the assurances of the ROK Representative that the ROK authorities will process the issuance of registration numbers expeditiously and will normally notify the United States recorder of the registration number to be assigned USFK personnel before the expiration of two working days.

19. The ROK Representative stated that paragraph 1, Article XXIV of the SOFA, provided that the Republic of Korea shall accept as valid, without a driving test or fee, the driving permit or license or military driving permit issued by the United States, or political subdivision thereof, to a member of the US armed forces, the civilian component, and their dependents. He stated that it was obvious that,for practical reasons, such licenses or permits should be converted into a form recognizable and readable by officials of the Republic of Korea. Therefore, the ROK Representative proposed assignment of a task to the Transportation Subcommittee to recommend ways and means to insure the aforementioned requirements (Inclosure 13). He further proposed that, in view of the close corelation between the licensing and registration of privately owned vehicles of personnel covered by the SOFA and the proposed task, the Transportation Subcommittee be instructed to complete

this task before the effective date of the licensing and registration procedures for privately owned vehicles so that the two procedures would go into effect at the same time.

20. The US Representative concurred in the assignment of this task to the Transportation Subcommittee. He noted that the Government of the Republic of Korea had agreed that it shall accept as valid, without a driving test or fee, the driving permit or license or military driving permit issued by the United States, or political subdivision thereof, to a member of the US armed forces, the civilian component, and their dependents. The United States Forces, Korea have been planning to issue a revised military driving permit, which would be in both English and Korean, to facilitate its recognition and use by ROK officials. The US Representative also expressed the hope that this task could be expeditiously completed and timely recommendations made to enable the bi-lingual driving permit to be available prior to the implementation of the new procedures for licensing and registration of privately owned United States Forces, Korea vehicles, on 1 October 1968.

21. The US Representative stated that, at the eleventh meeting of the US-ROK Joint Committee on 13 July 1967, it was agreed that the Governments of the Republic of Korea and the United States would establish a permanent joint investigative organization for the purpose of effecting close US-ROK cooperation in the enforcement of all laws and regulations relating to abuse of privileges and illegal transactions.

22. The US Representative stated that the US and ROK SOFA Secretaries, in consultation with other appropriate officials in their respective Governments, developed "Operating Instructions for ROK-US Joint Investigations." These operating instructions were approved by the US and ROK Representatives at the nineteenth meeting of the Joint Committee on 21 December 1967. In the implementation of the Joint Committee procedures for the operation of the ROK-US Joint Investigative Teams, questions arose concerning the disposition of goods confiscated by the Joint Investigative Teams. The US and ROK SOFA Secretaries held extensive consultations with appropriate officials in their respective Governments, in an effort to achieve mutual US-ROK agreement on procedures relating to disposition of goods confiscated by the Joint Investigative Teams. The result of the consultations was a proposed "Supplement to the Operating Instructions for ROK-US Joint Investigations," which has been developed during numerous conferences between US and ROK officials (Inclosure 14).

23. The US Representative stated that these supplemental instructions, which were believed to be fair and in the mutual interests of both the ROK and US Governments, were based on a careful analysis of the provisions of Article IX of the ROK-US SOFA. The US Representative expressed the belief that these supplemental instructions would greatly assist in the resolution of problems relating to difficult questions on disposition of goods confiscated by the Joint Investigative Teams. It was hoped that such questions could be resolved in a way which promoted ROK-US friendship and understanding, and which upheld the spirit of mutual cooperation in the defense

69

of the ROK as embodied in the SOFA. The US Representative proposed Joint Committee approval of the "Supplement to the Operating Instructions for ROK-US Joint Investigations."

24. The ROK Representative stated he was pleased to concur in Joint Committee approval of the recommendations. However, he indicated he would like to emphasize that mere definitions, demarcations or clarifications, however precise and concrete they might be, could not by themselves insure success in this kind of operation. Friendship, spirit of cooperation, and above all mutual respect were essential elements for smooth working, as the US Representative had already mentioned. There was another aspect which called for equal emphasis. Customs laws or controls have ~~had~~ an exclusiveness inherent to the concept of customs zones. This exclusiveness of customs matters was clearly recognized by the SOFA. It was to be noted that while Article VII referred to "the duty to respect local law," Article IX, which dealt specifically with customs duties, provided in paragraph 1 that save as provided in the Agreement, members of the US armed forces, the civilian component, and their dependents shall be subject to the laws and regulations administered by the customs authorities of the Republic of Korea. The ROK Representative expressed the hope that, in the implementation of the SOFA, the special nature of customs laws and regulations would always be kept in mind.

11

170

25. The ROK Representative presented a written memorandum on the subject of interpretation of Article XVI, paragraph 1, of the ROK-US SOFA (Inclosure 15). This memorandum was a formal reply to a US memorandum presented at the twenty-seventh meeting of the Joint Committee on 7 June, in which the US Representative expressed the view that restrictions supposedly contained in ROK Law 979 were inconsistent with the purpose and language of paragraph 1, Article XVI of the SOFA.

26. The ROK Representative wished to make the following points with regard to Law 979:

a. The Law does not provide for special licensing for performance of contracts with the US/UN armed forces. What the law provides for is simple registration for such contractors. Documents required for the registration are those needed to ensure minimum standards of responsibility for performance of contracts and also for minimum financial responsibility. For prospective contractors without past records a provisional registration status was provided for. As the detailed analysis given in the written memorandum indicates, the registration was not designed for any restrictive purpose, and was not restrictive in its nature.

b. The purpose of the law was to promote and encourage expansion of performance of contracts with the US/UN armed forces, and in order to achieve this objective the law envisaged:

(1) Establishment of a special committee to advise the Minister;

(2) Formation of associations of contractors by field of activity, in order to allow mutual cooperation and canalized representation;

71

(3) Publication of plans, which would provide a rational basis for individual planning and help eliminating uncertainties;

(4) Inspection of supplies for quality control when necessary;

(5) Award of special subsidies or compensations; and,

(6) Special exemptions from import restrictions.

c. It is to be noted that other administrative supports, not specifically mentioned in Law 979, such as assignment of special priorities in electricity and water supply, transportation, for labor, etc., are needed for orderly and efficient performance of procurement contracts, and the registration provided the framework for such administrative assistance.

d. The Law imposed on the registered contractors these obligations:

(1) Collecting contract payments within 30 days after completion of contracts through exchange banks in accordance with prescribed procedures, and to receive approval of the Minister of Commerce and Industry for disposition of sums remaining due at that date. Such a provision was inevitable under the current system of exchange controls, and was considered a legitimate concern of the Government of the Republic of Korea.

(2) Submission of reports as may be required by the Minister. These reports serve as a basis for rational formulation of policy and were considered not to constitute interference with the procurement activities of the USFK.

13

72

e. The only clause of the Law which may seem restrictive in appearance, Article VIII, provided for prior approval of the Minister on supply contracts of certain goods. This provision was conceived to preclude contracts detrimental to the economy or security of the Republic of Korea, and this concern was in conformity with the provisions of paragraph 2, Article XVI, of the SOFA. However, the provision proved unnecessary and remains unapplied. The Cabinet Ordinance referred to in the Law has not been formulated.

27. The ROK Representative, in summary, stated that it is the view of the Government of the ROK that Law 979 was not restrictive in its purpose or nature, and therefore there was no inconsistency between the Law and Article XVI of the SOFA. The Government of the ROK believed that the Law is in conformity with the best interests of both the ROK and US.

28. The US Representative thanked the ROK Representative for his memorandum and for his presentation regarding the interpretation of paragraph 1 of Article XVI. The US Representative stated he would reply in detail to the Republic of Korea presentation at an early meeting of the Joint Committee. It was obvious from the presentations of the US and ROK Representatives at the last two Joint Committee meetings that there were some differences of interpretation on this subject. Fortunately, Agreed Minute 2 to Article XVI provided:

"2. The problem of a satisfactory settlement of difficulties with respect to procurement contracts arising out of differences between economic laws and business practices of the Republic of Korea and the United States will be studied by the Joint Committee or other appropriate representatives."

The US Representative noted that in the interpretation of the Government of the Republic of Korea, "Law 979 is not restrictive in purpose or nature...". The US Representative expressed the belief that it was in the best interests of both the ROK and the US that the right of the US to contract in Korea "without restriction" be upheld. It was hoped that a mutually satisfactory resolution of the differences on this question could be achieved.

174

15

공 란

공 란

37. The US Representative presented memoranda to the Joint Committee informing the ROK Government of the designation of three new invited contractors under Article XV of the SOFA. After consultation with ROK Commerce Subcommittee personnel, the USFK has designated Lyon Associates, Incorporated (Inclosure 21); Daniel, Mann, Johnson & Mendenhall (Inclosure 22); and Trans-Asia Engineering Associates, Incorporated (Inclosure 23) as US invited contractors. The US Representative stated that pertinent data concerning employees of these invited contractors will be provided to the Government of the Republic of Korea in accordance with mutually approved procedures.

38. The ROK Representative acknowledged the US notification on the designation of USFK invited-contractors of three US firms; namely, Daniel, Mann, Johnson & Mendenhall; Lyon Associates, Inc., and Trans-Asia Engineering Associates, Inc. He stated he was happy to confirm that agreed procedures on consultation had been observed in these designations.

39. The ROK Representative presented recommendations of the Commerce Subcommittee. He stated that the city of Inchon was planning to have the services of Trans-Asia Engineering Associates, Inc., a USFK invited contractor, in connection with expansion of water supply system and active negotiations are underway (Inclosure 24). The plan raised the question of restriction contained in paragraph 2(b), Article XVI, SOFA. The Commerce Subcommittee recommended that, in this instance, the interpretation of the clause on which precedent was established with regard to Collins Radio Company at the twelfth meeting of the Joint Committee on 14 August 1967, and which removes the incompatibility between the invited contractor status and the other business with the ROK Government ~~being considered by~~ be applied to the Trans-Asia Engineering Associates, Inc. The ROK Representative proposed Joint Committee approval of the Subcommittee recommendations.

40. The US Representative concurred in the recommendation of the Commerce Subcommittee. He noted that the additional personnel working on contracts for the ROK Government will not be entitled to logistical support and privileges under the SOFA.

19

78

41. The ROK Representative stated that the next agenda item concerned implementation of Article XIII, SOFA, on which subject the ROK Representative presented a formal memorandum (Inclosure 25).

42. The ROK Representative noted that paragraph 1(a), Article XIII provided that military exchanges, messes, social clubs, theaters, newspapers and other nonappropriated fund organizations authorized and regulated by the US military authorities may be established by the US armed forces for the use of members of such forces, the civilian component and their dependents. He also noted that the Agreed Minute to Article XIII provides that the US armed forces may grant the use of the organizations referred to in paragraph 1 of Article XIII to:

a. Other officers or personnel of the US Government ordinarily accorded such privileges;

b. Those other non-Korean armed forces in the ROK under the Unified Command which receive logistical support from the US armed forces, and their members;

c. Those non-Korean persons whose presence in the ROK is solely for the purpose of providing contract services financed by the US Government.

d. Those organizations which are present in the ROK primarily for the benefit and service of the US armed forces, such as the American Red Cross and the United Service Organizations, and their non-Korean personnel;

e. Dependents of the foregoing; and

f. Other persons and organizations with the express consent of the ROK Government.

43. The ROK Representative referred to the Eighth United States Army Regulation Number 60-1 (EA Reg. 60-1) of 22 February 1968, which embodied the best efforts of the US authorities to control abuse of PX privileges. Inclosure 1 to the regulation, "Post Exchange Ration Card Eligibility List and Issuing Agencies of Ration Cards," included the following categories of persons:

"(11) Retired US military personnel."

"(14) Widows (US citizens) who have not remarried and their dependents of the following: Members of the uniformed services, who die on extended active duty; members of reserve components, inactive duty for training, or inactive duty training; and retired personnel, provided they are authorized the use of MPC."

"(15 d) Dependents of US military personnel whose sponsor is not stationed in Korea. (With limitations, 16, 17, and 18)."

"(15 j) Dependents of retired military personnel."

"(15 k) Dependents otherwise authorized exchange and MPC privileges who are transient in Korea. Privileges will be limited to a period not exceeding 90 days."

80

44. The ROK Representative stated that, while recognizing human or humanitarian considerations involved in granting PX privileges to these categories of persons the Government of the ROK hardly finds relevant provisions in Article XIII, SOFA, which may be applicable for each of the categories. The ROK Representative requested that the US will take one of the following alternative actions for each of the categories;

a. To give satisfactory explanations for applicability of the SOFA provisions; or

b. To request express consent of the ROK Government in accordance with paragraph (f) of the Agreed Minutes to Article XIII.

45. The US Representative stated he was pleased to receive the views of the ROK Representative regarding the categories of personnel eligible to utilize Post Exchanges, in accordance with the Agreed Minute to Article XIII. The US armed forces in Korea have made every effort to cooperate closely with the ROK Government in the implementation of the SOFA in general, and specifically in this case, in the implementation of the Agreed Minute to Article XIII. It has been the United States' interpretation that the categories of personnel provided PX privileges, which is questioned in paragraph 3 of the ROK Representative's memorandum, in general are covered by subparagraph (a) of the Agreed Minute to Article XIII. As the chief US SOFA negotiator informed the ROK negotiators, at the twenty-first negotiating session on 3 May 1963, the phrase "ordinarily accorded such privileges" was the binding one in this subparagraph. He

specifically indicated that this phrase included retired military personnel, who were ordinarily accorded the privilege of utilizing nonappropriated fund facilities. The other categories of personnel questioned by the ROK Representative were also "ordinarily accorded such privileges." The US Representative stated his belief that implementation of this SOFA language had been accomplished by the USFK with prudence and careful consideration to all factors involved. However, the US component was happy for the opportunity to review these matters with officials of the ROK Government. If desired, the ROK and US SOFA Secretaries could arrange a meeting between appropriate officials in the two Governments, at which time US armed forces personnel could explain in detail the basis for the US position on these matters and views could be exchanged on this question.

46. The US component of the Joint Committee had taken the general position that it would not request the "express consent of the ROK Government" for exceptions in the granting of the privilege of using nonappropriated fund facilities, in subparagraph (f) of the Agreed Minute to Article XIII. The ROK Government has taken a generally similar position on this question, with the result that the number of individuals granted the privilege of the use of the nonappropriated fund organizations, in accordance with paragraph (f) of the Agreed Minute of Article XIII, has been extremely limited.

-24-

82

46. The ROK Representative thanked the US Representative for his explanation and indicated that he thought that the problem could be worked out with an amicable understanding. The US Representative indicated that many types of organizations had made requests for privileges ~~and the standard USFK reply was that it could not be granted.~~ He expressed the hope that any differences of opinion could be resolved through mutual consultation.

47. The US Representative noted for the record that the US SOFA Secretary has furnished the following information to the ROK SOFA Secretary in accordance with the provisions of the SOFA and Joint Committee decisions:

a. Five copies of reports on the US armed forces disposition of cases for the month of May 1968.

b. Twenty copies of the report of US armed forces personnel, the civilian component, invited contractors, and dependents entering or departing the ROK during the month of May 1968.

c. Two copies of revised lists of Korean employees of the Eighth US Army and US Navy, Korea, who are deemed essential in the event of a national emergency. These lists are furnished in advance to the ROK, in accordance with the provisions of paragraph 5(b) of SOFA Article XVII. Revised lists of those Korean employees deemed essential, who are working for the US Air Forces, Korea, and US invited contractors in Korea, will be furnished in the near future.

~~25~~

83

49. The ROK Representative stated that he was pleased to confirm that the ROK SOFA Secretary had duly received the documents enumerated, from the US SOFA Secretary.

50. The US Representative concurred in the proposal to hold the next meeting of the Joint Committee on Wednesday, 14 August, in the US SOFA Conference Room. He stated that he also would like to propose that any urgent actions which develop before the next meeting be handled as exigency actions by the two Representatives, in accordance with established procedures. In this connection, he noted that there was an urgent requirement for the completion of a task assigned to the Commerce Subcommittee on 28 April 1967 on the subject: "Tax Exemption on Procurement in the Republic of Korea, Article XVI." He expressed the hope that the recommendations on this task from the Subcommittee could be obtained prior to the next Joint Committee meeting, and that the two Representatives will approve the recommendations as an exigency action, if possible.

51. The ROK Representative agreed that actions on the task referred to, as well as other long pending tasks, should be expedited, and recommendations ~~such recommendations, as well as other urgent actions, would~~ could be dealt with as exigency matters, in accordance with Joint Committee procedures.

52. The ROK Representative proposed approval of the joint press release as developed by the US and ROK SOFA Secretaries. The US Representative agreed to accept the press release as proposed.

53. The meeting was adjourned at 1655 hours.

26 Inclosures

ROBERT J. FRIEDMAN YOON HA JONG

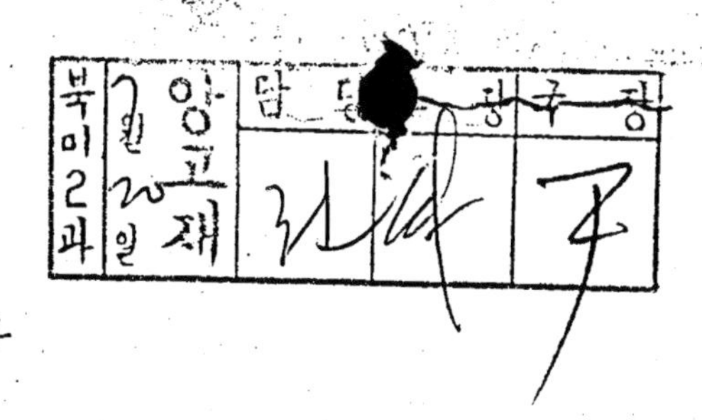

외 무 부

미이 720-　　　　　　　　　　　　1968. 7. 20.

수 신 : 배부처참조

참 조 :

제 목 : 한.미 합동위원회 회의록 송부

1. 한.미간 군대지위협정에 의하여 1968. 7. 3.에 개최된 한.미 합동위원회 제28차 회의의 회의록을 별첨 송부하오니 참고 하시기 바랍니다.

2. 본 회의록은 한.미 양측의 합의에 의하여서만 공개할 수 있는 문서이오니 유념하시기 바랍니다.

첨부 : 합동위원회 제28차 회의록　　부.

외 무 부 장 관

배부처 : 법무부장관 (법무실장, 검찰국장), 국방부장관 (기획국장, 시설국장), 재무부장관 (세관국장, 세제국장), 상공부장관 (상역국장), 노동청장 (노정국장), 교통부장관 (항공국장), 내무부장관 (치안국장), 주미 주일, 주중, 주비대사, 경제기획원장관(경제기획국장)

85

공　　란

공 란

공 란

공 란

17. The ROK Representative stated that the Joint Committee, at the Second Preliminary Meeting of the Working Group on 19 January 1967, directed development of procedures governing licensing and registration of privately owned vehicles pursuant to Article XXIV, paragraph 3, of the SOFA. The Transportation Subcommittee has finally presented its recommendations (Inclosure 12). The considerable delay was due mainly, among other things, to arrangements relative to insurance coverage of such vehicles. The ROK Representative noted that it is mutually understood that the expression "as expeditiously as possible," used in the last sentence of paragraph 5 of the recommended procedures in connection with the ROK notification after receipt of registration information, normally means within one or two working days. The ROK Representative proposed Joint Committee approval of the recommendation of the Transportation Subcommittee which was to take effect from the first day of the third month following the date of approval.

18. The US Representative stated he was happy to approve the recommendations of the Transportation Subcommittee with regard to procedures for licensing and registration of privately owned vehicles under Article XXIV. The US Representative is also pleased to note the assurances of

the ROK Representative that the ROK authorities will process the issuance of registration numbers expeditiously and will normally notify the United States recorder of the registration number to be assigned USFK personnel before the expiration of two working days.

19. The ROK Representative stated that paragraph 1, Article XXIV of the SOFA, provided that the Republic of Korea shall accept as valid, without a driving test or fee, the driving permit or license or military driving permit issued by the United States, or political subdivision thereof, to a member of the US armed forces, the civilian component, and their dependents. He stated that it was obvious that, for practical reasons, such licenses or permits should be converted into a form recognizable and readable by officials of the Republic of Korea. Therefore, the ROK Representative proposed assignment of a task to the Transportation Subcommittee to recommend ways and means to insure the aforementioned requirements (Inclosure 13). He further proposed that, in view of the close corelation between the licensing and registration of privately owned vehicles of personnel covered by the SOFA and the proposed task, the Transportation Subcommittee be instructed to complete this task before the effective date of the licensing and registration procedures for privately owned vehicles so that the two procedures would go into effect at the same time.

20. The US Representative concurred in the assignment of this task to the Transportation Subcommittee. He noted that the Government of the Republic of Korea had agreed that it shall accept as valid, without a driving test or fee, the driving permit or license or military driving permit issued by the United States, or political subdivision thereof, to a member of the US armed forces, the civilian component, and their dependents. The United States Forces, Korea have been planning to issue a revised military driving permit, which would be in both English and Korean, to facilitate its recognition and use by ROK officials. The US Representative also expressed the hope that this task could be expeditiously completed and timely recommendations made to enable the bilingual driving permit to be available prior to the implementation of the new procedures for licensing and registration of privately owned United States Forces, Korea vehicles, on 1 October 1968.

21. The US Representative stated that, at the eleventh meeting of the US-ROK Joint Committee on 13 July 1967, it was agreed that the Governments of the Republic of Korea and the United States would establish a permanent joint investigative organization for the purpose of effecting close US-ROK cooperation in the enforcement of all laws and regulations relating to abuse of privileges and illegal transactions.

22. The US Representative stated that the US and ROK SOFA Secretaries, in consultation with other appropriate officials in their respective Governments, developed "Operating Instructions for ROK-US Joint Investigations." These operating instructions were approved by the US and ROK Representatives at the nineteenth meeting of the Joint Committee on 21 December 1967. In the implementation of the Joint Committee procedures for the Operation of the ROK-US Joint Investigative Teams, questions arose concerning the disposition of goods confiscated by the Joint Investigative Teams. The US and ROK SOFA Secretaries held extensive consultations with appropriate officials in their respective Governments, in an effort to achieve mutual US-ROK agreement on procedures relating to disposition of goods confiscated by the Joint Investigative Teams. The result of the consultations was a proposed "Supplement to the Operating Instructions for ROK-US Joint Investigations," which has been developed during numerous conferences between US and ROK officials (Inclosure 14).

23. The US Representative stated that these supplemental instructions, which were believed to be fair and in the mutual interests of both the ROK and US Governments, were based on a careful analysis of the provisions of Article IX of the ROK-US SOFA. The US Representative expressed the belief that these supplemental instructions would greatly assist in the resolution of problems relating to difficult questions on disposition of goods confiscated by the Joint Investigative Teams. It was hoped that such questions could be resolved in a way which promoted ROK-US friendship and understanding, and which upheld the spirit of mutual cooperation in the defense of the ROK as embodied in the SOFA. The US Representative proposed Joint Committee approval of the "Supplement to the Operating Instructions for ROK-US Joint Investigations."

24. The ROK Representative stated he was pleased to concur in Joint Committee approval of the recommendations. However, he indicated he would like to emphasize that mere definitions, demarcations or clarifications, however precise and concrete they might be, could not by themselves insure success in this kind of operation. Friendship, spirit of cooperation, and above all mutual respect were essential elements for smooth working, as the US Representative had already mentioned. There was another aspect which called for equal emphasis. Customs laws or controls have an exclusiveness inherent to the concept of customs zones. This exclusiveness of customs matters was clearly recognized by the SOFA. It was to be noted that while Article VII referred to "the duty to respect local law," Article IX, which dealt specifically with customs duties, provided in paragraph 1 that save as provided in the Agreement, members of the US armed forces, the civilian component, and their dependents shall be subject to the laws and regulations administered by the customs authorities of the Republic of Korea. The ROK Representative expressed the hope that, in the implementation of the SOFA, the special nature of customs laws and regulations would always be kept in mind.

25. The ROK Representative presented a written memorandum on the subject of interpretation of Article XVI, paragraph 1, of the ROK-US SOFA (Inclosure 15). This memorandum was a formal reply to a US memorandum presented at the twenty-seventh meeting of the Joint Committee on 7 June, in which the US Representative expressed the view that restrictions supposedly contained in ROK Law 979 were inconsistent with the purpose and language of paragraph 1, Article XVI of the SOFA.

26. The ROK Representative wished to make the following points with regard to Law 979:

a. The Law does not provide for special licensing for performance of contracts with the US/UN armed forces. What the law provides for is simple registration for such contractors. Documents required for the registration are those needed to ensure minimum standards of responsibility for performance of contracts and also for minimum financial responsibility. For prospective contractors without past records a provisional registration status was provided for. As the detailed analysis given in the written memorandum indicates, the registration was not designed for any restrictive purpose, and was not restrictive in its nature.

b. The purpose of the law was to promote and encourage expansion of performance of contracts with the US/UN armed forces, and in order to achieve this objective the law envisaged:

(1) Establishment of a special committee to advise the Minister;

(2) Formation of associations of contractors by field of activity, in order to allow mutual cooperation and canalized representation;

(3) Publication of plans, which would provide a rational basis for individual planning and help eliminating uncertainties;

(4) Inspection of supplies for quality control when necessary;

(5) Award of special subsidies or compensations; and,

(6) Special exemptions from import restrictions.

c. It is to be noted that other administrative supports, not specifically mentioned in Law 979, such as assignment of special priorities in electricity and water supply, transportation, for labor, etc., are needed for orderly and efficient performance of procurement contracts, and the registration provided the framework for such administrative assistance.

d. The Law imposed on the registered contractors these obligations:

(1) Collecting contract payments within 30 days after completion of contracts through exchange banks in accordance with prescribed procedures, and to receive approval of the Minister of Commerce and Industry for disposition of sums remaining due at that date. Such a provision was inevitable under the current system of exchange controls, and was considered a legitimate concern of the Government of the Republic of Korea.

(2) Submission of reports as may be required by the Minister. These reports serve as a basis for rational formulation of policy and were considered not to constitute interference with the procurement activities of the USFK.

e. The only clause of the Law which may seem restrictive in appearance, Article VIII, provided for prior approval of the Minister on supply contracts of certain goods. This provision was conceived to preclude contracts detrimental to the economy or security of the Republic of Korea, and this concern was in conformity with the provisions of paragraph 2, Article XVI, of the SOFA. However, the provision proved unnecessary and remains unapplied. The Cabinet Ordinance referred to in the Law has not been formulated.

27. The ROK Representative, in summary, stated that it is the view of the Government of the ROK that Law 979 was not restrictive in its purpose or nature, and therefore there was no inconsistency between the Law and Article XVI of the SOFA. The Government of the ROK believed that the Law is in conformity with the best interests of both the ROK and US.

28. The US Representative thanked the ROK Representative for his memorandum and for his presentation regarding the interpretation of paragraph 1 of Article XVI. The US Representative stated he would reply in detail to the Republic of Korea presentation at an early meeting of the Joint Committee. It was obvious from the presentations of the US and ROK Representatives at the last two Joint Committee meetings that there were some differences of interpretation on this subject. Fortunately, Agreed Minute 2 to Article XVI provided:

> "2. The problem of a satisfactory settlement of difficulties with respect to procurement contracts arising out of differences between economic laws

These minutes are considered as official documents pertaining to both Governments and will not be released without mutual agreement.

and business practices of the Republic of Korea and the United States will be studied by the Joint Committee or other appropriate representatives."

The US Representative, in noting that in the interpretation of the Government of the Republic of Korea, "Law 979 is not restrictive in purpose or nature...," hoped that a mutually satisfactory resolution of the differences on this question could be achieved.

95

공 란

39. The ROK Representative presented recommendations of the Commerce Subcommittee. He stated that the city of Inchon was planning to have the services of Trans-Asia Engineering Associates, Inc., a USFK invited contractor, in connection with expansion of water supply system and active negotiations are underway (Inclosure 24). The plan raised the question of restriction contained in paragraph 2(b), Article XVI, SOFA. The Commerce Subcommittee recommended that, in this instance, the interpretation of the clause on which precedent was established with regard to Collins Radio Company at the twelfth meeting of the Joint Committee on 14 August 1967, and which removes the incompatibility between the invited contractor status and the other business with the ROK Government be applied to the Trans-Asia Engineering Associates, Inc. The ROK Representative proposed Joint Committee approval of the Subcommittee recommendations.

40. The US Representative concurred in the recommendation of the Commerce Subcommittee. He noted that the additional personnel working on contracts for the ROK Government will not be entitled to logistical ~~support and~~ privileges under the SOFA.

41. The ROK Representative stated that the next agenda item concerned implementation of Article XIII, SOFA, on which subject the ROK Representative presented a formal memorandum (Inclosure 25).

42. The ROK Representative noted that paragraph 1(a), Article XIII provided that military exchanges, messes, social clubs, theaters, newspapers and other nonappropriated fund organizations authorized and regulated by the US military authorities may be established by the US armed forces for the use of members of such forces, the civilian component and their dependents. He also noted that the Agreed Minute to Article XIII provides that the US armed forces may grant the use of the organizations referred to in paragraph 1 of Article XIII to:

a. Other officers or personnel of the US Government ordinarily accorded such privileges;

b. Those other non-Korean armed forces in the ROK under the Unified Command which receive logistical support from the US armed forces, and their members;

c. Those non-Korean persons whose presence in the ROK is solely for the purpose of providing contract services financed by the US Government.

d. Those organizations which are present in the ROK primarily for the benefit and service of the US armed forces, such as the American Red Cross and the United Service Organizations, and their non-Korean personnel;

e. Dependents of the foregoing; and

f. Other persons and organizations with the express consent of the ROK Government.

43. The ROK Representative referred to the Eighth United States Army Regulation Number 60-1 (EA Reg. 60-1) of 22 February 1968, which embodied the best efforts of the US authorities to control abuse of Post Exchange privileges. Inclosure 1 to the regulation, "Post Exchange Ration Card Eligibility List and Issuing Agencies of Ration Cards," included the following categories of persons:

"(11) Retired US military personnel."

"(14) Widows (US citizens) who have not remarried and their dependents of the following: Members of the uniformed services, who die on extended active duty;

members of reserve components, inactive duty for training, or inactive duty training; and retired personnel, provided they are authorized the use of MPC."

"(15 d) Dependents of US military personnel whose sponsor is not stationed in Korea. (With limitations, 16, 17, and 18)."

"(15 j) Dependents of retired military personnel."

"(15 k) Dependents otherwise authorized exchange and MPC privileges who are transient in Korea. Privileges will be limited to a period not exceeding 90 days."

44. The ROK Representative stated that, while recognizing human or humanitarian considerations involved in granting PX privileges to these categories of persons the Government of the ROK hardly finds relevant provisions in Article XIII, SOFA, which may be applicable for each of the categories. The ROK Representative requested that the US will take one of the following alternative actions for each of the categories;

a. To give satisfactory explanations for applicability of the SOFA provisions; or

b. To request express consent of the ROK Government in accordance with paragraph (f) of the Agreed Minutes to Article XIII.

45. The US Representative stated he was pleased to receive the views of the ROK Representative regarding the categories of personnel eligible to utilize Post Exchanges, in accordance with the Agreed Minute to Article XIII. The US armed forces in Korea have made every effort to cooperate closely with the ROK Government in the implementation of the SOFA in general, and specifically in this case, in the implementation of the Agreed Minute to Article XIII. It has been the United States' interpretation that the categories of personnel provided PX privileges, which is questioned in paragraph 3 of the ROK Representative's memorandum, in general are covered by subparagraph (a) of the Agreed Minute to Article XIII. As the chief US SOFA negotiator informed the ROK negotiators, at the twenty-first negotiating session on 3 May 1963, the phrase "ordinarily accorded such privileges" was the binding one in this subparagraph. He specifically indicated that this phrase included retired military personnel, who were ordinarily accorded the privilege of utilizing non-appropriated fund facilities. The other categories of personnel questioned by the ROK Representative were also "ordinarily accorded such privileges."

The US Representative stated his belief that implementation of this SOFA language had been accomplished by the USFK with prudence and careful consideration to all factors involved. However, the US component was happy for the opportunity to review these matters with officials of the ROK Government. If desired, the ROK and US SOFA Secretaries could arrange a meeting between appropriate officials in the two Governments, at which time US armed forces personnel could explain in detail the basis for the US position on these matters and views could be exchanged on this question.

46. The US component of the Joint Committee had taken the general position that it would not request the "express consent of the ROK Government" for exceptions in the granting of the privilege of using nonappropriated fund facilities, in subparagraph (f) of the Agreed Minute to Article XIII. The ROK Government has taken a generally similar position on this question, with the result that the number of individuals granted the privilege of the use of the nonappropriated fund organizations, in accordance with paragraph (f) of the Agreed Minute of Article XIII, has been extremely limited.

47. The ROK Representative thanked the US Representative for his explanation and indicated that he thought that the problem could be worked out with an amicable understanding. He further stated that as far as the ROK Government was concerned, it did not matter if USFK requested "express consent" of the ROK Government for exceptional granting of access to the nonappropriated fund organizations under paragraph (f) of the Agreed Minute to Article XIII. The US Representative indicated that many types of organizations had made requests for privileges but were denied in each instance. He expressed the hope that any differences of opinion could be resolved through mutual consultation.

48. The US Representative noted for the record that the US SOFA Secretary has furnished the following information to the ROK SOFA Secretary in accordance with the provisions of the SOFA and Joint Committee decisions:

a. Five copies of reports on the US armed forces disposition of cases for the month of May 1968.

b. Twenty copies of the report of US armed forces personnel, the civilian component, invited contractors, and dependents entering or departing the ROK during the month of May 1968.

c. Two copies of revised lists of Korean employees of the Eighth US Army and US Navy, Korea, who are deemed essential in the event of a national emergency. These lists are furnished in advance to the ROK, in accordance with the provisions of paragraph 5(b) of SOFA Article XVII. Revised lists of those Korean employees deemed essential, who are working for the US Air Forces, Korea, and US invited contractors in Korea, will be furnished in the near future.

49. The ROK Representative stated that he was pleased to confirm that the ROK SOFA Secretary had duly received the documents enumerated, from the US SOFA Secretary.

50. The US Representative concurred in the proposal to hold the next meeting of the Joint Committee on Wednesday, 14 August, in the US SOFA Conference Room. He stated that he also would like to propose that any urgent actions which develop before the next meeting be handled as exigency actions by the two Representatives, in accordance with established procedures. In this connection, he noted that there was an urgent requirement for the completion of a task assigned to the Commerce Subcommittee on 28 April 1967 on the subject: "Tax Exemption on Procurement in the Republic of Korea, Article XVI." He expressed the hope that the recommendations on this task from the Subcommittee could be obtained prior to the next Joint Committee meeting, and that the two Representatives will approve the recommendations as an exigency action, if possible.

51. The ROK Representative agreed that actions on the task referred to, as well as other long-pending tasks, should be expedited and recommendations could be dealt with as exigency matters, in accordance with Joint Committee procedures.

52. The ROK Representative proposed approval of the joint press release as developed by the US and ROK SOFA Secretaries. The US Representative agreed to accept the press release as proposed.

53. The meeting was adjourned at 1655 hours.

26 Inclosures

YOON HA JONG REPUBLIC OF KOREA REPRESENTATIVE	for ROBERT J. FRIEDMAN LIEUTENANT GENERAL UNITED STATES AIR FORCE UNITED STATES REPRESENTATIVE

28th JC
3 July 68

101

These minutes are considered as official documents pertaining to both Governments and will not be released without mutual agreement.

AGENDA FOR THE TWENTY-EIGHTH MEETING OF THE ROK-US JOINT COMMITTEE 1500 HOURS, 3 JULY 1968, ROK CAPITOL BUILDING

I Assignment of Additional Tasks to Facilities and Areas Subcommittee

1. Seven normal and eight exigency tasks - US Presentation
2. One task - ROK Presentation

II Assignment of Task to Criminal Jurisdiction Subcommittee - US Presentation

III Recommendations of Facilities and Areas Subcommittee

1. Two recommendations - ROK Presentation
2. Eight recommendations - US Presentation

IV Recommendations of the Transportation Subcommittee - ROK Presentation

V Assignment of Task to Transportation Subcommittee - ROK Presentation

VI Recommendations to Joint Committee on Disposition of Goods Confiscated by Joint Investigative Teams - US Presentation

VII ROK Reply to US Memorandum to Joint Committee on Interpretation of Paragraph 1, Article XVI - ROK Presentation

VIII US Memorandum on ROK Exercise of Criminal Jurisdiction - US Presentation

IX US Memoranda on Designation of USFK Invited Contractors - US Presentation

28th JC (Incl 1)
3 July 68

102

These minutes are c●sidered as official documents ●taining to both Governments and will not be released without mutual agreement.

X Recommendations of Commerce Subcommittee - Trans-Asia Engineering Associates, Inc. - ROK Presentation

XI ROK Memorandum on Implementation of Article XIII - ROK Presentation

XII Memoranda Presented to the ROK Government by the US in the Implementation of the SOFA - US Presentation

XIII Proposed Time of Next Meeting - Wednesday, 14 August 1968, US SOFA Conference Room

XIV Agreement on Joint Press Release

XV Adjourn

28th JC (Incl 1)
3 July 68

103

공 란

공 란

공 란

공 란

공　　란

These minutes are considered as official documents pertaining to both Governments and will not be released without mutual agreement.

JOINT COMMITTEE
UNDER
THE REPUBLIC OF KOREA AND THE UNITED STATES
STATUS OF FORCES AGREEMENT

3 July 1968

MEMORANDUM TO: Chairmen, Criminal Jurisdiction Subcommittee

SUBJECT: Situation in the vicinity of Osan Air Base

1. Reference is made to the minutes of the twenty-sixth meeting of the Joint Committee, which was specifically called to discuss the situation in the vicinity of Osan Air Base.

2. It is requested that you review the matters presented at the twenty-sixth meeting of the Joint Committee and submit to the Joint Committee recommendations which you consider appropriate.

YOON HA JONG	for ROBERT J. FRIEDMAN
Republic of Korea Representative	Lieutenant General
	United States Air Force
	United States Representative

28th JC (Incl 5)
3 July 68

공 란

공 란

공 란

공　　　란

공 란

공 란

공 란

COPY

These minutes are considered as official documents pertaining to both Governments and will not be released without mutual agreement.

MINISTRY OF TRANSPORTATION

27 April 1968

AIR SPACE 1555.5

SUBJECT: Request for Coordination Concerning Limitation on Construction of Aviation Obstacles

TO: Distribution

1. Reference is made to TAA 1555.5-11739, 22 September 1967.

2. We have made considerable achievement so far regarding limitation on construction of aviation obstacles. However, it is recognized that implementation of the regulation has not been satisfactory in some aspects, as you will read in the letter attached. Therefore, when you need to construct building near the airfield, you are requested to obtain approval from this Ministry prior to the construction, in order to help each other through mutual efforts for safe aviation to protect human lives and properties in this country.

Incl: 1. RE 947.01-1119, 16 April 1968 (1 copy)

2. Letter from USFK (1 copy)

3. Joint Committee Memo (1 copy)

4. Map of Standard Limitation on Aviation Obstacles (1 copy)

MINISTER OF TRANSPORTATION

117

28th JC (Incl 1 to Incl 8)
3 July 68

COPY

These minutes are considered as official documents pertaining to both Governments and will not be released without mutual agreement.

MINISTRY OF TRANSPORTATION

3 May 1968

AIR SPACE 1555.5-717

SUBJECT: Request for Preventive Measures on Construction of Obstructing Facilities Near Airfield Area

TO: Minister of National Defense

1. This is a reply to your letter, RE 947.01-1119, 16 April 1968.

2. In accordance with Article 40, 41, and the Implementing Regulation Article 133, 134, 135 and 140, of the ROK Aviation Law, it is under responsibility of this Ministry to control over aviation obstacles;

3. You are being informed that we have notified to authorities concerned, regarding securing of safe approach zone at the A-805 Airfield, Taegu;

4. And you will be notified as to the actions taken by the authorities concerned.

Incl: 1. Air Space 1555.5-669, April 28, 1968 (1 copy)

2. Map of Standard Limitation on Aviation Obstacles (1 copy)

MINISTER OF TRANSPORTATION

28th JC (Incl 7 to Incl 8)
3 July 68

118

These minutes are considered as official documents pertaining to both Governments and will not be released without mutual agreement.

REPUBLIC OF KOREA - UNITED STATES
FACILITIES AND AREAS SUBCOMMITTEE

20 June 1968

MEMORANDUM FOR: THE JOINT COMMITTEE

1. Subcommittee members:

United States	Republic of Korea
COL I. M. Rice, Chairman	MG KIM Mook, Chairman
LTC J. B. Carrick, USAFCSK	Mr. SONG Yong Tai
LTC Robert E. Graf, J4, USFK	Mr. SHIN Chung Sup
MAJ James B. Hoodenpyle, USAF	Mr. LEE Kihl Choo
Mr. Francis K. Cook, J5, USFK	Mr. LEE Soon Dong
Mr. Richard Rose, USAEDFE	Mr. LEE Moon Sup
Mrs. Betty H. Bowman, 8th Army	Mr. LEE Man Chun
	Mr. CHANG Kyong Shik
	Mr. CHA Sang Chun
	Mr. KIM Byoung Chan
	Mr. CHONG Young Hoon
	Mr. CHOI Chung Hwan
	Mr. NO Yong Goo
	Mr. PARK Moh Soo
	LTC KANG Jong Kuk
	Mr. KANG Hong Suk

2. Subject of Recommendation: Request to Convert to an Exclusive Use Basis Land Currently Held as a Perpetual Restrictive Easement (Reference Joint Committee Memorandum, same subject, dated 17 May 1968).

3. Recommendation: Request to convert to an exclusive use basis 0.643 acre of land currently held as a perpetual restrictive easement (portion of SAC-685) located at Bakdal-ni, Anyang-up, Shihung-gun, Kyonggi-do, has been accepted by the Ministry of National Defense. This real estate is required to construct a helicopter landing pad. Preliminary approval for construction was given by the Ministry of National Defense on 31 May 1968. The Ministry of National Defense and the Far East District Engineer will be requested to prepare the necessary documents. It is recommended that the Joint Committee, SOFA, approve this conversion.

119

28th JC (Incl 9)
3 July 68

4. Security Classification:

Unclassified.

COLONEL I. M. RICE
Chairman, United States Component
Facilities and Areas Subcommittee

for MAJOR GENERAL KIM Mook
Chairman, Republic of Korea Component
Facilities and Areas Subcommittee

APPROVED BY THE JOINT COMMITTEE ON
3 JULY 1968 AT TWENTY-EIGHTH MEETING

YOON HA JONG
Republic of Korea Representative

for ROBERT J. FRIEDMAN
Lieutenant General
United States Air Force
United States Representative

2

120

28th JC (Incl 9)
3 July 68

These minutes are considered as official documents pertaining to both Governments and will not be released without mutual agreement.

REPUBLIC OF KOREA - UNITED STATES
FACILITIES AND AREAS SUBCOMMITTEE

20 June 1968

MEMORANDUM FOR: THE JOINT COMMITTEE

1. Subcommittee members:

United States	Republic of Korea
COL I. M. Rice, Chairman	MG KIM Mook, Chairman
LTC J. B. Carrick, USAFCSK	Mr. SONG Yong Tai
LTC Robert E. Graf, J4, USFK	Mr. SHIN Chung Sup
MAJ James B. Hoodenpyle, USAF	Mr. LEE Kihl Choo
Mr. Francis K. Cook, J5, USFK	Mr. LEE Soon Dong
Mr. Richard Rose, USAEDFE	Mr. LEE Moon Sup
Mrs. Betty H. Bowman, 8th Army	Mr. LEE Man Chun
	Mr. CHANG Kyong Shik
	Mr. CHA Sang Chun
	Mr. KIM Byoung Chan
	Mr. CHONG Young Hoon
	Mr. CHOI Chung Hwan
	Mr. NO Yong Goo
	Mr. PARK Moh Soo
	LTC KANG Jong Kuk
	Mr. KANG Hong Suk

2. Subject of Recommendation: Request for Acquisition of Real Estate, Acquisition of Temporary Use Permits, and Extension of Temporary Use Permits (Reference Joint Committee Memorandum, para 3b, same subject, dated 25 April 1968).

3. Recommendation: Request for acquisition of a temporary use permit for 17.60 acres of land at Hwajon-ni, Shindo-myon, Koyang-gun, Kyonggi-do, for the conduct of air landing exercises during the period 1 May 1968 through 30 April 1969, has been mutually agreed upon by the Ministry of National Defense and the Eighth US Army in accordance with the jointly signed agreement attached as Inclosure 1. The Ministry of National Defense and the Far East District will be requested to prepare the necessary documents. It is recommended that the Joint Committee, SOFA, approve acquisition of this temporary use permit.

28th JC (Incl 10)
3 July 68

121

4. Security Classification:

Unclassified.

COLONEL I. M. RICE
Chairman, United States Component
Facilities and Areas Subcommittee

for MAJOR GENERAL KIM Mook
Chairman, Republic of Korea Component
Facilities and Areas Subcommittee

1 Incl
Conditions of Agreement

APPROVED BY THE JOINT COMMITTEE ON
3 JULY 1968 AT TWENTY-EIGHTH MEETING

YOON HA JONG
Republic of Korea Representative

for ROBERT J. FRIEDMAN
Lieutenant General
United States Air Force
United States Representative

28th JC (Incl 10)
3 July 68

122

These minutes are considered as official documents pertaining to both Governments and will not be released without mutual agreement.

HEADQUARTERS
EIGHTH UNITED STATES ARMY
APO 96301

27 May 1968

EAEN-RE

SUBJECT: Conditions of Agreement for Suseak Airfield - Task 193
제 목: 수색 비행장 협정에 대한 조건 과제 193호

FASC, US Component 수신: 미국 시설및 지역 분과 위원회
ATTN: Secretary 참조: 비서실
APO 96301 군우: 96301

1. PURPOSE: The purpose of this mutually agreeable proposal is to set forth certain conditions for temporary acquisition of Suseak airstrip.
목적: 본 상호 협정 요청의 목적은 수색 비행장 임시 취득의 조건을 설정하는데 있음.

2. AUTHORITY: US authorization for preparation of this proposal is contained in SOFA Meeting Minutes of 7 May 1968, Task 193.
권한: 본 요청서 작성의 미국측 권한은 1968년 5월 7일 군대 지위 협정 의사록 제 193항에 수해 있음.

3. AGREEMENT: This agreement was developed between the working group membership representing both ROK and US Chairmen. This agreement is submitted to the FASC, subject to their review and approval.
협정: 본 협정은 한미 양측 작업위원장의 참석하에 체결 되었음. 본 협정서는 검토와 승인을 받기 위하여 시설및 지역 분과 위원회에 제출함.

4. CONDITIONS: Acquisition of the area will be acquired under the following stipulations:
조건: 차 지역의 취득은 아래와 같은 조건하에 취득 될것임.

28th JC (Incl 1 to Incl 10)
3 July 68

123

EAEN-RE 27 May 1968

SUBJECT: Conditions of Agreement for Suseak Airfield - Task 193

a. That the acquisition of this landing strip will not interfere
가. 활주로의 취득은 국립 항공학교의 훈련이나 기타 다른 활동에
with the training or other National Aviation College activities.
지장을 주지 않을것임.

b. Use of the landing strip will only be used when an occasion arises,
나. 활주로의 사용은 한미 군대 지위협정 시설및 지역 분과위원장이
which would be considered as urgent by the US and ROK Chairmen of the
긴박하다고 인정되는 사건이 발생하였을 때에만 사용함.
Facilities and Areas Subcommittee.

c. In the event that an occasional landing is necessary, coordination
다. 특별한 착륙 비행이 필요할시에는 사전에 미국측과 국립 항공학교간에
between the US and the Aviation College will be made prior to the landing.
협의를 할것임.

d. The area to be acquired will contain 14.77 acres as per attached
마. 본 취득지역은 별첨도면과 같이 14.77에이카에 한함.
map.

-27. 68

Mr. CHO Young Kun
ROK Chairman
조 영 근

27 May 68

Mr. Stanley F. O'HOP
US Chairman
에스. 에프. 오합

2.

124

These minutes are considered as official documents pertaining to both Governments and will not be released without mutual agreement.

REPUBLIC OF KOREA - UNITED STATES
FACILITIES AND AREAS SUBCOMMITTEE

20 June 1968

MEMORANDUM FOR: THE JOINT COMMITTEE

1. Subcommittee members:

United States	Republic of Korea
COL I. M. Rice, Chairman	MG KIM Mook, Chairman
LTC J. B. Carrick, USAFCSK	Mr. SONG Yong Tai
LTC Robert E. Graf, J4, USFK	Mr. SHIN Chung Sup
MAJ James B. Hoodenpyle, USAF	Mr. LEE Kihl Choo
Mr. Francis K. Cook, J5, USFK	Mr. LEE Soon Dong
Mr. Richard Rose, USAEDFE	Mr. LEE Moon Sup
Mrs. Betty H. Bowman, 8th Army	Mr. LEE Man Chun
	Mr. CHANG Kyong Shik
	Mr. CHA Sang Chun
	Mr. KIM Byoung Chan
	Mr. CHONG Young Hoon
	Mr. CHOI Chung Hwan
	Mr. NO Yong Goo
	Mr. PARK Moh Soo
	LTC KANG Jong Kuk
	Mr. KANG Hong Suk

2. Subject of Recommendation: Requests for Acquisition of Real Estate and Extension of a Temporary Use Permit (Reference Joint Committee Memorandum, paras 2a, c, e, g, and 3, same subject, dated 7 June 1968).

3. Recommendations:

a. Request for acquisition of 1.19 acres of land at San, 152, 262-1, Lim Bukun-ni, Hajum-myon, Kanghwa-gun, Kyonggi-do, required for erection of a security fence around the existing STRATCOM communications site has been accepted by the Ministry of National Defense. The Ministry of National Defense and the Far East District Engineer will be requested to prepare the necessary documents. It is recommended that the Joint Committee, SOFA, approve this acquisition.

28th JC (Incl 11)
3 July 68

125

b. Request for acquisition of 1.98 acres of cultivated land at #322 Chung-dong, Tongnae-ku, Pusan City, required for a storage area has been accepted by the Ministry of National Defense. The Ministry of National Defense and the Far East District Engineer will be requested to prepare the necessary documents. It is recommended that the Joint Committee, SOFA, approve this acquisition.

c. Request for acquisition of 0.23 acre of land at Kanung-dong, Uijongbu-si, Kyonggi-do, required for expansion of Camp Albany Compound (IC-164), has been accepted by the Ministry of National Defense. The Ministry of National Defense and the Far East District Engineer will be requested to prepare the necessary documents. It is recommended that the Joint Committee, SOFA, approve this acquisition.

d. Request for acquisition of an easement for 0.85 acre of land located near the village of Pangchung-ni, Kwangtan-myon, Paju-gun, Kyonggi-do, has been accepted by the Ministry of National Defense. This easement is required for accomplishment of an erosion control project. The Ministry of National Defense and the Far East District Engineer will be requested to prepare the necessary documents. It is recommended that the Joint Committee, SOFA, approve this acquisition.

e. Request for extension of a Temporary Use Permit, CAV-T-9, consisting of 145 acres of land, from 7 May 1968 to 6 May 1969 for continued use as a field training area has been accepted by the Ministry of National Defense. The Ministry of National Defense and the Far East District Engineer will be requested to prepare the necessary documents. It is recommended that the Joint Committee, SOFA, approve this extension.

4. Security Classification: Unclassified.

I. M. Rice	Song Yong Tai
COLONEL I. M. RICE	for MAJOR GENERAL KIM Mook
Chairman, United States Component	Chairman, Republic of Korea Component
Facilities and Areas Subcommittee	Facilities and Areas Subcommittee

APPROVED BY THE JOINT COMMITTEE ON 3 JULY 1968 AT TWENTY-EIGHTH MEETING

Yoon Ha Jong	M. McMassie Capt. USN
YOON HA JONG	for **ROBERT J. FRIEDMAN**
Republic of Korea Representative	**Lieutenant General**
	United States Air Force
	United States Representative

28th JC (Incl 11)
3 July 68

126

These minutes are considered as official documents pertaining to both Governments and will not be released without mutual agreement.

US-ROK Transportation Subcommittee
Under the
US-ROK Joint Committee
Established by Article XXVIII of the
Status of Forces Agreement (SOFA)

13 June 1968

TO: US-ROK SOFA JOINT COMMITTEE

1. Subcommittee Members:

United States	Republic of Korea
COL R. R. Fishel, USAF	Mr. KIM Wan Soo
LTC B. L. Ross, USAF	Mr. KIM Doo Bang
LTC P. E. Jones, USAF	Mr. JUHN Hung Woo
LTC Walter Duke, Jr., USA	Mr. LEE Yong Kul
LTC H. A. Mailander, USAF	Mr. WON Chi Ong
LTC J. E. Dunn, USAF	Mr. KIM Mun Sun
LTC D. T. Craighead, USA	Mr. PARK Jin Sun
LTC F. E. Collier, USAF	Mr. LIM Young Taek
CDR C. J. Cush, USN	Mr. SEO Sang Moon
MAJ J. G. Devlin, USAF	Mr. KO Chung Sam
CPT R. R. Rubel, USAF	Mr. KIM Jae Yun
Mr. Darrel Charest	Mr. HUH Hyuk Jong
	LT COL LEE Chin Sung, ROKA
	Mr. NOH Sung Ho
	LT COL LEE Jin Woo, ROKAF
	Mr. OH Myong Too

2. Subject of recommendation: Procedures governing licensing and registration of privately owned vehicles pursuant to Article XXIV, para 3, of the Status of Forces Agreement. The United States and Republic of Korea Representatives on 19 January 1967 directed development of these procedures.

3. Recommendation: The Transportation Subcommittee recommends that the conditions and procedures set forth in the attachment be approved.

28th JC (Incl 12)
3 July 68

127

These minutes are considered as official documents pertaining to both Governments and will not be released without mutual agreement.

4. Security Classification: None.

for KIM WAN SOO Republic of Korea Chairman Transportation Subcommittee	ROBERT R. FISHEL Colonel, USAF United States Chairman Transportation Subcommittee

1 Attachment
as

APPROVED BY THE JOINT COMMITTEE ON
3 JULY 1968 AT TWENTY-EIGHTH MEETING

YOON HA JONG Republic of Korea Representative	for ROBERT J. FRIEDMAN Lieutenant General United States Air Force United States Representative

2

28th JC (Incl 12)
3 July 68

128

These minutes are considered as official documents pertaining to both Governments and will not be released without mutual agreement.

LICENSING AND REGISTRATION OF PRIVATELY OWNED VEHICLES OF UNITED STATES FORCES, KOREA, PERSONNEL

주한 미군요원 사유차량 면허 및 등록

1. Introduction. Licensing and registration of vehicles privately owned
1. 서언. 미 합중국 군대 구성원, 군속 및 그들의 가족의 사유
by members of the United States armed forces, the civilian component,
차량의 면허 및 등록은 한미 군대지위협정 제 24조에 따라 행한다.
and their dependents will be accomplished in accordance with Article

XXIV of the Republic of Korea - United States Status of Forces Agree-

ment. In implementation of the provisions of this Article, the following
동조의 규정을 시행함에 있어서 하기조건, 절차 및 문서기록 방식을
conditions, procedures, and documentation will apply.
적용한다.

2. License Plates and Seals. The Government of the Republic of Korea
2. 면허감찰 및 봉인. 대한민국 정부는 그가 정하는 모양과 규격에
will produce a requisite number of license plates and seals to a design
따라 필요한 수의 면허감찰과 봉인을 만든다.
and specification of its choice. The license plates and seals will be
면허감찰과 봉인은 대한민국 정부의
furnished to appropriate authorities of United States Forces, Korea, by
관계당국이 주한 미군 관계당국에 제공하되 제작실비를 초과하지않는 가격으로
appropriate authorities of the Republic of Korea at a price not to exceed
제공한다.
the actual cost of manufacture.

3. Insurance. Liability insurance in an amount not less than that specified
3. 보험. 사유차량을 등록함에 있어서는 대한민국 법령에 규정되어 있는
in Republic of Korea law is required for registration of privately owned
액면이상의 배상책임 보험에 들어야 한다.
vehicles. Such insurance will be with a Republic of Korea or United
그와같은 보험은 대한민국의 보험회사 또는 대한민국을 배상업무
States insurance company which extends claims coverage to the Republic
대상지역으로 하고있으며 또 한국내 업무 대상자로서 대한민국 정부가 인정하는
of Korea and is represented in the Republic of Korea by a company or
회사 또는 대리인을 가진 미 합중국의 보험회사에 가입하여야 한다.
agent accredited by the Government of the Republic of Korea. The name
보험회사
of the insurance company representative, the policy number, and the
대표자명, 가입번호 및 유효기간을 대한민국 정부에 제공하는 등록서류에
expiration date will be reflected on the registration information furnished
표시하여야 한다.
to the Republic of Korea.

28th JC (Incl 1 to Incl 12)
3 July 68

129

ATTACHMENT 1

4. Safety Inspections. Privately owned vehicles will be inspected in
4. 안전 검사. 사유차량은 대한민국 법령에 따라 검사를 한다.
accordance with Republic of Korea law. The inspections will be performed
차량검사는 인천, 서울, 부산,
on United States facilities at Inchon, Seoul, Pusan, or Taegu by inspectors
대구소재 미군시설에서 대한민국 정부당국 또는 미 합중국 정부당국에 의해서
certified by authorities of the Republic of Korea Government or by
자격인정을 받은 검사관이 행한다.
authorities of the United States Government. The inspector will issue a
검사관은 검사를 완료하였다는
certificate to the owner indicating that the vehicle inspection has been
증명서를 소유자에게 발부한다 (별첨 1 참조).
accomplished (Inclosure 1). A list of the names of those inspectors
미 합중국 당국은 미 합중국 당국에 의해서
certified by authorities of the United States Government will be furnished
자격인정을 받은 이들 검사관의 명단을 교통부에 있는 대한민국 정부당국자에게
by authorities of the United States Government to the Republic of Korea
제출한다.
authorities in the Ministry of Transportation.

5. Procedures to Register Privately Owned Vehicles of United States
5. 주한 미군요원의 사유차량 등록절차.
Forces, Korea, Personnel. Within ten days after acceptance of the vehicle
차량소유자 또는 소유자로 부터 권한을
by the owner or his authorized agent at the port of entry, the owner or his
위임받은 대리인은 입국항에서 차량을 수령한후 10일 이내에 인천, 서울, 부산,
authorized agent will take the vehicle to one of the United States Forces,
대구에 위치한 주한 미군 차량기록관에게 차량과 함께 출두하여야 한다.
Korea, motor vehicle recorders who will be located at Inchon, Seoul,

Pusan, and Taegu. The owner or his agent must have in his possession
소유자 또는 그의 대리인은 당해차량의 소유증명서 및
proof of ownership and insurance policy. At the recorder location, the
보험가입증서를 소지하여야 한다. 기록장소에서 안전검사를
safety inspection will be accomplished and the information necessary for
실시하며 차량등록에 필요한 사항을 첨부한 양식에 기재한다 (별첨 2 참조).
vehicle registration will be recorded on the attached form (Inclosure 2).

The recorder will forward the registration information to the Republic of
기록관은 등록관계 자료를 대한민국 당국앞으로 제출하면 대한민국 당국자는
Korea authorities who will review and record the information and will, as
이를 검토하고 기록한후, 가능한한 신속히 미 합중국 기록관에게 해당차량의
expeditiously as possible, notify the United States recorder of the registration
등록번호 또는 등록에 필요한 자료가운데 불비한 점이 있을 때에는 그것을
number to be assigned or of any deficiencies noted in the registration
통고한다.
information.

28th JC (Incl 1 to Incl 12)
3 July 68

170

6. Cancellation of Registration. Vehicle registration under this Agreement
6. 등록 취소. 본 합의에 의한 등록은 다음과 같은 경우에
will be cancelled when:
취소된다:

(1) The owner departs the Republic of Korea and desires to
(1) 차량소유자가 대한민국을 출국하면서 그 차량을 수출하고져
export his vehicle;
할때,

(2) The vehicle is stolen, abandoned, lost, or dismantled (exclud-
(2) 차량이 도난, 유기망실 또는 분해된 경우 (개조 또는 분해검사를
ing dismantling for remodeling or overhauling);
위해서 분해할 경우는 제외),

(3) Use of the vehicle is discontinued;
(3) 차량사용이 정지될 경우,

(4) The body of the vehicle is different from that at the time of
(4) 차량의 차체가 등록당시의 것과 상이할때, 또는
previous registration; or

(5) The vehicle is transferred to another person not entitled to
(5) 군대지위 협정에 의하여 비과세·수입특권이 부여되어 있지 않은
duty-free import privileges under the Status of Forces
자에게 차량이 양도될 경우.
Agreement.

7. Transfer of Title. When transfer of ownership is to be accomplished
7. 명의 이전. 미 합중국 군대 구성원, 군속 및 그들의 가족사이에서
between members of the United States armed forces, the civilian component,
차량의 소유권이 이전되는 경우, 양 당사자는 주한 미군 차량기록소 사무실에
or their dependents, both persons will report to the United States Forces,
보고하여야 하며 그곳에서 전 소유자는 대한민국 당국에 제출할 등록취소
Korea, motor vehicle recorder office where the previous owner will prepare
신청서를 작성하며, 새로운 소유자는 제 5항에 의하여 신규등록 신청을 한다.
a request for cancellation of registration to be forwarded to the Republic

of Korea authorities and the new owner will apply for new registration as

outlined in paragraph 5.

8. Mutilated or Lost License Plates. When plates have been mutilated to
8. 훼손 또는 망실된 면허감찰. 표식이 분별할수 없을정도로,
the extent that identifying information is not discernible, or one or more
감찰이 훼손되거나, 또는 하나 또는 그 이상의 감찰이 망실 되었을때, 소유자
plates are lost, the owner or his authorized agent will be required to appear
또는 그의 대리인은 주한 미군 차량기록관 사무실에 출두하여야 한다.
at an office of the United States Forces, Korea, motor vehicle recorder.

28th JC (Incl 1 to Incl 12)
3 July 68

1371

New registration will be accomplished in accordance with paragraph 5.
신규등록은 제 5항의 절차에 따라 이루워 진다.

9. License Plate Seals. Within ten days after vehicle license plates and
9. 면허감찰 봉인. 차량면허 감찰 및 봉인이 발급되고난 후 10일
seals are issued, the owner or his authorized agent will take the vehicle
이내에 차량소유자 또는 그의 대리인은 대한민국 정부가 지정한 대표자가
to a designated representative of the Republic of Korea Government to have
있는곳에 차량과 함께 출두하여 정식 봉인을 받는다.
the official seals affixed thereon. Affixing of the seals will complete the
봉인부착으로서 사유차량의 정식등록이
official registration of a privately owned vehicle. The official seals will
완료된다. 정식 봉인부착은
be affixed at no charge to the owner. Republic of Korea Government
무료로 한다. 대한민국 정부의 대표는 인천,
representatives will perform this service at Inchon, Seoul, Pusan, and
서울, 부산 및 대구에서 봉인업무를 행한다.
Taegu.

10. Reporting Vehicle Registration Information to the Republic of Korea.
10. 대한민국에의 차량등록 자료 보고.
At the close of business each day, United States Forces, Korea, authorities
매 근무일이 끝날무렵, 주한 미군 관계 당국자는 매 신규 신청서 및 취소문서를
will send documentation of each new application and cancellation to Republic
대한민국 당국으로 발송한다.
of Korea authorities. A consolidated list of names of owners of privately
사유차량의 소유자의 종합명단과 여기에서 그와같은
owned vehicles and other information required herein to effect the licensing
차량의 면허 및 등록에 필요하다고 정한 기타자료는 미 8군 헌병사령관을 통하여
and registration of such vehicles shall be furnished monthly to the Republic
대한민국 당국앞으로 월 별로 제출한다.
of Korea authorities through the Provost Marshal, Eighth United States Army.

11. Effective Date. The effective date for the implementation of the above
11. 발효일자. 상기 절차의 시행 발효일은 합동위원회에서 승인이 난
procedures will be the first day of the third month following the date of
날자로 부터 셋째번째 달의 첫날로부터 한다.
approval by the Joint Committee.

28th JC (Incl 1 to Incl 12)
3 July 68

132

제33호서식
(Form No. 33)

제 호
(No.)

자 동 차 검 사 증
(VEHICLE INSPECTION CERTIFICATE)

년 월 일
(Year) (Month) (Day)

도로운송 차량법의 소정규정에 의하여 검사를 받았음을 증명함.
(This is to certify that this vehicle has been duly inspected in accordance with the ROK Vehicle Law.)

서명권한자: ______________ 인
(Signature of Certifying Official) (Seal)

자동차등록번호 또는 차량번호: (Registration No.)		용 도: (Purpose of Use)	_사업용(Business Use) _관 용(Official Use) _자가용(Private Use)
차 량 중 량: (Weight)	Kg	차 명: (Make)	
차 량 정 원: (Passenger Capacity)		형 식: (Body Type and Year)	
최대 적재량: (Maximum Loading Capacity)	Kg	자동차의 종별: (Classification)	
차량 중량: (Weight of Vehicle)	Kg	원동기 형식: (Motor Type)	
길 이: (Length)	M	총배기량및정격출력: (Exhaust Capacity or Horse Power)	
넓 이: (Width)	M	기 통 수: (No. of Cylinders)	
높 이: (Height)	M	차 대 번 호: (Body No.)	
특수자동차인경우: (Special vehicle)			

유 효 기 간: (Effective Date)	자 년 월 일 (From)(Year)(Month)(Day)	지 년 월 일 (To) (Year) (Month) (Day)
		28th JC (Incl 1 to Incl 1 to Incl 12) 3 July 68

133 132

소유자의 성명 또는 명칭 및 주소: (Name and Address of Owner)	
사용 본거지: (Place of Use of Vehicle))	
법 41조에 의한 조치 내용: (Actions taken in accordance with Article 41 of the ROK Vehicle Law)	
비 고: (Remarks)	

134

These minutes are considered as official documents pertaining to both Governments and will not be released without mutual agreement.

APPLICATION FOR ☐ REGISTRATION ☐ CANCELLATION OF REGISTRATION OF USFK PRIVATELY OWNED VEHICLES			
1. APPLICANT'S NAME AND ADDRESS 신청자(차량 소유자)의 주소 성명			
NAME (Last, First, & MI) 성 명	RANK & SN 계급 및 군번	DOB 생년월일	ADDRESS 주 소
2. VEHICLE STATUS 차량 사항			
MAKE & YEAR OF CAR 차량명 및 제조일자	MOTOR NO. 엔진 번호	BODY TYPE & COLOR 형식 및 도색	DATE & PLACE OF SAFETY INSPECTION 안전검사 시행일자 및 장소
3. LICENSE STATUS 면허 사항			
OFFICE OF REGISTRATION 등록지	AREA OF OPN 운행구역	DATE & PLACE LICENSE PLATE SEAL AFFIXED 번호판 부착일자 및 장소	
LICENSE PLATE NO. 번호판 번호	USFK DRIVER LICENSE NO. & EXP DATE 주한미군 운전면허 번호 및 일자	DATE OF CANCELLATION OF REGIS. 등록취소일자	
4. INSURANCE STATUS 보험 사항			
DATE EXPIRES 만기일자	NAME OF LOCAL INSURANCE CO. 보험회사명	POLICY NAME & NO. 보험종류 및 번호	

USFK Form 29
25 May 68

28th JC (Incl 2 to Incl 1 to Incl 12)
3 July 68

135

5. CUSTOMS CLEARANCE STATUS 통관 사항

DATE OF CLEARANCE 통관일자	PORT OF ENTRY 군세수속담당

6. SIGNATURE 서명

DATE 신청일자	SIGNATURE OF APPLICANT 신청자 서명	SIGNATURE OF RECORDER: 기록자 서명

REMARKS:

136

These minutes are considered as official documents pertaining to both Governments and will not be released without mutual agreement.

JOINT COMMITTEE
UNDER
THE REPUBLIC OF KOREA AND THE UNITED STATES
STATUS OF FORCES AGREEMENT

3 July 1968

MEMORANDUM TO: Chairmen, Transportation Subcommittee

SUBJECT: Drivers' Licenses of the Members of the United States Armed Forces, the Civilian Component, and Their Dependents

1. Paragraph 1, Article XXIV of the Status of Forces Agreement provides that the Republic of Korea shall accept as valid, without a driving test or fee, the driving permit or license or military driving permit issued by the United States, or political subdivision thereof, to a member of the United States armed forces, the civilian component, and their dependents.

2. It is requested that the Transportation Subcommittee make recommendations to the Joint Committee on ways and means to insure that the US driving permits or licenses referred to in paragraph 1 of Article XXIV are in a form recognizable and readable to officials of the Government of the Republic of Korea.

YOON HA JONG
Republic of Korea Representative

for ROBERT J. FRIEDMAN
Lieutenant General
United States Air Force
United States Representative

28th JC (Incl 13)
3 July 68

137

These minutes are considered as official documents pertaining to both Governments and will not be released without mutual agreement.

JOINT COMMITTEE
UNDER
THE REPUBLIC OF KOREA AND THE UNITED STATES
STATUS OF FORCES AGREEMENT

28 June 1968

MEMORANDUM FOR: The Joint Committee
한.미 합동위원회에 대한 각서

SUBJECT : Operating Instructions for US-ROK Joint Investigations

제 목 한.미 합동수사반 운영지침

1. Reference is made to paragraph 8, Minutes of the nineteenth meeting of the ROK-US Joint Committee, 21 December 1967 and inclosure 12 thereto, pertaining to the subject of abuses of privileges, illegal transactions involving duty-free imports, and the establishment of permanent joint investigative organization. The purpose of the investigative organization is to effect close cooperation in the enforcement of ROK and US laws and regulations, and SOFA provisions, relating to abuse of privileges.

1. 관세 면제 수입물자에 관련하는 특권의 남용 및 부정거래 및 상설 합동수사기구 설치건에 관한 1967년 12월 21일 한.미 합동위원회 제19차 회의 회의록 제8항 및 동 회의록 부록 12를 참조 바람. 동 수사기구의 목적은 특권 남용에 관한 한.미 양국 법규 및 군대지위협정 시행에 있어 긴밀한 협조를 기함에 있음.

28th JC (Incl 14)
3 July 68

1378

2. It was found that the operating instructions
2. 전항에서 언급된 운영 지침은 압수물자 처리에 관하여 보완
referred to in the preceding paragraph needed amplification
을 요 함이 판명되었음.
with regard to disposition of seized goods and property.

In view of the original assignment, US and ROK SOFA
원 과제 부여 사실을 감안하여 군대지위협정 한.미 양측 간사는 기타
Secretaries proceeded to consult with other appropriate
관계관들과의 협의를 행 하였는바 본 건에 관한 상호 합의에 도달한 것으로
officials and it is believed that mutual agreement has
사료함.
been attained on the subject.

3. It is recommended that the Joint Committee
3. 합동위원회 제19차 회의에서 한.미 양국 대표가 승인한바
approve the attached supplement to the operating instructions
있는 운영 지침에 대한 별첨 추가 지침을 합동위원회가 승인할 것을 건의함.
approved by the US and ROK Representatives at the nineteenth
meeting of the Joint Committee.

1 Incl
as
첨부 1 : 상기 보충 지침

Robert A. Kinney
ROBERT A. KINNEY
United States Secretary
ROK-US Joint Committee

Chung Sup Shin
SHIN CHUNG SUP
Republic of Korea Secretary
ROK-US Joint Committee

2

179

These minutes are considered as official documents pertaining to both Governments and will not be released without mutual agreement.

SUPPLEMENT TO THE OPERATING INSTRUCTIONS
FOR US-ROK JOINT INVESTIGATIONS

한.미 합동수사반 운영 지침 추가

1. Reference: Paragraph 8, minutes of the nineteenth meeting of the ROK-US Joint Committee, 21 December 1967, and inclosure 12 thereto, pertaining to the subject of abuses of privileges, illegal transactions involving duty-free imports and the establishment of a permanent joint investigative organization to assist in enforcing ROK laws and regulations.

1. 참 조 : 관세면제 수입에 관련하는 특권 남용 및 부정 거래 및 한국 법규시행 조력을 목적으로 하는 상설 합동수사 기구 설치에 관한 1967년 12월 21일 한.미 합동위원회 제19차 회의 회의록 제8항 및 동 회의록 부록 12.

2. Section V, paragraph B of the Operating Instructions for conducting ROK-US Joint Investigations, which were approved by the Joint Committee on 21 December 1967, is hereby amplified by the addition of the following provisions:

2. 1967년 12월 21일 합동위원회가 승인한 한.미 합동수사 운영 지침 제5절"나"항에 다음 규정을 추가 보충한다.

INCLOSURE 1

28th JC (Incl 1 to Incl 14)
3 July 68

140

"(1) General policies
(1) 일반 방침

(a) Paragraph 1, Article IX, SOFA,
(ㄱ) 군대지위협정 제9조 1항은 합중국 군대
provides that save as provided in that Agreement, members
의 구성원, 군속 및 그들의 가족은 본 협정에서 규정된 경우를 제외
of the United States armed forces, the civilian component,
하고는 대한민국 세관 당국이 집행하고 있는 법령에 따라야 한다고
and their dependents shall be subject to the laws and
규정하고 있음.
regulations administered by the customs authorities of
the Republic of Korea.

(b) Subparagraph (a), paragraph 9, Article IX,
(ㄴ) 군대지위협정 제9조 9항 (가)는 대한민국 당국과
SOFA, provides that in order to prevent offenses against
합중국 군대는 대한민국 정부의 세관 당국이 집행하는 법령에 위반하는
laws and regulations administered by the customs authorities
행위를 방지하기 위하여 조사의 실시 및 증거의 수집에 있어서 상호 협조하여야
of the Government of the Republic of Korea, the authorities
한다고 규정하고 있음.
of the Republic of Korea and the United States armed forces
shall assist each other in the conduct of inquiries and
the collection of evidence.

(c) Subparagraph (b), paragraph 9 of
(ㄷ) 군대지위협정 제9조 9항 (나)는 합중국 군대는
Article IX, provides that the United States armed forces
대한민국 정부의 세관 당국에 의하여 또는 이에 대신하여 행하여 지는

shall render all assistance within their power to ensure
압류될 물품을 인도 하도록 확보하기 위하여 그의 권한내의 모든 원조를
that articles liable to seizure by, or on behalf of, the
제공하여야 한다고 규정하고 있음.
customs authorities of the Government of the Republic

of Korea are handed over to those authorities.

(d) Subparagraph (e), paragraph 9 of
(라) 군대지위협정 제9조 9항 (마)는
Article IX, provides that vehicles and articles belonging
합중국 군대에 속하는 차량 및 물품으로서 대한민국
to the United States armed forces seized by the customs
정부의 관세 또는 재무에 관한 법령에 위반하는 행위에 관련하여
authorities of the Government of the Republic of Korea
대한민국 정부의 세관 당국이 압류한 것은 관계 부대 당국에 인도
in connection with an offense against its customs or
하여야 한다고 규정하고 있음.
fiscal laws or regulations shall be handed over to the

appropriate authorities of such forces.

(e) Article XXII, paragraph 6(a) provides
(마) 제22조 6항 (가)는
that: 'The authorities of the Republic of Korea and the
"대한민국 당국과 합중국 군 당국은 범죄에 대한 모든
military authorities of the United States shall assist
필요한 수사의 실시 및 증거의 수집과 제출 (범죄에 관련된 물건의
each othr in the carrying out of all necessary investigations
압수 및 상당한 경우에는 그의 인도를 포함한다) 에 있어서 상호
into offenses, and in the collection and production of
조력하여야 한다.
evidence, including the seizure and, in proper cases,

the handing over of objects connected with an offense.

The handing over of such objects may, however, be made
그러나 이러한 물건은 인도를 하는 당국이 정하는 기간내에 환부할
subject to their return within the time specified by
것을 조건으로 인도할 수 있다" 고 규정하고 있음.
the authority delivering them.'

(f) The authorities of the Republic of
(바) 대한민국 및 합중국 군대 당국은 압류물자의
Korea and the United States armed forces will maintain
보관에 관하여 임시 저장 시설 제공을 포함한 긴밀한 협조를 유지한다.
close cooperation pertaining to the custody of seized

property, including provision of temporary storage

facilities.

(g) Appropriate records will be maintained
(사) 압류자산에 관한 적절한 기록을 작성 비치한다.
of the seized property. All actions pertaining to seized
이관 및 검사 요청을 포함한 압수물자에 관한
property, including transferes and request for inspection,
모든 조치는 문서로서 행한다.
will be executed in writing.

(h) To facilitate the identification and
(아) 도난된 미국 정부 재산의 식별과 회수에 이바지하기
recovery of stolen US property, the US authorities will
위하여 미국 당국은 망실인지 후 24시간 내에 재산 망실을 보고하는
establish a system of reporting loss of property within
제도를 수립하며 동 보고의 사본을 각 합동수사반에 송부한다.

24 hours after any loss is recognized, and copies of such reports will be furnished to the Joint Investigation Teams.

(2) Initial Custody
(2) 최초 보관

Subject to the provisions of paragraph (1)
전 (1)항의 제 규정을 적용하되 군대지위협정 적용
above, property seized from the possession or control of
대상이 아닌자의 소유 또는 통제 상태에서 압수된 물자는 대한민국
other than SOFA personnel will be subject to initial
당국이 보관하며, 반대로 군대지위협정 적용대상자의 소유 또는
custody by the ROK authorities and, conversely, property
통제상태에서 압수된 물자는 미국 당국이 제1차적으로 보관한다.
seized from the possession or control of SOFA personnel
will be subject to the initial custody of the US authorities.

(3) Availability for inspection or as evidence
(3) 검사 또는증거품으로서의 제시

Seized property held for initial custody, as
전 (2) 규정에 의하여 최초 보관상태에 있는 압수물자
provided for under (2) above, will be made available by
는 검사대상 또는 계류중인 사건 처리상의 증거로서 보관자가 이를
the custodian for inspection or as evidence in pending
공여한다.
proceedings. Requests for such property should be made
이러한 물자에 대한 요청은 문서로서 관리자에게

28th JC (Incl 1 to Incl 14)
3 July 68

144

in writing to the custodian and should indicate the
행하며 소요물품 내용과 검사일자 또는소요기간을 표시
identity of the property desired and the date or period
하여야 한다.
of time during which the property will be inspected or required.

The authorities furnished the property in accordance
본항 규정에 의하여 물품의 공여를 받은 관계당국은 별도 약정의
herewith will be responsible to return such property to
합의가 없는한 보관자에게 관계 물품을 반환하는 책임을 진다.
the custodian unless other arrangements are agreed upon.

(4) Final disposition
(4) 최종 처리

(a) Subject to all provisions above,
(ㄱ) 전기한 모든 규정을 적용하되 검사 또는
property no longer required for inspection or as evidence
증거로서, 또는 기타 상당한 목적으로 계속 보관할 필요가 없게됨
or required to be retained for other reasonable purpose
물품은 대한민국 및 합중국의 관계법령에 의거하여 한.미 양국 당국이
may be finally disposed of by the ROK and US authorities
이를 최종 처리할 수 있다.
in accordance with applicable laws and regulations of the
ROK and US.

(b) Of the property under initial US
(ㄴ) 미측의 최초보관 물품중
custody (subject to the provisions of subparagraph (1) (d)
(전기 1 (ㄹ)항이 적용되는 경우는 제외)
above), when the US and ROK authorities agree that it was
한.미 양국 당국이 기수 또는 미수의 관세법 위반에 관련됨

6

145

involved in an attempted or consummated customs violation
것으로 합의하고 대한민국 법에 의하여 몰수가 허용되는 것으로
and it appears that confiscation is authorized by
간주되는 경우에는 몰수를 위하여 한국측에 이관한다.
ROK law, it will be handed over to ROK custody for

confiscation. The US authorities will at the same time
미국 당국은 동시에 해당 소유주에게 이관 사실
notify the owner(s) of the transfer, and advise that
을 통고하고 소유자가 통고 후 10일 이내에 한국 법정의 재판권을
unless the owner or owners contest the decision, voluntarily
자진 수락 하면서 동 결정에 이의를 제기하지 않는한 몰수가
accepting the jurisdiction of the ROK judicial courts within
확정됨을 통지한다.
ten days of the notification, the confiscation becomes

definitive.

(5) Doubtful cases
(5) 이의가 있는 사안

Should disagreement arise in a particular
개별 사안에 관하여 이의가 발생하는 경우에는
case, the Director, Bureau of Customs, Ministry of Finance
재무부 세관국장과 미 제8군 헌병부장 또는 공군 헌병부장이 이견
and the Eighth US Army Provost Marshal and/or the Air
해소에 노력하여 적절한 지시를 시달한다.
Force Chief of Security Police will attempt to resolve

the question and issue appropriate instructions in the case.

If such resolution is not possible the case may be
그러한 해결이 불가능한 경우에는 사안을 한.미 합동위원회에

submitted to US-ROK Joint Committee. The property will
회부할 수 있다. 계류된 물품은

not be finally disposed of by either side pending the
재무부 세관국장, 미8군 헌병부장 또는공군 헌병부장, 또는

receipt of instructions as provided for either by the
합동위원회의 지시를 접수할때 까지 어느측도 최종 처분을 하지

Director, Bureau of Customs, Ministry of Finance; Eighth
아니한다."

US Army Provost Marshal and/or the Air Force Chief

of Security Police; or by the Joint Committee, as

appropriate."

APPROVED BY THE JOINT COMMITTEE ON
3 JULY 1968 AT TWENTY-EIGHTH MEETING

Ha Jong Yoon — for J. M. Massie Capt. USN

YOON HA JONG
Republic of Korea Representative

for ROBERT J. FRIEDMAN
Lieutenant General
United States Air Force
United States Representative

28th JC (Incl 1 to Incl 14)
3 July 68

8

147

공 란

공 란

공 란

공　　　란

공 란

These minutes are considered as official documents pertaining to both Governments and will not be released without mutual agreement.

JOINT COMMITTEE
UNDER
THE REPUBLIC OF KOREA AND THE UNITED STATES
STATUS OF FORCES AGREEMENT

5 April 1968

Dear Mr. Yoon:

Inclosed, for your information, is a copy of a letter sent by the Staff Judge Advocate of the United States Forces, Korea, to the Minister of Justice in regard to the exercise of jurisdiction by the Republic of Korea over SP4 Shindorff, CPL Henderson, and PVT Capanelli.

This matter was discussed with Lieutenant General Friedman, the US Representative on the SOFA Joint Committee, prior to his departure from Seoul. General Friedman shares the view that the circumstances surrounding the alleged offenses are not such that these cases can be categorized as matters of "particular importance" under the Status of Forces Agreement. In addition, there is concern that these cases may indicate a departure from that "utmost restraint" with which the Foreign Minister, on 7 July 1966, indicated the Republic of Korea would exercise its jurisdiction, and which was discussed at the eleventh meeting of the Joint Committee on 13 July 1967. Because of these considerations, he trusts that the Republic of Korea will allow the United States Army to make appropriate disposition of the three cases in question.

I regret that General Friedman is not here to correspond personally with you, but I believe that you would prefer this matter be brought to your attention without delay.

Sincerely,

Original signed by

M. R. MASSIE
CAPT USN
Alternate US Representative
SOFA Joint Committee

Mr. YOON Ha Jong
Republic of Korea Representative
SOFA Joint Committee

153

28th JC (Incl 16)
3 July 69

공 란

공 란

공 란

공 란

공 란

공 란

공 란

공 란

공 란

공 란

공　　란

공 란

공 란

공 란

공　　란

공 란

공 란

These minutes are considered as official documents pertaining to both Governments and will not be released without mutual agreement.

JOINT COMMITTEE
UNDER
THE REPUBLIC OF KOREA AND THE UNITED STATES
STATUS OF FORCES AGREEMENT

20 June 1968

MEMORANDUM FOR: THE JOINT COMMITTEE

SUBJECT: Designation of US Invited Contractor under Article XV, Status of Forces Agreement

1. References:

a. Paragraph 2, Article XV, Status of Forces Agreement.

b. US Commerce Subcommittee Memorandum of Consultation, dated 14 May 1968, subject as above (Inclosure 1).

c. ROK Commerce Subcommittee Memorandum of Consultation, dated 16 May 1968, subject as above (Inclosure 2).

2. The United States, after consultation with the ROK Commerce Subcommittee and after having duly considered their views, has designated Lyon Associates, Inc. as a US Invited Contractor for execution of Contract #DACA81-68-C-0059 for the design of various airfields in Korea.

3. Pertinent data concerning US citizen employees will be provided to the Joint Secretariat in the established periodic arrival and departure format.

2 Incl
as

ROBERT J. FRIEDMAN
Lieutenant General
United States Air Force
United States Representative
Joint Committee

28th JC (Incl 21)
3 July 68

171

These minutes are considered as official documents pertaining to both Governments and will not be released without mutual agreement.

REPUBLIC OF KOREA - UNITED STATES
COMMERCE SUBCOMMITTEE

14 May 1968

SUBJECT: Designation of US Invited Contractor under Article XV, Status of Forces Agreement

ROK Chairman, Commerce Subcommittee

1. Reference: Paragraph 2, Article XV of the Status of Forces Agreement.

2. The Government of the Republic of Korea is informed through this written consultive process that the United States Forces, Korea, proposes to extend invited contractor status to the successful negotiated bidder among qualified US firms on the contract described in paragraph 3 below.

3. The following data is provided:

a. Company Name:
1. Lyon Associates, Inc.
2. Daniel, Mann, Johnson & Mendenhall
3. Adrian Wilson Associates
4. Sverdrup and Parcel
5. Quinton Engineers
6. Bechtel Corp.

b. Local Address:
1. APO 96331
2. Fuchu Air Station, Japan, APO 96525
3. JCA, 3-ka, 1 Yongsan-dong, Yongsan-ku, Seoul, APO 96301
4. 417 Montgomery St., San Francisco, Calif.
5. 812 W. Eighth St., Los Angeles, Calif.
6. 220 Bush St., San Francisco, Calif.

c. Identification of US Citizen Employees: To be supplied after award of contract.

d. Number of US and ROK Employees: Number of US citizens and Koreans is not known at this time and will be supplied upon conclusion of negotiations.

172

28th JC (Incl 1 to Incl 21)
3 July 68

14 May 1968

SUBJECT: Designation of US Invited Contractor under Article XV, Status of Forces Agreement

e. Reasons for Designation of an Invited Contractor: Open competitive bidding among local contractors is not practicable due to the following:

(1) Security considerations.

(2) Technical qualifications of the contractors involved.

f. Location of Contract: Various locations in Korea.

g. Type of Contract: Lump Sum Contract for Architect-Engineer Services for Design of various airfields in Korea.

h. Length of Contract: Approximately 60 days.

i. Sponsoring Component Command: CGUSAEIGHT.

FLOYD R. WALTZ, JR.
Colonel, United States Army
Assistant Chief of Staff, J 4

These minutes are considered as official documents pertaining to both Governments and will not be released without mutual agreement.

MINISTRY OF COMMERCE AND INDUSTRY
REPUBLIC OF KOREA
SEOUL, KOREA

16 May 1968

SUBJECT: Designation of US Invited Contractor under Article XV, Status of Forces Agreement.

TO : Chairman, US Commerce Subcommittee

1. References:

a. Paragraph 2, Article XV, Status of Forces Agreement.

b. US Commerce Subcommittee Memorandum of Consultation, Dated 14 May 1968, subject as above, pertaining to contract for architect-engineer services for design of various airfields in Korea.

2. The US memorandum, reference 1b above, has been reviewed and the Government of the Republic of Korea fully understands the requirement for an invited contractor in this instance.

for [signature]
Chairman
ROK Commerce Subcommittee

28th JC (Incl 2 to Incl 21)
3 July 68

174

These minutes are considered as official documents pertaining to both Governments and will not be released without mutual agreement.

JOINT COMMITTEE
UNDER
THE REPUBLIC OF KOREA AND THE UNITED STATES
STATUS OF FORCES AGREEMENT

20 June 1968

MEMORANDUM FOR: THE JOINT COMMITTEE

SUBJECT: Designation of US Invited Contractor under Article XV, Status of Forces Agreement

1. References:

a. Paragraph 2, Article XV, Status of Forces Agreement.

b. US Commerce Subcommittee Memorandum of Consultation, dated 27 March 1968, subject as above (Inclosure 1).

c. ROK Commerce Subcommittee Memorandum of Consultation, dated 2 April 1968, subject as above, (Inclosure 2).

2. The United States, after consultation with the ROK Commerce Subcommittee and after having duly considered their views, has designated Daniel, Mann, Johnson & Mendenhall as a US Invited Contractor for execution of Contract #DACA81-68-C-0062 for architect and engineering services.

3. Pertinent data concerning US citizen employees will be provided to the Joint Secretariat in the established periodic arrival and departure format.

2 Incl
as

ROBERT J. FRIEDMAN
Lieutenant General
United States Air Force
United States Representative
Joint Committee

28th JC (Incl 22)
3 July 68

1175

These minutes are considered as official documents pertaining to both Governments and will not be released without mutual agreement.

REPUBLIC OF KOREA - UNITED STATES
COMMERCE SUBCOMMITTEE

27 March 1968

SUBJECT: Designation of US Invited Contractor under Article XV, Status of Forces Agreement

Chairman, ROK Commerce Subcommittee

1. Reference: Paragraph 2, Article XV of the Status of Forces Agreement.

2. The Government of the Republic of Korea is informed through this written consultive process that the United States Forces, Korea, proposes to extend invited contractor status to the successful negotiated bidder among qualified US firms on the contract described in paragraph 3 below.

3. The following data is provided:

a. Company Name: 1. Lyon Associates, Inc.
2. Daniel, Mann, Johnson & Mendenhall
3. Adrian Wilson Associates

b. Local Address: 1. APO 96331
2. Fuchu Air Station, Japan, APO 96525
3. JCA, 3 ka-1, Yongsan-dong, Yongsan-ku, Seoul, APO 96301

c. Identification of US Citizen Employees: To be supplied upon conclusion of negotiations.

d. Number of US and ROK Employees: Number of US Citizens and Koreans is not known at this time and will be supplied upon conclusion of negotiations.

e. Reasons for Designation of an Invited Contractor: Open competitive bidding among local contractors is not practicable due to the following:

(1) Security considerations.

(2) Limited technical qualifications of the contractors involved.

f. Location of Contract: Kunsan AB, Korea.

28th JC (Incl 1 to Incl 22)
3 July 68

1176

27 March 1968

SUBJECT: Designation of US Invited Contractor under Article XV, Status of Forces Agreement

g. Type of Contract: Lump Sum Contract for Architect-Engineer Services for Design of Water Supply Treatment Plant & Mains.

h. Length of Contract: Approximately 3 months.

i. Sponsoring Component Command: CGUSAEIGHT.

4. The United States certifies that the successful bidder or named contractor is present in the Republic of Korea solely for the purpose of executing contracts with the United States, for the benefit of the United States Armed Forces or other armed forces under the Unified Command receiving logistical support from the United States Forces.

5. The views of the Government of the Republic of Korea are earnestly solicited prior to United States selection and designation of an invited contractor to perform the work outlined above. You may be assured that your views will be considered carefully.

6. Your early reply will be greatly appreciated.

FLOYD R. WALTZ, JR.
Colonel, United States Army
US Chairman, Commerce Subcommittee

1117

28th JC (Incl 1 to Incl 22)
3 July 68

These minutes are considered as official documents pertaining to both Governments and will not be released without mutual agreement.

MINISTRY OF COMMERCE AND INDUSTRY
REPUBLIC OF KOREA
SEOUL, KOREA

2 April 1968

SUBJECT: Designation of US Invited Contractor under Article XV, Status of Forces Agreement.

TO : Chairman, US Commerce Subcommittee

1. References:

a. Paragraph 2, Article XV, Status of Forces Agreement.

b. US Commerce Subcommittee Memorandum of Consultation, dated 27 March 1968, subject as above, pertaining to contract for Architect-Engineer Services Design of Water Supply Treatment Plant & Mains.

2. The US memorandum, reference 1b above, has been reviewed and the Government of the Republic of Korea fully understands the requirement for an invited contractor in this instance.

For Han Byung Il
Chairman
ROK Commerce Subcommittee

178

28th JC (Incl 2 to Incl 22)
3 July 68

These minutes are considered as official documents pertaining to both Governments and will not be released without mutual agreement.

JOINT COMMITTEE
UNDER
THE REPUBLIC OF KOREA AND THE UNITED STATES
STATUS OF FORCES AGREEMENT

7 June 1968

MEMORANDUM FOR: The Joint Committee

SUBJECT: Designation of US Invited Contractor under Article XV, Status of Forces Agreement

1. References:

a. Paragraph 2, Article XV, Status of Forces Agreement.

b. US Commerce Subcommittee Memorandum of Consultation, dated 28 May 1968, subject as above (Inclosure 1).

c. ROK Commerce Subcommittee Memorandum of Consultation, dated 7 June 1968, subject as above (Inclosure 2).

2. The United States, after consultation with the ROK Commerce Subcommittee and after having duly considered their views, has designated Trans-Asia Engineering Associates, Inc., as a US invited contractor for execution of Contract #F62087-68-C-0104 for Architect and Engineering services.

3. Pertinent data concerning US citizen employees will be provided to the Joint Secretariat in the established periodic arrival and departure format.

2 Incl
as stated

ROBERT J. FRIEDMAN
Lieutenant General
United States Air Force
United States Representative
Joint Committee

1179

28th JC (Incl 23)
3 July 68

These minutes are considered as official documents pertaining to both Governments and will not be released without mutual agreement.

REPUBLIC OF KOREA - UNITED STATES
COMMERCE SUBCOMMITTEE

28 May 1968

SUBJECT: Designation of US Invited Contractor under Article XV, Status of Forces Agreement

ROK Chairman, Commerce Subcommittee

1. Reference: Paragraph 2, Article XV of the Status of Forces Agreement.

2. The Government of the Republic of Korea is informed through this written consultive process that the United States Forces, Korea, proposes to extend invited contractor status to the qualified US firm on the contract described in paragraph 3 below.

3. The following data is provided:

a. Company Name: Trans-Asia Engineering Associates Inc.

b. Local Address: Bldg 1510, APO 96301

c. Identification of US Citizen Employees: To be supplied after award of contract.

d. Number of US and ROK Employees:

U.S. - 5
ROK - 5

e. Reasons for Designation of an Invited Contractor: Open competitive bidding among local contractors is not practicable due to the following:

(1) Security considerations.

(2) Technical qualifications of the contractor involved.

f. Location of contract: Taegu Air Base and Osan Air Base, Korea.

180

28th JC (Incl 1 to Incl 23)
3 July 68

These minutes are considered as official documents pertaining to both Governments and will not be released without mutual agreement.

SUBJECT: Designation of US Invited Contractor under Article XV, Status of Forces Agreement

g. Type of Contract: Architect-Engineering services.

h. Length of Contract: Approximately 30 days.

i. Sponsoring Component Command: Commander, Air Forces, Korea (Headquarters 6314th Support Wing (PACAF)).

FLOYD R. WALTZ, JR.
Colonel, United States Army
Assistant Chief of Staff, J 4

181

28th JC (Incl 1 to Incl 23)
3 July 68

These minutes are considered as official documents pertaining to both Governments and will not be released without mutual agreement.

MINISTRY OF COMMERCE AND INDUSTRY
REPUBLIC OF KOREA
SEOUL, KOREA

7 June 1968

SUBJECT: Designation of US Invited Contractor under Article XV, Status of Forces Agreement.

TO : Chairman, US Commerce Subcommittee.

1. References:

a. Paragraph 2, Article XV, Status of Forces Agreement.

b. US Commerce Subcommittee Memorandum of Consultation, Dated 28 May 1968, subject as above, pertaining to contract for architect-engineering services in the Taegu and Osan Air Base construction projects.

2. The US memorandum, reference 1b above, has been reviewed and the Government of the Republic of Korea fully understands the requirement for an invited contractor in this instance.

For [signature]
Chairman
ROK Commerce Subcommittee

182

28th JC (Incl 2 to Incl 23)
3 July 68

These minutes are considered as official documents pertaining to both Governments and will not be released without mutual agreement.

REPUBLIC OF KOREA - UNITED STATES
COMMERCE SUBCOMMITTEE

under the

REPUBLIC OF KOREA - UNITED STATES
JOINT COMMITTEE, SOFA

20 June 1968

MEMORANDUM FOR: THE JOINT COMMITTEE

SUBJECT: Status of Trans-Asia Engineering Associates, Inc. performing certain contracts for the Republic of Korea.

1. Subcommittee Members:

United States	
COL Floyd R. Waltz, Jr., Chairman	Mr. SHIM Ui Hwan, Chairman
COL John T. Horrocks, Alt. Chairman	Mr. HAN Byung Il, Secretary
LTC Walter A. Brown, Jr., Secretary	Mr. MOON Ki Sang, Member
COL Norman I. Radin, Member	Mr. PARK Pil Soo, Member
LTC James A. Jolley, Member	Mr. RHEE Eun Tak, Member
Major Edmund P. Murphy, Member	Mr. LEE Chang Ha, Member
Major Frederick Chapman, Member	Mr. LEE Woong Soo, Member
Mr. Oliver J. Kennedy, Member	Mr. IM Young Duk, Member
Mr. Charles E. Coleman, Member	Mr. NAMKOONG Chull, Member
Mr. Lawrence D. Hillyer, Jr., Member	Mr. KIM Sae Kwon, Member
Mr. Samuel Pollack, Member	Mr. SONG Ju In, Member
	Mr. DOKKO Young, Member
	Mr. KIM Bong Kyun, Member
	Mr. OH Myong Too, Member

2. Subject of Recommendation: Interpretation of paragraph 2(b), Article XV, SOFA, in regard to the Trans-Asia Engineering Associates, Inc. Reference Minutes of Joint Committee Meeting #12, dated 14 Aug 1967, concerning Collins Radio Company.

3. Proposal that Trans-Asia Engineering Associates, Inc. engaged in business activities in the Republic of Korea pertaining immediately and directly to the Government of the Republic of Korea would not be in violation of paragraph 2(b), Article XV, SOFA, because in this instance and under the special facts appearing, the provision may and should be construed so as to favor those certain business activities which do also bear an indirect yet reasonably close pertaining relation to the United States Armed Forces. This construction of the provision will allow

28th JC (Incl 24)
3 July 68

183

These minutes are considered as official documents pertaining to both Governments and will not be released without mutual agreement.

20 June 1968

SUBJECT: Status of Trans-Asia Engineering Associates, Inc. performing certain contracts for the Republic of Korea.

those Trans-Asia Engineering Associates, Inc. employees, presently in the Republic of Korea, for the purpose of performing contracts with the U.S. Armed Forces to retain the privileges and immunities granted under SOFA, even though the Trans-Asia Engineering Associates, Inc. is performing certain contracts with additional personnel, for the Republic of Korea. Invited contractor privileges and immunities granted under SOFA will not be extended to the additional personnel of Trans-Asia Engineering Associates, Inc. employed on the contract with the Republic of Korea.

4. Recommendation: It is recommended that the construction as outlined in paragraph 3 above be adopted.

For Han Byung Il
SHIM UI HWAN, Chairman
Republic of Korea Chairman
Commerce Subcommittee

Floyd R. Waltz
COL FLOYD R. WALTZ, JR., USA
United States Chairman
Commerce Subcommittee

APPROVED BY THE JOINT COMMITTEE ON 3 JULY 1968 AT TWENTY-EIGHTH MEETING

YOON HA JONG
Republic of Korea Representative

for ROBERT J. FRIEDMAN
Lieutenant General
United States Air Force
United States Representative

28th JC (Incl 24)
3 July 68

2

184

These minutes a[illegible] considered as official docume[illegible] pertaining to both Governments and will not be released without mutual agreement.

JOINT COMMITTEE
UNDER
THE REPUBLIC OF KOREA AND THE UNITED STATES
STATUS OF FORCES AGREEMENT

3 July 1968

MEMORANDUM TO: The Joint Committee

SUBJECT : Interpretation of Article XIII, Status of Forces Agreement

1. a. Paragraph 1(a), Article XIII provides that military exchanges, messes, social clubs, theatres, newspapers and other non-appropriated fund organizations authorized and regulated by the United States military authorities may be established by the United States armed forces for the use of members of such forces, the civilian component and their dependents.

b. Agreed Minutes to Article XIII provides that the United States armed forces may grant the use of the organizations referred to in paragraph 1 of Article XIII to:

(a) other officers or personnel of the Government of the United States ordinarily accorded such privileges;

(b) those other non-Korean armed forces in the Republic of Korea under the Unified Command which receive logistical support from the United States armed forces, and their members;

(c) those non-Korean persons whose presence in the Republic of Korea is solely for the purpose of providing contract services financed by the Government of the United States;

28th JC (Incl 25)
3 July 68

(d) those organizations which are present in the Republic of Korea primarily for the benefit and service of the United States armed forces, such as the American Red Cross and the United Service Organizations, and their non-Korean personnel;

(e) dependents of the foregoing; and

(f) other persons and organizations with the express consent of the Government of the Republic of Korea.

2. Reference is made to the Eighth United States Army Regulation Number 60-1 (EA 60-1) of 22 February 1968 which embodies best efforts of the US authorities to control abuse of PX privileges.

3. According to Inclosure 1 to the regulation referred to in the preceding paragraph, "Post Exchange Ration Card Eligibility List and Issuing Agencies of Ration Cards" includes the following categories of persons:

(11) Retired US military personnel

(14) Widows (US citizens) who have not remarried and their dependents of the following: Members of the uniformed services, who die on extended active duty; members of Reserve components, inactive duty for training, or inactive duty training; and retired personnel, provided they are authorized the use of MPC.

(15 d) Dependents of US military personnel whose sponsor is not stationed in Korea. (with limitations, 16, 17 and 18)

(15 j) Dependents of retired military personnel.

(15 k) Dependents otherwise authorized exchange and MPC privileges who are transient in Korea. Privileges will be limited to a period not exceeding 90 days.

4. While recognizing human or humanitarian considerations involved in granting PX privileges to the categories of persons enumerated in paragraph 3 above, the Government of

28th JC (Incl 25)
3 July 68

186

the Republic of Korea hardly finds relevant provisions in Article XIII, SOFA which may be applicable to each of the above enumerated categories.

5. It is therefore requested that the United States authorities will take one of the following alternative actions for each of the categories:

(a) to give satisfactory explanations for applicability of the SOFA provisions; or

(b) to request express consents of the ROK Government in accordance with paragraph (f) of the Agreed Minutes to Article XIII.

YOON HA JONG
Republic of Korea
Representative

28th JC (Incl 25)
3 July 68

187

These minutes [illegible] considered as official docum[illegible]s pertaining to both Governments and will not be released without mutual agreement.

JOINT ROK - US PRESS RELEASE
TWENTY-EIGHTH ROK-US JOINT COMMITTEE MEETING
3 JULY 1968

The ROK-US Joint Committee approved new procedures covering the licensing and registration of the privately owned vehicles of personnel of the US armed forces in Korea at the twenty-eighth meeting of the Joint Committee on 3 July. The Joint Committee also adopted procedures for the disposition of goods and property seized by the ROK-US Joint Investigative Teams, in accordance with applicable laws and regulations of the ROK and the US, and the provisions of the ROK-US SOFA.

The Joint Committee on 3 July also approved ten recommendations of its Facilities and Areas Subcommittee and assigned sixteen new tasks to the Subcommittee, including urgent actions to strengthen the Joint ROK-US defense posture in the Republic of Korea.

The ROK and US Representative also presented memoranda relating to interpretations of several articles of the SOFA, concerning nonappropriated fund organizations, local procurement, and criminal jurisdiction.

Mr. YOON Ha Jong, Director of the Eurpope and America Bureau of the Foreign Ministry, presided at this Joint Committee meeting which was held at the ROK Capitol Building. The next meeting of the ROK-US Joint Committee is scheduled for Wednesday, 14 August in the US SOFA Conference Room in Yongsan.

28th JC (Incl 26)
3 July 68

188

MINISTRY OF FOREIGN AFFAIRS
REPUBLIC OF KOREA

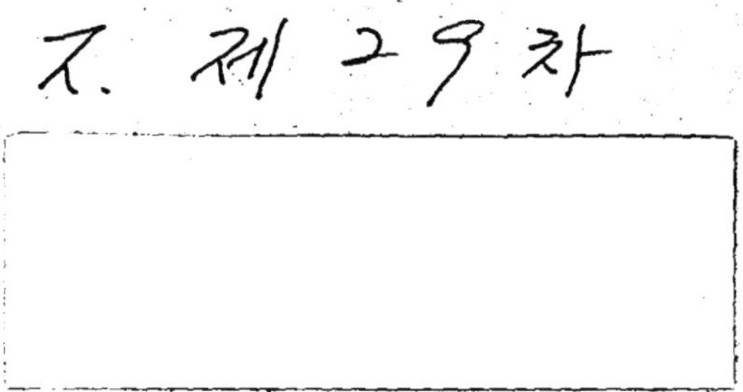

189

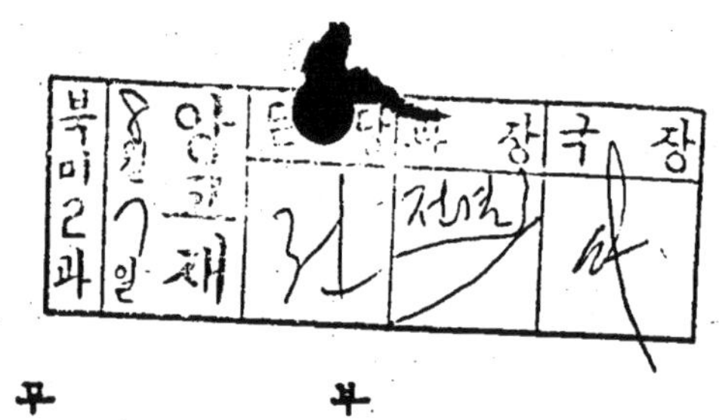

외 무 부

외미이 723- 1968. 8. 7.

수신: 배부처 참조

제목: 한미합동위원회 회의 개최 통지

1. 오는 1968년 8월 14일 (수요일) 15:00시에 ~~중앙청 제1회의실~~, 주한미군사령부 회의실에서 한미합동위원회 제29차 회의가 개최될 예정이오니 각 위원의 참석을 바랍니다.

2. 한편, 동 회의에 대비한 한국 대표단의 대책회의를 오는 8월 13일(화요일) 10:00시에 중앙청 5층 528회의실에서 개최하오니 참석 하시기 바랍니다. 끝.

외 무 부 장 관

배부처: 법무부장관(법무실장, 검찰국장), 국방부장관 (기획국장, 시설국장), 재무부장관(세관국장), 상공부장관(상역국장), 교통부장관(항공국장), 노동청장(노정국장), 경제기획원장관(경제기획국장).

190

한.미 합동위원회 제29차 회의

대책회의 의제

1968. 8. 13. 10:00시

중앙청 회의실

1. 시설구역 분과위원회에 대한 추가 과제부여 5건 — 미측 설명 —
충북 진천군 소재 0.8056 에이커의 취득, 경기도 평택군 소재 0.50 에이커의 취득, 강원도 원성군 소재 2.824 에이커의 취득,
7X -T -11 및 K-E-T-6 의 임시사용 허가 연장
2. 형사재판권 분과위원회에 대한 추가 과제부여 2건
가. 한국측 설명 — 협정 제22조 3(가)항에 의거한 한국측의 재판권 행사기간 15일의 계산방법
나. 미측 설명 — 재판절차 완결 후의 신병 인도 절차
3. 시설구역 분과위원회의 건의 13건
가. 한국측 설명 — 5건 — SAC-616, SAC-715, PAC-152, Camp Yuma 의 일부 등의 반환, AAC-391 의 합동사용
나. 미측설명 — 8건 — 경기도 의정부 소재 0.8 에이커, 용산구 소재 0.01 에이커의 취득, 용산구 소재 0.019 에이커의 영구제한 지역권 취득, 경기도 양주군 소재 0.186 에이커 및 포천군 소재 2.796 에이커의 임시취득, 경기도 양주군 소재 IC-T-41 및

191

경기도 연천면 및 창공면 소재 7X - T - 15
의 임시사용 허가 연장

4. 형사재판권 분과위원회의 건의 2건

가. 한국측 설명 — 한국수사 당국에 참고인이나 피의자를 출석케 하는 절차 (합의 의견 14)

나. 미측 설명 — 전속적 및 제1차적 재판권에 관한 문제의 해결절차 (합의 의견 15)

5. 주한 미군 초청계약자 지명 10건에 관한 미측 각서 — 미측 설명

— Tectonics Asia, Inc., Huwin Corporation, Trans-Asia Engineering Associates, Inc., Daniel, Mann, Johnson & Mendenhall (F62087-69-C-0003, DACA 81-C-0075, F 62087-68-C-0130), Lyon Associates, Inc., Adrian Wilson Associates, R.M. Towill Corporation, Maintenance & Repair Service

6. SOFA 시행상 미측으로 부터 한국 정부에 제출하는 각서 — 미측 설명

7. 차기회의 일시 — 1968. 9.12 (목), 중앙청 회의실

8. 공동발표문 채택

9. 기 타

192

한.미 합동위원회 제29차 회의 의제

1968. 8. 14. 15:00시

미국 SOFA 회의실

1. 시설구역 분과위원회에 대한 과제부여 — 미측설명
2. 형사재판권 분과위원회에 대한 추가 과제부여
   가. 한국측 설명 1건
   나. 미측 설명 1건
3. 시설구역 분과위원회의 건의
   가. 한국측 설명 5건
   나. 미측 설명 8건
4. 형사재판권 분과위원회의 건의
   가. 한국측 설명 1건
   나. 미측 설명 1건
5. 주한 미군 초청계약자의 지명에 관한 각서 — 미측 설명
6. SOFA 시행상 미측이 한국 정부에 제출하는 각서 — 미측 설명
7. 차기회의 예정 — 1968. 9. 12. (목) 중앙청 회의실
8. 공동발표문 채택
9. 폐 회

197

한.미 군대지위협정 합동위원회

제 29 차 회의

1968. 8. 14.

한 국 대 표

발 언 취 지 (안)

194

(의 제 1 - 시설구역 분과위원회 과제부여)

(미국측 설명)

감사합니다.

대한민국 대표는 5건의 과제를 시설구역 분과위원회에 부여 하는데 동의하는 바입니다.

195

(의 제 2 - 형사관할권 분과위원회에 대한 추가 과제부여)

1. 한국측 설명 1건

(미국대표, 한국대표의 설명을 요청)

감사합니다.

제1차 관할권의 행사 및 포기에 관한 제22조 3 "나" 항에 관한 합의의사록 규정의 시행규칙을 정한 1966. 7. 9. 자한.미간 교환 서한은 법무장관이 문서로서 대한민국이 통고접수 기타의 방법으로 그의 제1차 관할권에 속하는 범죄 발생을 인지한 후 15일 이내에 관할권을 행사하겠다는 대한민국의 결정을 관계 미군당국에 통고할 것을 규정하고 있읍니다.

이 문제는 본시 범죄관련자가 군대지위협정 규제대상이라는 점과 관계 범죄가 군대지위협정이 규정한바의 제1차 관할권에 속함을 전제조건으로 하고 있으므로 수사 시초단계에서 군대지위협정 규제 대상여부 또는 관할권의 성질에 문제점이 있는 사건에 있어서는 전기 15일 기한이 언제 시작되느냐에 관하여 문제가 제기되며, 범죄 관련자의 신원이 불명이거나 오인된 사건이나 추후 합의의견 15호로서 건의의 대상이되고 있는바와 같이 관할권의 성질에 관하여 의문이 제기되는 사건까지도 포함하여 이 문제에 관한 상호 합의된 지침이 필요하다고 사료됩니다.

따라서 형사관할권 분과위원회에 한.미 군대지위협정 제22조 3 "나" 항에 해당하는 사건에 있어 관할권 행사에 관한 15일 기한이 시작되는 시기에 관한 지침을 작성하는 과제를 부여할 것을 제의하는 바입니다.

(미측 동의 표시)

감사합니다.

196

2. 미측 설명 1건

(재판 절차가 완결된 후의 신병 인도 절차)

(미측 설명과 동의 요청)

형사관할권 분과위원회에 부여할 것으로 제의된 과제는 가장 적절한 것으로 한국 대표는 동 과제부여에 동의하는 바입니다.

197

공 란

공 란

(의제 4 - 형사관할권 분과위원회 건의)

1. 한국측 설명 - 1건

(미국대표, 한국대표의 설명을 요청)

감사합니다.

합동위원회 1967. 9. 28. 개최된 제15차 회의에서 전속 관할권과 제1차 관할권 구분 정의할 것을 목적으로, 전반적 연구분야에 관한 최초 작업으로서 형사관할권 분과위원회에 관세 및 교통법규 분야에서의 관할권에 관한 합의된 지침에 도달할 것을 목표로 동 분야의 관계법규를 비교 검토하는 과제를 부여한바 있읍니다.

동 분과위원회는 관세 및 차량교통이나 여타 분야에 관한 한국 및 미국 법률이 광범하고 복잡하며 끊임없이 개정 또는 해석 변경 과정에 있으며, 따라서 장차 발생할 사건에 대한 유효한 지침으로서의 기능을 다 할수 있는 정확한 규칙을 작성하는 것이 불가능하고 개개의 범죄가 발생할때마다 당시 유효한 제 법률과 시행 규칙에 의거하여 검토하여야 한다는 결론에 도달하였읍니다.

동 분과위원회는 이러한 판정과 결론에 입각하여

(1) 관할권에 관한 문제는 발생시마다 개별적으로 해결할 것.

(2) 전속 및 경합관할권에 관한 문제의 해결 방법으로 합의의견 15호를 채택할 것.

을 건의하고 있읍니다.

동 합의의견 15호의 취지는 다음과 같읍니다.

200

(1) 전속 관할권에 관한 문제가 제기되면 우선 이를 형사관할권 분과위원회 한.미 양 위원장에게 회부하여 협의 해결케 하며, 양 분과위원장 간의 합의 도달이 불가능한 경우에는 그 어느쪽이든 합동위원회에 이를 제기회부한다.

(2) 전기 절차가 진행중에는 쌍방이 관할권을 행사하지 아니하며 제1차 관할권 행사 통고에 관한 15일간의 기한은 시작되지 않은 것으로 간주한다.

(3) 전기 절차에 의한 합의가 불가능한 경우에는 다른 경로에 의하여 별도 합의가 이루어질 때까지 전속 관할권을 주장하는 쪽이 관할권을 행사할 수 있다.

본 건 문제의 극도의 복잡성을 감안할때 전기 건의는 대단히 온당한 것입니다. 그러나 사법 절차의 안정성이란 견지에서 가능하다면 일정한 지침이 있는 것이 월등히 낫다는 것은 명백하고 또 모든관계자의 시간과 정력을 절약하게될 것입니다. 경험이 누적됨에 따라 여러지침이 자연적으로 점차 형성되고, 명시적인 지침의 작성이 가능하게될 시기가 도래할 것을 희망하는바입니다.

따라서 본 건 채택이 명시적 지침을 작성하겠다는 장차의 노력을 배제하지 않는다는 양해하에 형사관할권 분과위원회의 건의를 합동위원회가 채택할 것을 제안하는 바입니다.

201

2. 미측 설명 1건

(한국 수사기관을 위한 증인 또는 피의자 출두 절차)

(미측 설명)

감사합니다.

한국 대표는 합의의견 14호의 합동위원회 승인에 동의하는 바입니다.

202

(의 제 5 - 주한미군 초청계약자 지명에 관한 각서 - 미측 설명)

(미측 설명)

감사합니다.

한국 대표는 10개 초청계약자 지명에 관한 미측 통고 접수와 또 이들 지명에 있어 양측이 합의한 협의절차를 완전히 이행하였음을 확인하는 바입니다.

203

(의 제 6 - 미국측이 제출하는 각서)

(미국측 각서 열거)

감사합니다.

대한민국 대표는 열거하신 제 각서를 접수하였음을 확인하는 바입니다.

204

(의 제 7 - 차기회의)

(미국측 차기회의 일시 제안)

감사합니다.

대한민국 대표는 차기회의 일시와 장소에 대하여 동의하는 바입니다.

205

(의 제 8 - 공동발표문)

(미국측 제안)

대한민국 대표는 양측 간사가 준비한 신문 공동발표문 안을 채택하는데 동의하는 바입니다.

206

THE TWENTY-NINTH MEETING

THE ROK-US SOFA JOINT COMMITTEE 14 AUGUST 1968

NOTES

for

The Republic of Korea Representative

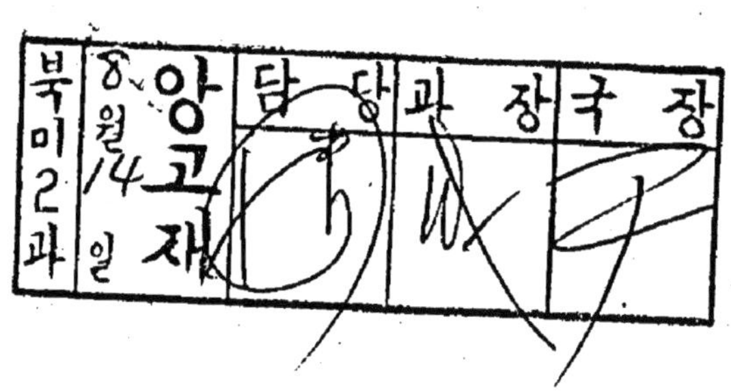

(Agenda I - Assignment of Tasks to Facilities & Areas Subcommittee)

(U.S. Representative will present)

Thank you.

The Republic of Korea Representative is pleased to concur in the assignment of 5 tasks to the Facilities and Areas Subcommittee.

208

(Agenda II - Assignment of Additional Tasks to Criminal Jurisdiction Subcommittee)

1. One Task - ROK Rresentation

(The US Representative invites presentation by the ROK Representative)

Thank you.

The Exchange of Letters between the Republic of Korea and the United States on 9 July 1966, which implement the provisions of the Agreed Minute Re Paragraph 3(b) Article XXII concerning exercise and waiver of primary jurisdiction, provides that the Minister of Justice will notify in writing the appropriate US military authorities of the ROK decision to exercise jurisdiction within fifteen (15) days after the Republic of Korea is notified or otherwise apprised of the commission of an offense falling within its primary jurisdiction.

Since the whole question presupposes that the persons involved in an offense are covered by the SOFA and the offense falls within primary jurisdiction as defined by the SOFA, there are problems as to when the said fifteen-day period should commence in cases where

209

either the SOFA coverage or the nature of jurisdiction is in question in the initial stages of investigation. It is felt that there should be mutually agreed guidelines as to this question to cover the cases where either the identity of the persons involved is unknown, doubtful or misunderstood, or where the nature of jurisdiction is in doubt, which is partly made a subject of specific recommendations to be presented later as Agreed View No. 15.

It is therefore proposed that Criminal Jurisdiction Subcommittee be assigned a task of formulating guidelines as to when the fifteen (15) day period for assuming jurisdiction commences in cases which fall under the provisions of Paragraph 3(b), Article XXII, ROK-US SOFA.

(US Concurrence)

Thank you very much.

210

2. One task - US Presentation

(Procedures for transfer of custody upon completion of all judicial proceedings)

(US presentation and request for concurrence)

The task proposed for the Criminal Jurisdiction Subcommittee is most pertinent, and the Republic of Korea Representative is happy to concur in the assignment of this task.

211

공 란

공 란

(Agenda III - 2)

(U.S. Presentation)

The Republic of Korea Representative is happy to approve the 8 recommendations of the Facilities and Areas Subcommittee.

214

(Agenda IV - Recommendations of the Criminal Jurisdiction Subcommittee)

1. One Recommendation - ROK Presentation

(The US Representative invites presentation by the ROK Representative)

Thank you, General Friedman.

The Joint Committee, at the fifteenth meeting on 28 September 1967, has assigned a task to the Criminal Jurisdiction Subcommittee, in order to define exclusive and primary jurisdictions and as an initial undertaking in the general area of study, of making a comparative review of pertinent laws and regulations relating to customs and traffic violations with a view to arriving at agreed guidelines as to jurisdiction in these specific areas.

The Subcommittee has found that the laws of the Republic of Korea and the United States relating to customs and vehicular traffic as well as in regard to other areas, are extensive, complicating and constantly subject to change and reinterpretation, and concluded

215

that it is not possible to formulate precise rules which would serve as effective guidelines for future cases, and therefore each offense must be studied at the time it occurs in the light of the laws and implementing regulations then in effect.

Based on these findings and conclusions the Subcommittee recommends:

(1) that questions of jurisdiction in all cases be resolved on a case by case basis as they arise.

(2) that Agreed View No. 15 be adopted for resolving questions of exclusive and concurrent jurisdiction.

Substance of the Agreed View No. 15 is as follows:

(1) When the question of exclusive jurisdiction is raised, the case will be first referred to two chairman of the Subcommittee for consultation and resolution; if agreement cannot be reached at that level, either chairman will refer the case to the Joint Committee.

(2) During the foregoing procedures neither side will exercise jurisdiction and the 15-day time-limit period for notification of the exercise of primary jurisdiction will be considered not to have commenced.

(3) Failing mutual agreement through the foregoing procedures, the State claiming exclusive jurisdiction may

216

exercise jurisdiction until a mutual agreement is reached through other channels.

Given the extreme complexity of the problem, the recommendation is a very reasonable one.

However, it is obviously much preferrable to have a set of guidelines, if it is possible, in the interest of stability in the judicial proceedings, and it will save time and effort for everyone concerned, And it is hoped that by accumulation of experience certain body of guidelines will gradually grow up naturally and perhaps it may become possible to formulate explicit guidelines.

It is therefore proposed that the Joint Committee adopt the recommendation of Criminal Jurisdiction Subcommittee with the understanding that the adoption does not preclude future effort to formulate explicit guidelines.

(US Concurrence)

Thank you very much.

217

2. One Recommendation - US Presentation

(Procedures for obtaining witnesses or suspects for ROK investigative authorities.)

(US Presentation)

Thank you.

The Republic of Korea Representative is pleased to agree to the Joint Committee approval of Agreed View No. 14.

218

(Agenda V - Memoranda on Designation of USFK Invited Contractors -- US Presentation)

(US Presentation)

Thank you, General Friedman.

The Republic of Korea Representative is pleased to acknowledge US notification on designation of ten Invited Contractors, and to confirm that mutually agreed procedures of consultation have duly been observed in these designations.

219

(Agenda VI - Memoranda Presented to the ROK Government by the U.S. in the Implementation of the SOFA)

(U.S. Representative will enumerate)

Thank you.

The Republic of Korea Representative is happy to acknowledge the receipt of the memoranda as enumerated.

220

(Agenda VII - Next Meeting)

(U.S. Representative will suggest the date of the Next Meeting)

Thank you.

The Republic of Korea Representative is pleased to accept the proposed time and place of the next meeting.

221

공 란

7. The ROK Representative presented a new task for the Criminal Jurisdiction Subcommittee (Inclosure 3). He stated that the exchange of letters between the Republic of Korea and the United States on 9 July

1966, which implement the provisions of the Agreed Minute Re Paragraph 3(b), Article XXII concerning exercise and waiver of primary jurisdiction, provided that the Minister of Justice would notify in writing the appropriate US military authorities of the ROK decision to exercise jurisdiction within 15 days after the Republic of Korea was notified or otherwise apprised of the commission of an offense falling within its primary jurisdiction. Since this whole question presupposed that the persons involved in an offense were covered by the SOFA and that the offense fell within primary jurisdiction as defined by the SOFA, there were problems as to when the said 15-day period should commence in cases where either the SOFA coverage or the nature of jurisdiction was in question in the initial stages of investigation. The ROK Representative stated that he felt there should be mutually agreed guidelines as to this question to cover the cases where either the identity of the persons involved was unknown, doubtful, or misunderstood, or where the nature of jurisdiction was in doubt (which was partly made a subject of specific recommendations to be presented later as Agreed View No. 15).

8. The ROK Representative proposed that the Criminal Jurisdiction Subcommittee be assigned a task of formulating guidelines as to when the 15-day period for assuming jurisdiction commenced in cases which fell under the Agreed Minute Re Paragraph 3(b) of Article XXII of the SOFA.

9. The US Representative concurred in the assignment of this task to the Criminal Jurisdiction Subcommittee. He stated that mutual agreement on this subject should facilitate the implementation of the provisions

of the SOFA relating to notification to the United States military authorities of the Government of the Republic of Korea's intention to exercise jurisdiction. The SOFA and the exchange of letters between the ROK Foreign Minister and the US Ambassador provide that the Government of the Republic of Korea would make its decision regarding exercise of jurisdiction within 15 days after it is notified or otherwise apprised of the commission of an offense falling within its primary jurisdiction. It is hoped that the Criminal Jurisdiction Subcommittee would be able to submit recommendations which would facilitate and expedite the effective implementation of these SOFA provisions.

10. The US Representative proposed the assignment of a task to the Criminal Jurisdiction Subcommittee relating to procedures for the transfer of custody of US personnel upon completion of all judicial proceedings (Inclosure 4). The SOFA provides that the custody of an accused member of the US forces, civilian component, invited contractor, or dependent, shall remain with the military authorities of the US pending the conclusion of all judicial proceedings and until custody was requested by the authorities of the Republic of Korea. The US Representative stated that this task to the Criminal Jurisdiction Subcommittee requested recommendations on procedures to implement the provisions of the SOFA relating to the transfer of custody. The recommended procedures should include the designation of ROK authorities who would make the request, the US military authorities to whom the request would be made, the documentation required

at the time of transfer, and the arrangements for the physical transfer of the individual concerned.

226

공 란

17. The ROK Representative stated that the Subcommittee found that the laws of the ROK and the US relating to customs and vehicular traffic, as well as in regard to other areas, are extensive, complicated, and constantly subject to change and re-interpretation. Consequently, the Subcommittee found that it was not possible to formulate precise rules which would serve as effective guidelines for future cases. Therefore, each offense must be studied at the time it occurs in the light of the laws and implementing regulations then in effect.

18. The ROK Representative stated that, based on these findings and conclusions, the Subcommittee recommended (Inclosure 12):

a. That questions of jurisdiction in all cases be resolved on a case-by-case basis as they arise.

b. That Agreed View No. 15 be adopted for resolving questions of exclusive and concurrent jurisdiction.

19. The ROK Representative summarized the substance of the Agreed View No. 15 (Inclosure 12), as follows:

228

a. When a question of exclusive jurisdiction is raised, the case will be first referred to two chairmen of the Subcommittee for consultation and resolution; if agreement cannot be reached at that level, either chairman may refer the case to the Joint Committee for resolution.

b. During the course of the foregoing procedures, neither side will exercise jurisdiction and the 15-day-time-limit period for notification of the exercise of primary jurisdiction will be considered not to have commenced until it is determined that the incident falls within the primary jurisdiction of the ROK.

c. When mutual agreement cannot be reached through the foregoing procedures, the State claiming exclusive jurisdiction may exercise jurisdiction over the specific offense until a mutual agreement is reached through other channels.

20. The ROK Representative stated that, given the extreme complexity of the problem, the recommendation of the Subcommittee was a very reasonable one. However, it was obviously much preferrable to have a set of guidelines, if it were possible, in the interests of stability in the judicial proceedings. Such guidelines would save time and effort for everyone concerned. The ROK Representative expressed the hope that by accumulation of experience a certain body of guidelines would gradually grow up naturally and perhaps it could become possible at some future time to formulate explicit guidelines. The ROK Representative, therefore, proposed that Joint Committee approve the recommendations of Criminal Jurisdiction

Subcommittee, with the understanding that the adoption of these recommendations does not preclude future efforts to formulate explicit guidelines.

21. The US Representative concurred in the approval of the recommendations of the Criminal Jurisdiction Subcommittee, including Agreed View No. 15. He stated that he felt these recommendations were both practical and realistic, but that of course Joint Committee approval of them at this time does not preclude further consideration of the question at some future time, if such appears desirable.

22. The US Representative proposed Joint Committee approval of the Criminal Jurisdiction Subcommittee's Agreed View No. 14, relating to procedures for obtaining US witnesses or suspects for ROK investigative authorities (Inclosure 13). The US Representative also expressed his appreciation to the Criminal Jurisdiction Subcommittee for its good work, as reflected in the recommendations presented in the implementation of the Criminal Jurisdiction Article, at this Joint Committee meeting. The ROK Representative concurred in Joint Committee approval of Agreed View No. 14.

23. The US Representative presented memoranda to the Joint Committee informing the ROK Government of the designation of ten new US invited contractors, in accordance with Article XV of the SOFA. After consultation with ROK Commerce Subcommittee personnel, the US Forces, Korea designated as US invited contractors Daniel, Mann, Johnson & Mendenhall (three contracts - Inclosures 14, 15, and 16); Trans-Asia Engineering Associates, Inc. (Inclosure 17); Lyon Associates, Inc. (Inclosure 18); Tectonics Asia (Inclosure 19); R.M. Towill Corp. (Inclosure 20);

2270

Huwin Corp. (Inclosure 21); Maintenance & Repair Services, Inc. (Inclosure 22); and Adrian Wilson Associates (Inclosure 23). The US Representative stated that pertinent data concerning employees of these invited contractors would be provided to the Government of the ROK in accordance with mutually approved procedures.

24. The ROK Representative stated that he was pleased to acknowledge US notification on designation of these ten US invited contractors. He confirmed that mutually agreed procedures of consultation had been duly observed in these designations.

25. The US Representative noted for the record that the US SOFA Secretary has furnished the following information to the ROK SOFA Secretary, in accordance with the provisions of the SOFA and Joint Committee decisions:

a. Five copies of reports on the US armed forces disposition of cases for the month of June 1968.

b. Twenty copies of the report of US armed forces personnel, the civilian component, invited contractors, and dependents entering or departing the ROK during the month of June 1968.

c. Eighteen copies of notices of arrivals, departures, and changes of addresses of US invited contractor personnel and their dependents, dated 2 August 1968.

26. The ROK Representative acknowledged the receipt of the memoranda, as enumerated.

27. The US Representative proposed that the next meeting of the Joint Committee be held on Thursday, 12 September 1968, in the ROK Capitol Building, as proposed by the Republic of Korea SOFA Secretariat. The ROK Representative agreed.

28. The US Representative proposed approval of the joint press release for the twenty-ninth Joint Committee meeting, as prepared by the ROK and US SOFA Secretaries (Inclosure 24). The ROK Representative concurred.

29. The US Representative stated that, before adjourning the twenty-ninth Joint Committee meeting, he wished to offer his congratulations to his Korean colleagues on the Joint Committee on the progress of their Nation, as they celebrate on 15 August the twenty-third anniversary of liberation from Japanese rule and the twentieth anniversary of the founding of the Government of the Republic of Korea. The ROK Representative thanked the US Representative for his congratulations and good wishes. The meeting was adjourned at 1550 hours.

24 Inclosures

ROBERT J. FRIEDMAN
LIEUTENANT GENERAL
UNITED STATES AIR FORCE
UNITED STATES REPRESENTATIVE

YOON HA JONG
REPUBLIC OF KOREA
REPRESENTATIVE

11

232

AGENDA FOR THE TWENTY-NINTH MEETING
OF THE ROK-US JOINT COMMITTEE
1500 HOURS, 14 AUGUST 1968, US SOFA CONFERENCE ROOM

I Assignment of Tasks to Facilities and Areas Subcommittee - US Presentation

II Assignment of Additional Tasks to Criminal Jurisdiction Subcommittee

1. One Task - ROK Presentation
2. One Task - US Presentation

III Recommendations of Facilities and Areas Subcommittee

1. Five Recommendations - ROK Presentation
2. Eight Recommendations - US Presentation

IV Recommendations of the Criminal Jurisdiction Subcommittee

1. One Recommendation - ROK Presentation
2. One Recommendation - US Presentation

V Memoranda on Designation of USFK Invited Contractors - US Presentation

VI Memoranda Presented to the ROK Government by the US in the Implementation of the SOFA - US Presentation

VII Proposed Time of Next Meeting - Thursday, 12 September 1968, in the ROK Capitol Building

VIII Agreement on Joint Press Release

IX Adjourn

223

공 란

공 란

JOINT COMMITTEE
UNDER
THE REPUBLIC OF KOREA AND THE UNITED STATES
STATUS OF FORCES AGREEMENT

14 August 1968

MEMORANDUM FOR: Chairmen, Criminal Jurisdiction Subcommittee

SUBJECT: Commencement of the 15 Day Period for the Republic of Korea to Exercise its Criminal Jurisdiction under Paragraph 3(b), Article XXII, US-ROK SOFA

1. The Exchange of Letters between the ROK and the US on 9 July 1966, implementing the provisions of the Agreed Minute Re Paragraph 3(b), Article XXII, provides that the Minister of Justice will notify in writing the appropriate US military authorities of the ROK decision to exercise jurisdiction within 15 days after the Republic of Korea is notified or otherwise apprised of the commission of an offense falling within its primary jurisdiction. A method of counting these 15 days should be devised which would apply not only in routine cases but also in those instances where the name of the suspect is unknown, or his status as a member of the US armed forces, civilian component, invited contractor, dependent, or Korean national employee is misunderstood, or it is uncertain whether US personnel were involved in any respect.

2. It is requested, therefore, that the Criminal Jurisdiction Subcommittee recommend guidelines as to when the 15 day period for assuming jurisdiction commences in cases which fall under the provisions of Paragraph 3(b), Article XXII, US-ROK SOFA.

YOON HA JONG
Republic of Korea Representative

ROBERT J. FRIEDMAN
Lieutenant General
United States Air Force
United States Representative

236

JOINT COMMITTEE
UNDER
THE REPUBLIC OF KOREA AND THE UNITED STATES
STATUS OF FORCES AGREEMENT

14 August 1968

MEMORANDUM FOR: Chairmen, Criminal Jurisdiction Subcommittee

SUBJECT: Procedure for Transfer of Custody upon Completion of All Judicial Proceedings

1. Paragraph 5(c), Article XXII, of the US-ROK Status of Forces Agreement provides that the custody of an accused member of the US armed forces, civilian component, invited contractor, or dependent shall remain with the military authorities of the United States pending the conclusion of all judicial proceedings and until custody is requested by the authorities of the Republic of Korea. However, the manner of such request by the ROK and the mechanics for transfer of custody at the conclusion of all judicial proceedings are not provided for in the SOFA.

2. A procedure for such transfer of custody is necessary to implement the above cited provision. The procedure should include the designation of the ROK authorities who will make the request, the US military authorities to whom such request will be made, the documentation required at the time of transfer and the arrangements for physical transfer of the individual concerned. Your recommendations as to such procedures are requested.

YOON HA JONG
Republic of Korea Representative

ROBERT J. FRIEDMAN
Lieutenant General
United States Air Force
United States Representative

227

공 란

공 란

공 란

공 란

공 란

공 란

공 란

공 란

공　　　란

공 란

공 란

공 란

공 란

공 란

공 란

공 란

공 란

공 란

공 란

공　　　란

공 란

CRIMINAL JURISDICTION SUBCOMMITTEE
ROK/US SOFA JOINT COMMITTEE

16 July 1968

SUBJECT: Recommendations of Criminal Jurisdiction Subcommittee

US-ROK SOFA Joint Committee

1. Subject of Recommendations. On 28 September 1967, the Joint Committee requested the Criminal Jurisdiction Subcommittee to "make a comparative review of pertinent laws and regulations relating to customs and traffic violations with a view to arriving at agreed guidelines as to jurisdiction in these two specific areas."

2. Such comparative review has been made. The laws of the Republic of Korea and the United States relating to customs and vehicular traffic, as well as in regard to other areas, are extensive, complicated, and constantly subject to change and reinterpretation. Consequently, it is not possible to formulate precise rules which would serve as effective guidelines for future cases. Each offense must be studied at the time it occurs in the light of the laws and implementing regulations then in effect.

3. Recommendations. a. That questions of jurisdiction in all areas be resolved on a case by case basis as they arise.

b. That the inclosed procedure set forth as Agreed View No. 15 be adopted for resolving questions of exclusive and concurrent jurisdiction.

4. Security Classification: None.

KIM, SUNG CHAE
Chairman, ROK Component
Criminal Jurisdiction Subcommittee

GERALD W. DAVIS
Colonel, JAGC
Chairman, US Component
Criminal Jurisdiction Subcommittee

259

CRIMINAL JURISDICTION

Agreed View No. 15

Procedures for the Resolution of Questions of Exclusive and Primary Jurisdiction

전속적및 제1차적 재판권에 관한 문제의 해결절차

1. When a question of the existence of exclusive jurisdiction is raised
대한민국 당국이나 미합중국 당국은 특정사건에 있어서 전속적 재판권의
in any particular case by ROK or US authorities, the matter will be referred
존재 여부에 관하여 문제가 생길때에는, 그문제를 형사 재판권 분과
to the US and ROK Chairmen of the Criminal Jurisdiction Subcommittee for
위원회의 한미 양국 위원장에게 회부하여 협의 해결토록한다.
consultation and resolution.

2. If agreement cannot be reached by mutual consultation between the
형사 재판 분과 위원회 위원장간의 상호 협의에 의하여 합의가
Chairmen of the Criminal Jurisdiction Subcommittee, either Chairman may
이루어지지 않을때에는, 어느 위원장이든지 그 문제를 합동 위원회에서
refer the matter to the SOFA Joint Committee for resolution in the Joint
해결하도록 합동 위원회에 회부할 수 있다.
Committee.

3. During the course of the foregoing procedures, neither the ROK nor
상기 절차가 진행되는 동안에는 대한민국이나 미합중국은 동 특정
the US will exercise its jurisdiction over the specific incident, and it
사건에 대하여 재판권을 행사하지 못하며, 형사 재판권 분과 위원회
is considered that the period for the notification by the ROK of a decision
위원장이나 합동 위원회에 의하여 동사건이 대한민국의 제 1 차적
to exercise its primary jurisdiction,as set forth in the exchange of
재판권에 속한다는 것이 결정될 때까지 1966 년 7 월 9일자의
letters of 9 July 1966,does not commence until it is determined, either
교환 서한에 규정된 대한민국의 제 1 차적 재판권 행사 결정 통고기간은
by the Chairmen of the CJ Subcommittee or by the Joint Committee, that the
시작되지 않는 것으로 본다.
incident falls within the primary jurisdiction of the ROK.

260

4. When mutual agreement cannot be reached through the procedures outlined
상기 제 1 항 및 제 2 항에 규정된 절차에 의해서도 상호합의가

in paragraphs 1 and 2, above, the State which claims exclusive jurisdiction
이루어지지 않을때는, 다른 경로를 통한 상호합의가 이루어 질 때까지

may exercise its jurisdiction over the specific offense in accordance with
전속적 재판권을 가지고 있다고 주장한 국가는 한미행정협정과 자국법령에

the US-ROK Status of Forces Agreement and its laws, until a mutual agreement,
따라 동 사건에 대하여 재판권을 행사 할 수 있다.

if possible, is reached through other channels.

The above procedure does not prohibit earlier consultation through the
상기 절차는 이 보다 앞선 합동위원회를 통한 협의나, 양국 실무자간의

Joint Committee, informal consultation between officials of both States
비공식적인 수시 협의 또는 합동위원회가 해결 할 수 없는 경우의

at any time, or a solution through diplomatic channels if the Joint Committee
외교적 경로를 통한 해결등을 금하는 것은 아니다.

is unable to resolve the matter.

268

CRIMINAL JURISDICTION SUBCOMMITTEE
ROK/US SOFA JOINT COMMITTEE

16 July 1968

SUBJECT: Recommendation of Criminal Jurisdiction Subcommittee

ROK/US SOFA Joint Committee

1. Subject of recommendations. On 23 February 1967, the Joint Committee requested the Criminal Jurisdiction Subcommittee to recommend "mutually agreed procedures for cooperation in the conduct of investigations and in the collection and production of evidence."

2. Recommendation. The Criminal Jurisdiction Subcommittee recommends, in partial fulfillment of this task, that the following agreed view be adopted by the Joint Committee:

Agreed View No. 14 - Procedures for Obtaining Witnesses or Suspects for ROK Investigative Authorities.

3. Security Classification: None.

KIM, SUNG CHAE
Chairman, ROK Component
Criminal Jurisdiction Subcommittee

GERALD W. DAVIS
Colonel, JAGC
Chairman, US Component
Criminal Jurisdiction Subcommittee

262

CRIMINAL JURISDICTION

Agreed View No. 14

Procedures for Obtaining Witnesses or Suspects for ROK Investigative Authorities

한국 수사당국에 참고인이나 피의자를 출석케하는 절차

Pursuant to the provisions of paragraph 6(a), Article XXII, and paragraph 2
한미 행정협정 제 22 조 제 6 항 (가) 및 동조 제 3 항 (나) 에
of the Agreed Understanding to the Agreed Minute Re Paragraph 3(b),
관한 합의 의사록에 대한 합의 양해사항 제 2 항의 규정에
Article XXII, ROK-US Status of Forces Agreement, the following procedure
의하여 한국 당국이 미 합중국 군대의 구성원, 군속, 가족 및
will apply when the cooperation of US authorities is necessary to obtain
초청계약자를 수사상 참고인이나 피의자로 출석토록 하는데 미군
a member of the United States armed forces, civilian component, a dependent,
당국의 협력이 필요한 경우에는 다음 절차를 적용한다.
or an US invited contractor as a witness or as a suspect at an investigation by ROK authorities:

1. The request for such witness or suspect will be in writing, if
동 참고인이나 피의자의 요청은 가능한한 서면으로 인근
possible, and delivered to the nearest area provost marshal/security police
헌병대장에게 하여야 하며, 동 요청서에는 한국당국이 필요로
officer. The request will contain the individual's name, organization,
하는 당사자의 성명, 소속과 출석장소 및 시간을 명시하여야 한다.
and the place and time that the ROK authorities desire the individual.

2. The area provost marshal/security police officer of his designee
요청서를 접수한 헌병대장이나 그 대리인은 당사자의 부대장,
will contact the commanding officer, supervisor, or employer of the
감독자나 고용인 또는 그 보호자에게 이를 통보한다.
individual, or the individual's sponsor.

263

3. The commanding officer, supervisor, or employer will make the necessary
부대장, 감독자 또는 고용인은 한국 당국의 요청에 응할 수

arrangements, including transportation, to comply with the ROK request.
있도록 교통편의를 포함한 필요한 조치를 한다.

4. If the individual is not available at the requested time because of
만일 당사자가 긴급한 군무나 질병, 기타 유사한 이유로

imperative military duties, illness, or other similar reason, the commanding
요청된 시간에 출석하지 못 할 때에는 부대장, 감독자 또는

officer, supervisor, or employer will propose to the ROK authorities, either
고용인은 직접 또는 헌병대장을 통하여 한국 당국에 참고인이나

directly or through the provost marshal/security police officer, a time
피의자가 출석할 수 있는 시간을 제시한다.

when the witness or suspect will be available.

Note: 주의

Procedures for obtaining witnesses and defendants at ROK trial proceedings
한국의 재판에 증인이나 피고인을 출석케 하는 절차는 한미

are set forth in unnumbered paragraph 2, 3, and 4 of paragraph 1 of the
행정협정 제 22 조 제 6 항에 관한 합의 의사록 제 1 항의

Agreed Minute Re Paragraph 6, Article XXII, US-ROK Status of Forces
제 2, 3 및 4 절에 규정되어 있다.

Agreement.

2

264

JOINT COMMITTEE
UNDER
THE REPUBLIC OF KOREA AND THE UNITED STATES
STATUS OF FORCES AGREEMENT

26 July 1968

MEMORANDUM FOR: The Joint Committee

SUBJECT: Designation of US Invited Contractor under Article XV, Status of Forces Agreement

1. References:

a. Paragraph 2, Article XV, Status of Forces Agreement.

b. US Commerce Subcommittee Memorandum of Consultation, dated 16 July 1968, subject as above (Inclosure 1).

c. ROK Commerce Subcommittee Memorandum of Consultation, dated 25 July 1968, subject as above (Inclosure 2).

2. The United States, after consultation with the ROK Commerce Subcommittee and after having duly considered their views, has designated Trans-Asia Engineering Associates, Inc. as a US invited contractor for execution of Contract #F62087-69-C-0004 for Architect and Engineering services.

3. Pertinent data concerning US citizen employees will be provided to the Joint Secretariat in the established periodic arrival and departure format.

2 Incl
as

ROBERT J. FRIEDMAN
Lieutenant General
United States Air Force
United States Representative
Joint Committee

265

REPUBLIC OF KOREA - UNITED STATES
COMMERCE SUBCOMMITTEE

16 July 1968

SUBJECT: Designation of US Invited Contractor under Article XV, Status of Forces Agreement

ROK Chairman, Commerce Subcommittee

1. Reference: Paragraph 2, Article XV of the Status of Forces Agreement.

2. The Government of the Republic of Korea is informed through this written consultive process that the United States Forces, Korea proposes to extend invited contractor status to the qualified US firm on the contract described in paragraph 3 below.

3. The following data is provided:

a. Company Name: Trans-Asia Engineering Associates, Inc.

b. Local Address: Bldg 1510, APO 96301.

c. Identification of US Citizen Employees: To be supplied after award of contract.

d. Number of US and ROK Employees:

US - 7
ROK - 12

e. Reasons for Designation of an Invited Contractor: Open competitive bidding among local contractors is not practicable due to the following:

(1) Security considerations.

(2) Technical qualifications of the contractor involved.

f. Location of Contract: Kunsan Air Base and Osan Air Base, Korea.

266

16 July 1968

SUBJECT: Designation of US Invited Contractor under Article XV, Status of Forces Agreement

g. Type of Contract: Architect-Engineering services contract consisting of Type A service of field surveys and preliminary investigations and Type B service of preparations and production of designs, plans, drawings, estimates and specifications.

h. Length of Contract: 30 days from date of notice to proceed.

i. Sponsoring Component Command: Commander, Air Forces, Korea.

John T. Horrocks

JOHN T. HORROCKS
Colonel, US Air Force
US Alternate Chairman
Commerce Subcommittee

2697

MINISTRY OF COMMERCE AND INDUSTRY
REPUBLIC OF KOREA
SEOUL, KOREA

25 July 1968

SUBJECT: Designation of US Invited Contractor under Article XV, Status of Forces Agreement.

TO : Chairman, US Commerce Subcommittee

1. References:

a. Paragraph 2, Article XV, Status of Forces Agreement.

b. US Commerce Subcommittee Memorandum of Consultation, Dated 16 July 1968, subject as above, pertaining to contract for Architect Engineering Services consisting of Type A and Type B.

2. The US memorandum, reference 1b above, has been reviewed and the Government of the Republic of Korea fully understands the requirement for an invited contractor in this instance.

For [signature]
Shim Ui Hwan
Chairman
ROK Commerce Subcommittee

268

JOINT COMMITTEE
UNDER
THE REPUBLIC OF KOREA AND THE UNITED STATES
STATUS OF FORCES AGREEMENT

26 July 1968

MEMORANDUM FOR: The Joint Committee

SUBJECT: Designation of US Invited Contractor under Article XV, Status of Forces Agreement

1. References:

a. Paragraph 2, Article XV, Status of Forces Agreement.

b. US Commerce Subcommittee Memorandum of Consultation, dated 16 July 1968, subject as above (Inclosure 1).

c. ROK Commerce Subcommittee Memorandum of Consultation, dated 25 July 1968, subject as above (Inclosure 2).

2. The United States, after consultation with the ROK Commerce Subcommittee and after having duly considered their views, has designated Daniel, Mann, Johnson & Mendenhall as a US Invited Contractor for execution of Contract #F62087-69-C-0003 for Architect and Engineering services.

3. Pertinent data concerning US citizen employees will be provided to the Joint Secretariat in the established periodic arrival and departure format.

2 Incl
as

ROBERT J. FRIEDMAN
Lieutenant General
United States Air Force
United States Representative
Joint Committee

269

REPUBLIC OF KOREA - UNITED STATES
COMMERCE SUBCOMMITTEE

16 July 1968

SUBJECT: Designation of US Invited Contractor under Article XV, Status of Forces Agreement

ROK Chairman, Commerce Subcommittee

1. Reference: Paragraph 2, Article XV of the Status of Forces Agreement.

2. The Government of the Republic of Korea is informed through this written consultive process that the United States Forces, Korea proposes to extend invited contractor status to the qualified US firm on the contract described in paragraph 3 below.

3. The following data is provided:

a. Company Name: Daniel, Mann, Johnson & Mendenhall.

b. Local Address: Bldg 1510, APO 96301.

c. Identification of US Citizen Employees: To be supplied after award of contract.

d. Number of US and ROK Employees:

US - 7
ROK - 12

e. Reasons for Designation of an Invited Contractor: Open Competitive bidding among local contractors is not practicable due to the following:

(1) Security considerations.

(2) Technical qualifications of the contractor involved.

f. Location of Contract: Kunsan Air Base and Osan Air Base, Korea.

270

16 July 1968

SUBJECT: Designation of US Invited Contractor under Article XV, Status of Forces Agreement.

g. Type of Contract: Architect-Engineering services contract consisting of Type A service of field surveys and preliminary investigations and Type B service of preparations and production of designs, plans, drawings, estimates and specifications.

h. Length of Contract: 30 days from date of notice to proceed.

i. Sponsoring Component Command: Commander, Air Forces, Korea.

John T. Horrocks
JOHN T. HORROCKS
Colonel, US Air Force
US Alternate Chairman
Commerce Subcommittee

271

MINISTRY OF COMMERCE AND INDUSTRY
REPUBLIC OF KOREA
SEOUL, KOREA

25 July 1968

SUBJECT: Designation of US Invited Contractor under Article XV, Status of Forces Agreement.

TO : Chairman, US Commerce Subcommittee

1. References:

a. Paragraph 2, Article XV, Status of Forces Agreement.

b. US Commerce Subcommittee Memorandum of Consultation, Dated 16 July 1968, subject as above, pertaining to contract for Architect Engineering Services consisting of Type A and Type B.

2. The US memorandum, reference 1b above, has been reviewed and the Government of the Republic of Korea fully understands the requirement for an invited contractor in this instance.

For [signature]
Shim Ui Hwan
Chairman
ROK Commerce Subcommittee

277

JOINT COMMITTEE
UNDER
THE REPUBLIC OF KOREA AND THE UNITED STATES
STATUS OF FORCES AGREEMENT

26 July 1968

MEMORANDUM FOR: The Joint Committee

SUBJECT: Designation of US Invited Contractor under Article XV, Status of Forces Agreement

1. References:

a. Paragraph 2, Article XV, Status of Forces Agreement.

b. US Commerce Subcommittee Memorandum of Consultation, dated 18 July 1968, subject as above (Inclosure 1).

c. ROK Commerce Subcommittee Memorandum of Consultation, dated 25 July 1968, subject as above (Inclosure 2).

2. The United States, after consultation with the ROK Commerce Subcommittee and after having duly considered their views, has designated Lyon Associates, Inc. as a US invited contractor for execution of Contract #DACA81-68-C-0067 for Architect and Engineering services.

3. Pertinent data concerning US citizen employees will be provided to the Joint Secretariat in the established periodic arrival and departure format.

2 Incl
as

ROBERT J. FRIEDMAN
Lieutenant General
United States Air Force
United States Representative
Joint Committee

273

REPUBLIC OF KOREA - UNITED STATES
COMMERCE SUBCOMMITTEE

18 July 1968

SUBJECT: Designation of US Invited Contractor under Article XV, Status of Forces Agreement

ROK Chairman, Commerce Subcommittee

1. Reference: Paragraph 2, Article XV of the Status of Forces Agreement.

2. The Government of the Republic of Korea is informed through this written consultive process that the United States Forces, Korea proposes to extend invited contractor status to the qualified US firm on the contract described in paragraph 3 below.

3. The following data is provided:

a. Company Name: Lyon Associates, Inc.

b. Local Address: 6175 Air Base Group, BCEEE
Kunsan AB, APO 96264

c. Identification of US Citizen Employees: To be supplied after award of contract.

d. Number of US and ROK Employees:

US - 2
ROK - 0

e. Reasons for Designation of an Invited Contractor: Open competitive bidding among local contractors is not practicable due to the following:

(1) Security considerations.

(2) Technical qualifications of the contractor involved.

f. Location of Contract: Kunsan AB, Korea.

274

18 July 1968

SUBJECT: Designation of US Invited Contractor under Article XV, Status of Forces Agreement

g. Type of Contract: Lump Sum Contract for Architect-Engineer services for Hydro-Geologic Study and Water Treatment and Distribution Alterations, Kunsan Air Base, Korea.

h. Length of Contract: Approximately 9 months.

i. Sponsoring Component Command: CGUSAEIGHT.

John T. Horrocks
JOHN T. HORROCKS
Colonel, US Air Force
US Alternate Chairman
Commerce Subcommittee

275

MINISTRY OF COMMERCE AND INDUSTRY
REPUBLIC OF KOREA
SEOUL, KOREA

25 July 1968

SUBJECT: Designation of US Invited Contractor under Article XV, Status of Forces Agreement.

TO : Chairman, US Commerce Subcommittee

1. References:

a. Paragraph 2, Article XV, Status of Forces Agreement.

b. US Commerce Subcommittee Memorandum of Consultation, Dated 18 July 1968, subject as above, pertaining to contract for architect-engineer services for Hydro-Geologic Study and Water Treatment and Distribution Alterations, Kunsan Air Base, Korea.

2. The US memorandum, reference 1b above, has been reviewed and the Government of the Republic of Korea fully understands the requirement for an invited contractor in this instance.

for/ [signature]
Shim Ui Hwan
Chairman
ROK Commerce Subcommittee

276

JOINT COMMITTEE
UNDER
THE REPUBLIC OF KOREA AND THE UNITED STATES
STATUS OF FORCES AGREEMENT

23 July 1968

MEMORANDUM FOR: The Joint Committee

SUBJECT: Designation of US Invited Contractor under Article XV, Status of Forces Agreement

1. References:

a. Paragraph 2, Article XV, Status of Forces Agreement.

b. US Commerce Subcommittee Memorandum of Consultation, dated 14 May 1968, subject as above (Inclosure 1).

c. ROK Commerce Subcommittee Memorandum of Consultation, dated 16 May 1968, subject as above (Inclosure 2).

2. The United States, after consultation with the ROK Commerce Subcommittee and after having duly considered their views, has designated Adrian Wilson Associates as a US invited contractor for execution of Contract #DACA81-68-C-0076 for Architect and Engineering services.

3. Pertinent data concerning US citizen employees will be provided to the Joint Secretariat in the established periodic arrival and departure format.

2 Incl
as

ROBERT J. FRIEDMAN
Lieutenant General
United States Air Force
United States Representative
Joint Committee

2717

REPUBLIC OF KOREA - UNITED STATES
COMMERCE SUBCOMMITTEE

14 May 1968

SUBJECT: Designation of US Invited Contractor under Article XV, Status of Forces Agreement

ROK Chairman, Commerce Subcommittee

1. Reference: Paragraph 2, Article XV of the Status of Forces Agreement.

2. The Government of the Republic of Korea is informed through this written consultive process that the United States Forces, Korea, proposes to extend invited contractor status to the successful negotiated bidder among qualified US firms on the contract described in paragraph 3 below.

3. The following data is provided:

a. Company Name:
1. Lyon Associates, Inc.
2. Daniel, Mann, Johnson & Mendenhall
3. Adrian Wilson Associates
4. Sverdrup and Parcel
5. Quinton Engineers
6. Bechtel Corp.

b. Local Address:
1. APO 96331
2. Fuchu Air Station, Japan, APO 96525
3. JCA, 3-ka, 1 Yongsan-dong, Yongsan-ku, Seoul, APO 96301
4. 417 Montgomery St., San Francisco, Calif.
5. 812 W. Eighth St., Los Angeles, Calif.
6. 220 Bush St., San Francisco, Calif.

c. Identification of US Citizen Employees: To be supplied after award of contract.

d. Number of US and ROK Employees: Number of US citizens and Koreans is not known at this time and will be supplied upon conclusion of negotiations.

2178

14 May 1968

SUBJECT: Designation of US Invited Contractor under Article XV, Status of Forces Agreement

e. Reasons for Designation of an Invited Contractor: Open competitive bidding among local contractors is not practicable due to the following:

(1) Security considerations.

(2) Technical qualifications of the contractors involved.

f. Location of Contract: Various locations in Korea.

g. Type of Contract: Lump Sum Contract for Architect-Engineer Services for Design of various airfields in Korea.

h. Length of Contract: Approximately 60 days.

i. Sponsoring Component Command: CGUSAEIGHT.

FLOYD R. WALTZ, JR.
Colonel, United States Army
Assistant Chief of Staff, J 4

279

MINISTRY OF COMMERCE AND INDUSTRY
REPUBLIC OF KOREA
SEOUL, KOREA

16 May 1968

SUBJECT: Designation of US Invited Contractor under Article XV, Status of Forces Agreement.

TO : Chairman, US Commerce Subcommittee

1. References:

a. Paragraph 2, Article XV, Status of Forces Agreement.

b. US Commerce Subcommittee Memorandum of Consultation, Dated 14 May 1968, subject as above, pertaining to contract for architect-engineer services for design of various airfields in Korea.

2. The US memorandum, reference 1b above, has been reviewed and the Government of the Republic of Korea fully understands the requirement for an invited contractor in this instance.

for [signature]
Chairman
ROK Commerce Subcommittee

280

JOINT COMMITTEE
UNDER
THE REPUBLIC OF KOREA AND THE UNITED STATES
STATUS OF FORCES AGREEMENT

16 July 1968

MEMORANDUM FOR: The Joint Committee

SUBJECT: Designation of US Invited Contractor under Article XV, Status of Forces Agreement

1. References:

a. Paragraph 2, Article XV, Status of Forces Agreement.

b. US Commerce Subcommittee Memorandum of Consultation, dated 11 July 1968, subject as above (Inclosure 1).

c. ROK Commerce Subcommittee Memorandum of Consultation, dated 15 July 1968, subject as above (Inclosure 2).

2. The United States, after consultation with the ROK Commerce Subcommittee and after having duly considered their views, has designated Daniel, Mann, Johnson & Mendenhall, as a US invited contractor for execution of Contract #DACA81-C-0075 for Architect and Engineering services.

3. Pertinent data concerning US citizen employees will be provided to the Joint Secretariat in the established periodic arrival and departure format.

2 Incl
as

ROBERT J. FRIEDMAN
Lieutenant General
United States Air Force
United States Representative
Joint Committee

281

REPUBLIC OF KOREA - UNITED STATES
COMMERCE SUBCOMMITTEE

11 July 1968

SUBJECT: Designation of US Invited Contractor under Article XV, Status of Forces Agreement

ROK Chairman, Commerce Subcommittee

1. Reference: Paragraph 2, Article XV of the Status of Forces Agreement.

2. The Government of the Republic of Korea is informed through this written consultive process that the United States Forces, Korea proposes to extend invited contractor status to the qualified US firm on the contract described in paragraph 3 below.

3. The following data is provided:

a. Company Name: Daniel, Mann, Johnson & Mendenhall.

b. Local Address: Osan AB, APO 96570

c. Identification of US Citizen Employees: To be supplied after award of contract.

d. Number of US and ROK Employees:

US - 6
ROK - 0

e. Reasons for Designation of an Invited Contractor: Open competitive bidding among local contractors is not practicable due to the following:

(1) Security considerations.

(2) Technical qualifications of the contractor involved.

f. Location of Contract: Various locations in Korea.

282

11 July 1968

SUBJECT: Designation of US Invited Contractor under Article XV, Status of Forces Agreement

g. Type of Contract: Lump Sum Contract for Architect-Engineer Services for Preparation of Definitive Data and Budget Estimates for Supplemental FY 68 Projects, Various Locations, Korea.

h. Length of Contract: 1 Month.

i. Sponsoring Component Command: CGUSAEIGHT.

FLOYD R. WALTZ, JR.
Colonel, United States Army
Assistant Chief of Staff, J 4

2

283

MINISTRY OF COMMERCE AND INDUSTRY
REPUBLIC OF KOREA
SEOUL, KOREA

15 July 1968

SUBJECT: Designation of US Invited Contractor under Article XV, Status of Forces Agreement.

TO : Chairman, US Commerce Subcommittee

1. References:

a. Paragraph 2, Article XV, Status of Forces Agreement.

b. US Commerce Subcommittee Memorandum of Consultation, dated 11 July 1968, subject as above, pertaining to contract for Architect-Engineer Services for Preparation of Definitive Data and Budget Estimates for Supplemental FY 68 Projects, Various Locations, Korea.

2. The US memorandum, reference 1b above, has been reviewed and the Government of the Republic of Korea fully understands the requirement for an invited contractor in this instance.

for: Shim Ui Hwan
Chairman
ROK Commerce Subcommittee

284

JOINT COMMITTEE
UNDER
THE REPUBLIC OF KOREA AND THE UNITED STATES
STATUS OF FORCES AGREEMENT

5 July 1968

MEMORANDUM FOR: The Joint Committee

SUBJECT: Designation of US Invited Contractor under Article XV, Status of Forces Agreement

1. References:

a. Paragraph 2, Article XV, Status of Forces Agreement.

b. US Commerce Subcommittee Memorandum of Consultation, dated 12 June 1968, subject as above (Inclosure 1).

c. ROK Commerce Subcommittee Memorandum of Consultation, dated 3 July 1968, subject as above (Inclosure 2).

2. The United States, after consultation with the ROK Commerce Subcommittee and after having duly considered their views, has designated Daniel, Mann, Johnson & Mendenhall as a US invited contractor for execution of Contract #F62087-68-C-0130 for architect and engineering services.

3. Pertinent data concerning US citizen employees will be provided to the Joint Secretariat in the established periodic arrival and departure format.

2 Incl
as

ROBERT J. FRIEDMAN
Lieutenant General
United States Air Force
United States Representative
Joint Committee

285

MINISTRY OF COMMERCE AND INDUSTRY
REPUBLIC OF KOREA
SEOUL, KOREA

3 July 1968

SUBJECT: Designation of US Invited Contractor under Article XV, Status of Forces Agreement.

TO : Chairman, US Commerce Subcommittee.

1. References:

a. Paragraph 2, Article XV, Status of Forces Agreement.

b. US Commerce Subcommittee Memorandum of Consultation, Dated 12 June 1968, subject as above, pertaining to contract for architect-engineering service in the Kunsan, Suwon and Osan Air Bases construction projects.

2. The US memorandum, reference 1b above, has been reviewed and the Government of the Republic of Korea fully understands the requirement for an invited contractor in this instance.

For [signature]
Chairman
ROK Commerce Subcommittee

286

REPUBLIC OF KOREA - UNITED STATES
COMMERCE SUBCOMMITTEE

12 June 1968

SUBJECT: Designation of US Invited Contractor under Article XV, Status of Forces Agreement

ROK Chairman, Commerce Subcommittee

1. Reference: Paragraph 2, Article XV of the Status of Forces Agreement.

2. The Government of the Republic of Korea is informed through this written consultive process that the United States Forces, Korea, proposes to extend invited contractor status to the qualified US firm on the contract described in paragraph 3 below.

3. The following data is provided:

a. Company Name: Daniel, Mann, Johnson and Mendenhall.

b. Local Address: Box 11, APO 96570.

c. Identification of US Citizen Employees: To be supplied after award of contract.

d. Number of US and ROK Employees:

U.S. - 7
ROK - 10

e. Reasons for Designation of an Invited Contractor: Open competitive bidding among local contractors is not practicable due to the following:

(1) Security considerations.

(2) Technical qualifications of the contractor involved.

f. Location of Contract: Kunsan, Suwon and Osan Air Bases, Korea.

287

12 June 1968

SUBJECT: Designation of US Invited Contractor under Article XV, Status of Forces Agreement

g. Type of Contract: Architect-Engineering services.

h. Length of Contract: Approximately 30 days.

i. Sponsoring Component Command: Commander, Air Forces, Korea. (Headquarters, 6314th Support Wing (PACAF)).

John T. Horrocks

JOHN T. HORROCKS
Colonel, United States Air Force
US Alternate Chairman, Commerce Subcommittee

288

JOINT COMMITTEE
UNDER
THE REPUBLIC OF KOREA AND THE UNITED STATES
STATUS OF FORCES AGREEMENT

13 July 1968

MEMORANDUM FOR: The Joint Committee

SUBJECT: Designation of US Invited Contractor under Article XV, Status of Forces Agreement

1. References:

a. Paragraph 2, Article XV, Status of Forces Agreement.

b. US Commerce Subcommittee Memorandum of Consultation, dated 6 July 1968, subject as above (Inclosure 1).

c. ROK Commerce Subcommittee Memorandum of Consultation, dated 11 July 1968, subject as above (Inclosure 2).

2. The United States, after consultation with the ROK Commerce Subcommittee and after having duly considered their views, has designated the Huwin Corporation as a US invited contractor for execution of Contract #DACA81-68-C-0065 for construction of access roads to AC&W sites.

3. Pertinent data concerning US citizen employees will be provided to the Joint Secretariat in the established periodic arrival and departure format.

2 Incl
as

ROBERT J. FRIEDMAN
Lieutenant General
United States Air Force
United States Representative
Joint Committee

289

MINISTRY OF COMMERCE AND INDUSTRY
REPUBLIC OF KOREA
SEOUL, KOREA

11 July 1968

SUBJECT: Designation of US Invited Contractor under Article XV, Status of Forces Agreement.

TO : Chairman, US Commerce Subcommittee

1. References:

a. Paragraph 2, Article XV, Status of Forces Agreement.

b. US Commerce Subcommittee Memorandum of Consultation, dated 6 July 1968, subject as above, pertaining to contract for construction of access roads to AC&W Sites, Korea.

2. The US memorandum, reference 1b above, has been reviewed and the Government of the Republic of Korea fully understands the requirement for an invited contractor in this instance.

for [signature]
Shim Ui Hwan
Chairman
ROK Commerce Subcommittee

290

REPUBLIC OF KOREA - UNITED STATES
COMMERCE SUBCOMMITTEE

6 July 1968

SUBJECT: Designation of US Invited Contractor under Article XV, Status of Forces Agreement

ROK Chairman, Commerce Subcommittee

1. Reference: Paragraph 2, Article XV of the Status of Forces Agreement.

2. The Government of the Republic of Korea is informed through this written consultive process that the United States Forces, Korea proposes to extend invited contractor status to the qualified US firm on the contract described in paragraph 3 below.

3. The following data is provided:

a. Company Name: Huwin Corporation

b. Local Address: 130 Chong No, 3rd Street, Chongno-ku, Seoul, Korea.

c. Identification of US Citizen Employees: To be supplied after award of contract.

d. Number of US and ROK Employees:

U.S.	-	5
ROK	-	6

e. Reasons for Designation of an Invited Contractor: Open competitive bidding among local contractors is not practicable due to the following:

Restrictions imposed by United States law, specifically the Foreign Assistance Act of 1961. Further guidance is contained in the Armed Services Procurement Regulation, paragraph 6-703.2, which states, in part "...Procurement for the Military Assistance Program shall be restricted to domestic concerns and to United States end products..."

291

6 July 1968

SUBJECT: Designation of US Invited Contractor under Article XV, Status of Forces Agreement

f. Location of Contract: Yongmun-san and Palgong-san, Korea.

g. Type of Contract: Construction of access roads to AC&W Sites, Korea.

h. Length of Contract: To be supplied upon conclusion of negotiation.

i. Sponsoring Component Command: CGUSAEIGHT.

Floyd R. Waltz

FLOYD R. WALTZ, JR.
Colonel, United States Army
Assistant Chief of Staff, J 4

JOINT COMMITTEE
UNDER
THE REPUBLIC OF KOREA AND THE UNITED STATES
STATUS OF FORCES AGREEMENT

15 July 1968

MEMORANDUM FOR: The Joint Committee

SUBJECT: Designation of US Invited Contractor under Article XV, Status of Forces Agreement

1. References:

a. Paragraph 2, Article XV, Status of Forces Agreement.

b. US Commerce Subcommittee Memorandum of Consultation, dated 29 March 1968, subject as above (Inclosure 1).

c. ROK Commerce Subcommittee Memorandum of Consultation, dated 15 July 1968, subject as above (Inclosure 2).

2. The United States, after consultation with the ROK Commerce Subcommittee and after having duly considered their views, has designated Tectonics Asia, Incorporated as a US invited contractor for execution of Contract #DAJB03-68-C-0489 for repair and utilities in the I Corps area.

3. Pertinent data concerning US citizen employees will be provided to the Joint Secretariat in the established periodic arrival and departure format.

2 Incl
as

ROBERT J. FRIEDMAN
Lieutenant General
United States Air Force
United States Representative
Joint Committee

293

REPUBLIC OF KOREA - UNITED STATES
COMMERCE SUBCOMMITTEE

29 March 1968

SUBJECT: Designation of US Invited Contractor under Article XV, Status of Forces Agreement

ROK Chairman, Commerce Subcommittee

1. Reference: Paragraph 2, Article XV of the Status of Forces Agreement.

2. The Government of the Republic of Korea is informed through this written consultive process that the United States Forces, Korea, proposes to extend invited contractor status to the successful negotiated bidder among qualified US firms on the contract described in paragraph 3 below.

3. The following data is provided:

a. Company Name:
1. Adrian Wilson Associates.
2. Associated American Engineers Overseas, Inc.
3. Barclay Overseas, Inc.
4. D. F. Fischer & Sons, Ltd.
5. Maintenance & Repair Services, Inc.
6. Pacific Architects & Engineers, Inc.
7. Universal American Enterprises, Inc.
8. Vinnel Corporation.
9. *Stolte-Korea Development Corporation.
10. *Huwin-Sam Whan.
11. *Cosmo Industry.
12. *Tetronics Asia Incorporated.

* Subject to approval of Accounting System by DCAA.

b. Local Address:
1. Eighth US Army/COMAFK, APO 96301.
2. Eighth US Army, APO 96301.
3. COMAFK, Sanryung Bldg., Room 302, Seoul.
4. Eighth US Army/COMAFK, APO 96301.
5. Eighth US Army, Bldg., 1510, Yongsan Mil Res, APO 96301.
6. Eighth US Army, APO 96302.
7. COMAFK, Osan AB, APO 96570.
8. Eighth US Army/COMAFK, CMR Box 521, APO 96570.

294

29 March 1968

SUBJECT: Designation of US Invited Contractor under Article XV, Status of Forces Agreement

9. #92 Kalwol Dong, Yongsan-Ku, Seoul.
10. #199-53, 2Ka, Ulchiro, Chung-Ku, Seoul.
11. #199-34, 2Ka, Ulchiro, Chung-Ku, Seoul.
12. Tongnam Bldg #97-2, Cho Dong, Chung-Ku, Seoul.

c. Identification of US Citizen Employees: To be supplied after award.

d. Number of US & ROK Employees (estimated):

(1) Camp Humphreys - US 25 ROK 925.

(2) I Corps - US 23 ROK 575.

e. Reasons for Designation of an Invited Contractor: Competitive bidding will be restricted to the above firms for the following reasons:

(1) Security considerations.

(2) Special management and technical skills are required.

(3) Experience in this type of operation is highly desirable.

(4) Limitations of US law regarding procurement.

f. Location of Contract: Camp Humphreys and I Corps.

g. Type of Contract: Cost-plus-fixed-fee.

h. Length of Contract: 1 July 68 thru 30 June 69 with 30 day transition period (13 months total).

i. Sponsoring Component Command: Commanding General, Eighth US Army.

4. The United States certifies that the successful bidder or named contractor is present in the Republic of Korea solely for the purpose of executing contracts with the United States, for the benefit of the United States Armed Forces or other armed forces under the Unified Command receiving logistical support from the United States Forces.

5. The views of the Government of the Republic of Korea are earnestly solicited prior to United States selection and designation of an invited

295

contractor to perform the work outlined above. You may be assured that your views will be considered carefully.

6. Your early reply will be greatly appreciated.

FLOYD R. WALTZ, JR.
Colonel, United States Army
US Chairman, Commerce Subcommittee

296

3

MINISTRY OF COMMERCE AND INDUSTRY
REPUBLIC OF KOREA
SEOUL, KOREA

15 July 1968

SUBJECT: Designation of US Invited Contractor under Article XV, Status of Forces Agreement.

TO : Chairman, US Commerce Subcommittee.

1. References:

a. Paragraph 2, Article XV, Status of Forces Agreement.

b. US Commerce Subcommittee Memorandum of Consultation, Dated 29 March 1968, subject as above, pertaining to contract for repair and utilities in Camp Humphreys and 1 Corps Area.

2. The US memorandum, reference 1b above, has been reviewed and the Government of the Republic of Korea fully understands the requirement for an invited contractor in this instance.

Shim Ui Hwan
Shim Ui Hwan
Chairman
ROK Commerce Subcommittee

297

JOINT COMMITTEE
UNDER
THE REPUBLIC OF KOREA AND THE UNITED STATES
STATUS OF FORCES AGREEMENT

23 July 1968

MEMORANDUM FOR: The Joint Committee

SUBJECT: Designation of US Invited Contractor under Article XV, Status of Forces Agreement

1. References:

a. Paragraph 2, Article XV, Status of Forces Agreement.

b. US Commerce Subcommittee Memorandum of Consultation, dated 6 July 1968, subject as above (Inclosure 1).

c. ROK Commerce Subcommittee Memorandum of Consultation, dated 11 July 1968, subject as above (Inclosure 2).

2. The United States, after consultation with the ROK Commerce Subcommittee and after having duly considered their views, has designated R. M. Towill Corporation as a US invited contractor for execution of Contract #DACA81-69-C-0001 for Architect and Engineering services for Aerial Photogrammetric Survey.

3. Pertinent data concerning US citizen employees will be provided to the Joint Secretariat in the established periodic arrival and departure format.

2 Incl
as

ROBERT J. FRIEDMAN
Lieutenant General
United States Air Force
United States Representative
Joint Committee

298

MINISTRY OF COMMERCE AND INDUSTRY
REPUBLIC OF KOREA
SEOUL, KOREA

11 July 1968

SUBJECT: Designation of US Invited Contractor under Article XV, Status of Forces Agreement.

TO : Chairman, US Commerce Subcommittee

1. References:

a. Paragraph ?, Article XV, Status of Forces Agreement.

b. US Commerce Subcommittee Memorandum of Consultation, dated 6 July 1968, subject as above, pertaining to contract for Architect-Engineer Services for Photogrammetric Surveys at various locations in Korea.

2. The US memorandum, reference 1b above, has been reviewed and the Government of the Republic of Korea fully understands the requirement for an invited contractor in this instance.

Shim Ui Hwan
Chairman
ROK Commerce Subcommittee

299

REPUBLIC OF KOREA - UNITED STATES
COMMERCE SUBCOMMITTEE

6 July 1968

SUBJECT: Designation of US Invited Contractor under Article XV, Status of Forces Agreement

ROK Chairman, Commerce Subcommittee

1. Reference: Paragraph 2, Article XV of the Status of Forces Agreement.

2. The Government of the Republic of Korea is informed through this written consultive process that the United States Forces, Korea proposes to extend invited contractor status to the qualified US firm on the contract described in paragraph 3 below.

3. The following data is provided:

a. Company Name: 1. Pacific Architects & Engineers, Inc.
2. Towill Corporation

b. Local Address: 1. APO 96302
2. Honolulu, Hawaii

c. Identification of US Citizen Employees: To be supplied after award of contract.

d. Number of US and ROK Employees: To be supplied after award of contract.

e. Reasons for Designation of an Invited Contractor: Open competitive bidding among local contractors is not practicable due to the following:

(1) Security Considerations.

(2) Technical qualifications of the contractor involved.

f. Location of Contract: Various locations in Korea.

700

6 July 1968

SUBJECT: Designation of US Invited Contractor under Article XV, Status of Forces Agreement

g. Type of Contract: Lump Sum Contract for Architect-Engineer Services for Photogrammetric Surveys at various locations in Korea.

h. Length of Contract: To be supplied upon conclusion of negotiations.

i. Sponsoring Component Command: CGUSAEIGHT.

Floyd R. Waltz

FLOYD R. WALTZ, JR.
Colonel, United States Army
Assistant Chief of Staff, J 4

2

701

JOINT COMMITTEE
UNDER
THE REPUBLIC OF KOREA AND THE UNITED STATES
STATUS OF FORCES AGREEMENT

15 July 1968

MEMORANDUM FOR: The Joint Committee

SUBJECT: Designation of US Invited Contractor under Article XV, Status of Forces Agreement

1. References:

a. Paragraph 2, Article XV, Status of Forces Agreement.

b. US Commerce Subcommittee Memorandum of Consultation, dated 29 March 1968, subject as above (Inclosure 1).

c. ROK Commerce Subcommittee Memorandum of Consultation, dated 15 July 1968, subject as above (Inclosure 2).

2. The United States, after consultation with the ROK Commerce Subcommittee and after having duly considered their views, has designated Maintenance & Repair Services, Inc. as a US invited contractor for execution of Contract #DAJB03-68-C-0490 for repair and utilities at Camp Humphreys.

3. Pertinent data concerning US citizen employees will be provided to the Joint Secretariat in the established periodic arrival and departure format.

2 Incl
as

ROBERT J. FRIEDMAN
Lieutenant General
United States Air Force
United States Representative
Joint Committee

702

JOINT COMMITTEE
UNDER
THE REPUBLIC OF KOREA AND THE UNITED STATES
STATUS OF FORCES AGREEMENT

15 July 1968

MEMORANDUM FOR: The Joint Committee

SUBJECT: Designation of US Invited Contractor under Article XV, Status of Forces Agreement

1. References:

a. Paragraph 2, Article XV, Status of Forces Agreement.

b. US Commerce Subcommittee Memorandum of Consultation, dated 29 March 1968, subject as above (Inclosure 1).

c. ROK Commerce Subcommittee Memorandum of Consultation, dated 15 July 1968, subject as above (Inclosure 2).

2. The United States, after consultation with the ROK Commerce Subcommittee and after having duly considered their views, has designated Maintenance & Repair Services, Inc. as a US invited contractor for execution of Contract #DAJB03-68-C-0490 for repair and utilities at Camp Humphreys.

3. Pertinent data concerning US citizen employees will be provided to the Joint Secretariat in the established periodic arrival and departure format.

2 Incl
as

ROBERT J. FRIEDMAN
Lieutenant General
United States Air Force
United States Representative
Joint Committee

303

MINISTRY OF COMMERCE AND INDUSTRY
REPUBLIC OF KOREA
SEOUL, KOREA

15 July 1968

SUBJECT: Designation of US Invited Contractor under Article XV, Status of Forces Agreement.

TO : Chairman, US Commerce Subcommittee.

1. References:

a. Paragraph 2, Article XV, Status of Forces Agreement.

b. US Commerce Subcommittee Memorandum of Consultation, Dated 29 March 1968, subject as above, pertaining to contract for repair and utilities in Camp Humphreys and 1 Corps Area.

2. The US memorandum, reference 1b above, has been reviewed and the Government of the Republic of Korea fully understands the requirement for an invited contractor in this instance.

Shin Ui Hwan
Chairman
ROK Commerce Subcommittee

304

REPUBLIC OF KOREA - UNITED STATES
COMMERCE SUBCOMMITTEE

29 March 1968

SUBJECT: Designation of US Invited Contractor under Article XV, Status of Forces Agreement

ROK Chairman, Commerce Subcommittee

1. Reference: Paragraph 2, Article XV of the Status of Forces Agreement.

2. The Government of the Republic of Korea is informed through this written consultive process that the United States Forces, Korea, proposes to extend invited contractor status to the successful negotiated bidder among qualified US firms on the contract described in paragraph 3 below.

3. The following data is provided:

a. Company Name:
1. Adrian Wilson Associates.
2. Associated American Engineers Overseas, Inc.
3. Barclay Overseas, Inc.
4. D. F. Fischer & Sons, Ltd.
5. Maintenance & Repair Services, Inc.
6. Pacific Architects & Engineers, Inc.
7. Universal American Enterprises, Inc.
8. Vinnel Corporation.
9. *Stolte-Korea Development Corporation.
10. *Huwin-Sam Whan.
11. *Cosmo Industry.
12. *Tetronics Asia Incorporated.

* Subject to approval of Accounting System by DCAA.

b. Local Address:
1. Eighth US Army/COMAFK, APO 96301.
2. Eighth US Army, APO 96301.
3. COMAFK, Sanryung Bldg., Room 30?, Seoul.
4. Eighth US Army/COMAFK, APO 96301.
5. Eighth US Army, Bldg., 1510, Yongsan Mil Res, APO 96301.
6. Eighth US Army, APO 96302.
7. COMAFK, Osan AB, APO 96570.
8. Eighth US Army/COMAFK, CMR Box 521, APO 96570.

305

29 March 1968

SUBJECT: Designation of US Invited Contractor under Article XV, Status of Forces Agreement

9. #92 Kalwol Dong, Yongsan-Ku, Seoul.
10. #199-53, 2Ka, Ulchiro, Chung-Ku, Seoul.
11. #199-34, 2Ka, Ulchiro, Chung-Ku, Seoul.
12. Tongnam Bldg #97-2, Cho Dong, Chung-Ku, Seoul.

c. Identification of US Citizen Employees: To be supplied after award.

d. Number of US & ROK Employees (estimated):

(1) Camp Humphreys - US 25 ROK 925.

(2) I Corps - US 23 ROK 575.

e. Reasons for Designation of an Invited Contractor: Competitive bidding will be restricted to the above firms for the following reasons:

(1) Security considerations.

(2) Special management and technical skills are required.

(3) Experience in this type of operation is highly desirable.

(4) Limitations of US law regarding procurement.

f. Location of Contract: Camp Humphreys and I Corps.

g. Type of Contract: Cost-plus-fixed-fee.

h. Length of Contract: 1 July 68 thru 30 June 69 with 30 day transition period (13 months total).

i. Sponsoring Component Command: Commanding General, Eighth US Army.

4. The United States certifies that the successful bidder or named contractor is present in the Republic of Korea solely for the purpose of executing contracts with the United States, for the benefit of the United States Armed Forces or other armed forces under the Unified Command receiving logistical support from the United States Forces.

5. The views of the Government of the Republic of Korea are earnestly solicited prior to United States selection and designation of an invited

2

706

29 March 1968

SUBJECT: Designation of US Invited Contractor under Article XV, Status of Forces Agreement

contractor to perform the work outlined above. You may be assured that your views will be considered carefully.

6. Your early reply will be greatly appreciated.

FLOYD R. WALTZ, JR.
Colonel, United States Army
US Chairman, Commerce Subcommittee

3

7109

대한민국 외무부
공보관실

보 도 자 료

— 호 이 기사는 제공처인 외무부를
1968년 8월 14일 시 분 발표 밝히고 보도할수 있음

JOINT ROK - US PRESS RELEASE
TWENTY-NINTH ROK-US JOINT COMMITTEE MEETING

The ROK-US Joint Committee adopted two recommendations of its Criminal Jurisdiction Subcommittee to facilitate implementation of the Criminal Jurisdiction procedures under the SOFA at its twenty-ninth meeting, held at the US SOFA Conference Room, on 14 August. The Joint Committee also assigned two new tasks to the Criminal Jurisdiction Subcommittee to clarify criminal jurisdiction procedures.

The Joint Committee also approved thirteen recommendations of its Facilities and Areas Subcommittee relating to the acquisition and release of facilities and areas by the US armed forces in Korea. Five additional tasks were assigned to the Facilities and Areas Subcommittee.

The US Representative, Lieutenant General Robert J. Friedman, presided at this meeting and designated ten US invited contractors, as recommended by the Commerce Subcommittee.

The next meeting of the ROK-US Joint Committee is scheduled for Thursday, 12 September, at the ROK Capitol Building.

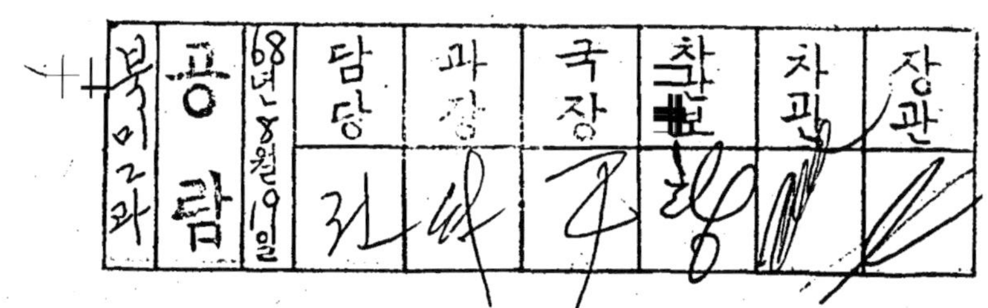

한.미 합동위원회 제29차 회의 회의록 (요약)

일 시 : 1968. 8. 14.

장 소 : 용산 미군 SOFA 회의실

1. 시설구역 분과위원회의 건의 채택 및 동 분과위원회에 대한 신규과제 부여

가. 건 의

건의내용	건 수	면 적 (에이커)
부동산 취득	2	0.81
지역권 취득	1	0.019
임시취득	2	2.982
임시사용허가 연장	3	8534.55
반 환	5	28.708 및 건물 1동
계	13	8567.069

나. 신규과제

과제내용	건 수	면 적
부동산취득	3	4.1296
임시사용허가 연장	2	77,708.97
계	5	77,713.0996

309

2. 형사재판권 분과위원회의 건의 채택 및 신규과제 부여

가. 건 의

(1) 전속적 및 제1차적 재판권에 관한 문제의 해결 절차

(2) 한국 수사당국에 참고인이나 피의자를 출석케 하는 절차

나. 신규과제

(1) 협정 제22조 3 (나)항에 의거한 한국측의 재판권 행사기간 15일의 기산 방법

(2) 재판 절차 완결후의 신병 인도 절차

3. 주한 미군 초청계약자 지명 10건.

310

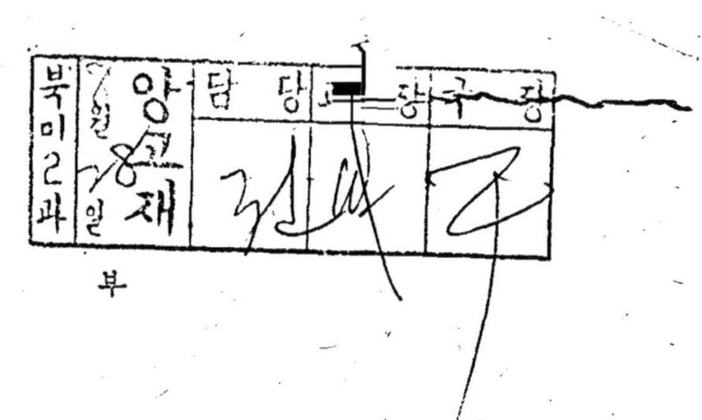

외 무 부

미이 720- 1968 . 8 . 28 .

수 신 : 배부처 참조

참 조 :

제 목 : 한.미 합동위원회 회의록 송부

1. 한.미간 군대지위협정에 의하여 1968 . 8 . 14 .에 개최된 한.미 합동위원회 제 29 차 회의의 회의록을 별첨 송부하오니 참고 하시기 바랍니다.

2. 본 회의록은 한.미 양측의 합의에 의하여서만 공개할 수 있는 문서이오니 유념하시기 바랍니다.

첨부 : 합동위원회 제 29 차 회의록 부. 끝

외 무 부 장 관

배부처 : 법무부장관 (법무실장, 검찰국장) 3부, 국방부장관 (기획국장, 시설국장) 2부, 재무부장관 (세관국장, 세제국장) 2부, 상공부장관 (상역국장), 노동청장 (노정국장), 교통부장관 (항공국장), 내무부장관 (치안국장), 주미 2부 주일, 주중, 주비대사, 경제기획원장관 (경제기획국장)

311

공 란

7. The ROK Representative presented a new task for the Criminal Jurisdiction Subcommittee (Inclosure 3). He stated that the exchange of letters between the Republic of Korea and the United States on 9 July 1966, which implement the provisions of the Agreed Minute Re Paragraph 3(b), Article XXII concerning exercise and waiver of primary jurisdiction, provided that the Minister of Justice would notify in writing the appropriate US military authorities of the ROK decision to exercise jurisdiction within 15 days after the Republic of Korea was notified or otherwise apprised of the commission of an offense falling within its primary jurisdiction. Since this whole question presupposed that the persons involved in an offense were covered by the SOFA and that the offense fell within primary jurisdiction as defined by the SOFA, there were problems as to when the said 15-day period should commence in cases where either the SOFA coverage or the nature of jurisdiction was in question in the initial stages of investigation. The ROK Representative stated that he felt there should be mutually agreed guidelines as to this question to cover the cases where either the identity of the persons involved was unknown, doubtful, or misunderstood, or where the nature of jurisdiction was in doubt (which was partly made a subject of specific recommendations to be presented later as Agreed View No. 15).

These minutes are considered as official documents pertaining to both Governments and will not be released without mutual agreement.

8. The ROK Representative proposed that the Criminal Jurisdiction Subcommittee be assigned a task of formulating guidelines as to when the 15-day period for assuming jurisdiction commenced in cases which fell under the Agreed Minute Re Paragraph 3(b) of Article XXII of the SOFA.

9. The US Representative concurred in the assignment of this task to the Criminal Jurisdiction Subcommittee. He stated that mutual agreement on this subject should facilitate the implementation of the provisions of the SOFA relating to notification to the United States military authorities of the Government of the Republic of Korea's intention to exercise jurisdiction. The SOFA and the exchange of letters between the ROK Foreign Minister and the US Ambassador provide that the Government of the Republic of Korea would make its decision regarding exercise of jurisdiction within 15 days after it is notified or otherwise apprised of the commission of an offense falling within its primary jurisdiction. It is hoped that the Criminal Jurisdiction Subcommittee would be able to submit recommendations which would facilitate and expedite the effective implementation of these SOFA provisions.

10. The US Representative proposed the assignment of a task to the Criminal Jurisdiction Subcommittee relating to procedures for the transfer of custody of US personnel upon completion of all judicial proceedings (Inclosure 4). The SOFA provides that the custody of an accused member of the US forces, civilian component, invited contractor, or dependent, shall remain with the military authorities of the US pending the conclusion of all judicial proceedings and until custody was requested by the authorities of the Republic of Korea. The US Representative stated that this task to the Criminal Jurisdiction Subcommittee requested recommendations on procedures to implement the provisions of the SOFA relating to the transfer of custody. The recommended procedures should include the designation of ROK authorities who would make the request, the US military authorities to whom the request would be made, the documentation required at the time of transfer, and the arrangements for the physical transfer of the individual concerned.

11. The ROK Representative stated that the task proposed for the Criminal Jurisdiction Subcommittee was most pertinent, and he was happy to concur in the assignment of this task.

12. The ROK Representative presented five recommendations of the Facilities and Areas Subcommittee, as follows:

29th JC
14 Aug 68

기14

These minutes are considered as official documents pertaining to both Governments and will not be released without mutual agreement.

a. Withdrawal of the request for release of real estate, SAC-616, consisting of 2.43 acres of land at Yangmal-san, Yoido, Yongdongpo-ku, Seoul for construction of Yoido circular dike (Inclosure 5). It was recommended that this request be included in the request for the release of the entire tract of K-16.

b. Release of a portion of SAC-715, comprising 1.64 acres located in Seoul City, in connection with a Seoul City development plan (Inclosure 6).

c. Withdrawal of the request for release of real estate, PAC-152, involving 23.90 acres of land located in Chilgok-gun, Kyungsangpuk-do (Inclosure 7).

d. Joint use of a portion of AAC-391, consisting of one building and 0.703 acre of land located within the area of Kimpo Air Base, for use by the Republic of Korea Air Force (Inclosure 8).

e. Release of a portion of Camp Yuma, consisting of 0.035 acre located at Inchon, in connection with the construction of a new highway from Seoul to Inchon (Inclosure 9).

13. The ROK Representative proposed approval of the five recommendations of the Facilities and Areas Subcommittee, as set forth in detail in Inclosures 5 through 9. The US Representative concurred.

14. The US Representative presented eight recommendations of the Facilities and Areas Subcommittee, as follows:

a. Acquisition of 0.8 acre of land in Uijongbu City to expand Hill 651 Compound (Inclosure 10).

b. Acquisition of 0.01 acre of land in Seoul City to construct a bridge at Camp Niblo (Inclosure 11).

c. Acquisition of perpetual restrictive easement in Seoul City involving 0.019 acre of land in Yongsan-ku, Seoul for an underground steam heating line between the North and South Posts of the Eighth US Army in Yongsan (Inclosure 11).

d. Acquisition of a temporary use permit for 0.186 acre of land in Yangju-gun, Kyonggi-do, to relocate and reconstruct Bayonet Bridge (Inclosure 11).

These minutes are considered as official documents pertaining to both Governments and will not be released without mutual agreement.

e. Acquisition of a temporary use permit for 2.796 acres of land in Pochon-gun, Kyonggi-do to reconstruct Old Faithful Bridge (Inclosure 11).

f. The extension of temporary use permits IC-T-41, 7X-T-15, and 7X-T-16 (Inclosure 11).

15. The US Representative proposed Joint Committee approval of these eight recommendations of the Facilities and Areas Subcommittee and the ROK Representative concurred.

16. The ROK Representative stated that the Joint Committee, at its fifteenth meeting on 28 September 1967, assigned a task to the Criminal Jurisdiction Subcommittee, to define exclusive and concurrent jurisdiction. As an initial undertaking in this general area of study, the Criminal Jurisdiction Subcommittee was requested to make a comparative review of pertinent laws and regulations relating to customs and traffic violations with a view to arriving at agreed guidelines as to jurisdiction in these specific areas.

17. The ROK Representative stated that the Subcommittee found that the laws of the ROK and the US relating to customs and vehicular traffic, as well as in regard to other areas, are extensive, complicated, and constantly subject to change and re-interpretation. Consequently, the Subcommittee found that it was not possible to formulate precise rules which would serve as effective guidelines for future cases. Therefore, each offense must be studied at the time it occurs in the light of the laws and implementing regulations then in effect.

18. The ROK Representative stated that, based on these findings and conclusions, the Subcommittee recommended (Inclosure 12):

a. That questions of jurisdiction in all cases be resolved on a case-by-case basis as they arise.

b. That Agreed View No. 15 be adopted for resolving questions of exclusive and concurrent jurisdiction.

19. The ROK Representative summarized the substance of the Agreed View No. 15 (Inclosure 12), as follows:

29th JC
14 Aug 68

316

These minutes are considered as official documents pertaining to both Governments and will not be released without mutual agreement.

a. When a question of exclusive jurisdiction is raised, the case will be first referred to the two chairmen of the Subcommittee for consultation and resolution; if agreement cannot be reached at that level, either chairman may refer the case to the Joint Committee for resolution.

b. During the course of the foregoing procedures, neither side will exercise jurisdiction and the 15-day-time-limit period for notification of the exercise of primary jurisdiction will be considered not to have commenced until it is determined that the incident falls within the primary jurisdiction of the ROK.

c. When mutual agreement cannot be reached through the foregoing procedures, the State claiming exclusive jurisdiction may exercise jurisdiction over the specific offense until a mutual agreement is reached through other channels.

20. The ROK Representative stated that, given the extreme complexity of the problem, the recommendation of the Subcommittee was a very reasonable one. However, it was obviously much preferable to have a set of guidelines, if it were possible, in the interests of stability in the judicial proceedings. Such guidelines would save time and effort for everyone concerned. The ROK Representative expressed the hope that by accumulation of experience a certain body of guidelines would gradually grow up naturally and perhaps it could become possible at some future time to formulate explicit guidelines. The ROK Representative, therefore, proposed that Joint Committee approve the recommendations of the Criminal Jurisdiction Subcommittee, with the understanding that the adoption of these recommendations does not preclude future efforts to formulate explicit guidelines.

21. The US Representative concurred in the approval of the recommendations of the Criminal Jurisdiction Subcommittee, including Agreed View No. 15. He stated that he felt these recommendations were both practical and realistic, but that of course Joint Committee approval of them at this time does not preclude further consideration of the question at some future time, if such appears desirable.

22. The US Representative proposed Joint Committee approval of the Criminal Jurisdiction Subcommittee's Agreed View No. 14, relating to procedures for obtaining US witnesses or suspects for ROK investigative

29th JC
14 Aug 68

These minutes are considered as official documents pertaining to both Governments and will not be released without mutual agreement.

authorities (Inclosure 13). The US Representative also expressed his appreciation to the Criminal Jurisdiction Subcommittee for its good work, as reflected in the recommendations presented in the implementation of the Criminal Jurisdiction Article, at this Joint Committee meeting. The ROK Representative concurred in Joint Committee approval of Agreed View No. 14.

23. The US Representative presented memoranda to the Joint Committee informing the ROK Government of the designation of ten new US invited contractors, in accordance with Article XV of the SOFA. After consultation with ROK Commerce Subcommittee personnel, the US Forces, Korea designated as US invited contractors Daniel, Mann, Johnson & Mendenhall (three contracts - Inclosures 14, 15, and 16); Trans-Asia Engineering Associates, Inc. (Inclosure 17); Lyon Associates, Inc. (Inclosure 18); Tectonics Asia (Inclosure 19); R. M. Towill Corp. (Inclosure 20); Huwin Corp. (Inclosure 21); Maintenance & Repair Services, Inc. (Inclosure 22); and Adrian Wilson Associates (Inclosure 23). The US Representative stated that pertinent data concerning employees of these invited contractors would be provided to the Government of the ROK in accordance with mutually approved procedures.

24. The ROK Representative stated that he was pleased to acknowledge US notification on designation of these ten US invited contractors. He confirmed that mutually agreed procedures of consultation had been duly observed in these designations.

25. The US Representative noted for the record that the US SOFA Secretary has furnished the following information to the ROK SOFA Secretary, in accordance with the provisions of the SOFA and Joint Committee decisions:

a. Five copies of reports on the US armed forces disposition of cases for the month of June 1968.

b. Twenty copies of the report of US armed forces personnel, the civilian component, invited contractors, and dependents entering or departing the ROK during the month of June 1968.

c. Eighteen copies of notices of arrivals, departures, and changes of addresses of US invited contractor personnel and their dependents, dated 2 August 1968.

29th JC
14 Aug 68

These minutes are considered as official documents pertaining to both Governments and will not be released without mutual agreement.

26. The ROK Representative acknowledged the receipt of the documents, as enumerated.

27. The US Representative proposed that the next meeting of the Joint Committee be held on Thursday, 12 September 1968, in the ROK Capitol Building, as proposed by the Republic of Korea SOFA Secretariat. The ROK Representative agreed.

28. The US Representative proposed approval of the joint press release for the twenty-ninth Joint Committee meeting, as prepared by the ROK and US SOFA Secretaries (Inclosure 24). The ROK Representative concurred.

29. The US Representative stated that, before adjourning the twenty-ninth Joint Committee meeting, he wished to offer his congratulations to his Korean colleagues on the Joint Committee on the progress of their Nation, as they celebrate on 15 August the twenty-third anniversary of liberation from Japanese rule and the twentieth anniversary of the founding of the Government of the Republic of Korea. The ROK Representative thanked the US Representative for his congratulations and good wishes. The meeting was adjourned at 1550 hours.

24 Inclosures

ROBERT J. FRIEDMAN
LIEUTENANT GENERAL
UNITED STATES AIR FORCE
UNITED STATES REPRESENTATIVE

YOON HA JONG
REPUBLIC OF KOREA
REPRESENTATIVE

29th JC
14 Aug 68

These minutes are [illegible]nsidered as official documents [illegible]rtaining to both Governments and will not be released without mutual agreement.

26. The ROK Representative acknowledged the receipt of the documents, as enumerated.

27. The US Representative proposed that the next meeting of the Joint Committee be held on Thursday, 12 September 1968, in the ROK Capitol Building, as proposed by the Republic of Korea SOFA Secretariat. The ROK Representative agreed.

28. The US Representative proposed approval of the joint press release for the twenty-ninth Joint Committee meeting, as prepared by the ROK and US SOFA Secretaries (Inclosure 24). The ROK Representative concurred.

29. The US Representative stated that, before adjourning the twenty-ninth Joint Committee meeting, he wished to offer his congratulations to his Korean colleagues on the Joint Committee on the progress of their Nation, as they celebrate on 15 August the twenty-third anniversary of liberation from Japanese rule and the twentieth anniversary of the founding of the Government of the Republic of Korea. The ROK Representative thanked the US Representative for his congratulations and good wishes. The meeting was adjourned at 1550 hours.

24 Inclosures

YOON HA JONG
REPUBLIC OF KOREA
REPRESENTATIVE

ROBERT J. FRIEDMAN
LIEUTENANT GENERAL
UNITED STATES AIR FORCE
UNITED STATES REPRESENTATIVE

29th JC
14 Aug 68

8

720

These minutes are considered as official documents pertaining to both Governments and will not be released without mutual agreement.

AGENDA FOR THE TWENTY-NINTH MEETING OF THE ROK-US JOINT COMMITTEE 1500 HOURS, 14 AUGUST 1968, US SOFA CONFERENCE ROOM

I Assignment of Tasks to Facilities and Areas Subcommittee - US Presentation

II Assignment of Additional Tasks to Criminal Jurisdiction Subcommittee

1. One Task - ROK Presentation
2. One Task - US Presentation

III Recommendations of Facilities and Areas Subcommittee

1. Five Recommendations - ROK Presentation
2. Eight Recommendations - US Presentation

IV Recommendations of the Criminal Jurisdiction Subcommittee

1. One Recommendation - ROK Presentation
2. One Recommendation - US Presentation

V Memoranda on Designation of USFK Invited Contractors - US Presentation

VI Memoranda Presented to the ROK Government by the US in the Implementation of the SOFA - US Presentation

VII Proposed Time of Next Meeting - Thursday, 12 September 1968, in the ROK Capitol Building

VIII Agreement on Joint Press Release

IX Adjourn

29th JC
14 Aug 68 (Incl 1)

321

공 란

공 란

공 란

These minutes are considered as official documents pertaining to both Governments and will not be released without mutual agreement.

JOINT COMMITTEE
UNDER
THE REPUBLIC OF KOREA AND THE UNITED STATES
STATUS OF FORCES AGREEMENT

14 August 1968

MEMORANDUM FOR: Chairmen, Criminal Jurisdiction Subcommittee

SUBJECT: Commencement of the 15 Day Period for the Republic of Korea to Exercise its Criminal Jurisdiction under Paragraph 3(b), Article XXII, US-ROK SOFA

1. The Exchange of Letters between the ROK and the US on 9 July 1966, implementing the provisions of the Agreed Minute Re Paragraph 3(b), Article XXII, provides that the Minister of Justice will notify in writing the appropriate US military authorities of the ROK decision to exercise jurisdiction within 15 days after the Republic of Korea is notified or otherwise apprised of the commission of an offense falling within its primary jurisdiction. A method of counting these 15 days should be devised which would apply not only in routine cases but also in those instances where the name of the suspect is unknown, or his status as a member of the US armed forces, civilian component, invited contractor, dependent, or Korean national employee is misunderstood, or it is uncertain whether US personnel were involved in any respect.

2. It is requested, therefore, that the Criminal Jurisdiction Subcommittee recommend guidelines as to when the 15 day period for assuming jurisdiction commences in cases which fall under the provisions of Paragraph 3(b), Article XXII, US-ROK SOFA.

YOON HA JONG
Republic of Korea Representative

ROBERT J. FRIEDMAN
Lieutenant General
United States Air Force
United States Representative

29th JC
14 Aug 68 (Incl 3)

325

공 란

공 란

공 란

공 란

공 란

공 란

공 란

공 란

공 란

공　　　란

공 란

공 란

공 란

공 란

공 란

공　　　　　란

공　　　란

공　　　란

공　　　란

공 란

공 란

공 란

These minutes are considered as official documents pertaining to both Governments and will not be released without mutual agreement.

CRIMINAL JURISDICTION SUBCOMMITTEE
ROK/US SOFA JOINT COMMITTEE

16 July 1968

SUBJECT: Recommendation of Criminal Jurisdiction Subcommittee

ROK/US SOFA Joint Committee

1. Subject of recommendations. On 23 February 1967, the Joint Committee requested the Criminal Jurisdiction Subcommittee to recommend "mutually agreed procedures for cooperation in the conduct of investigations and in the collection and production of evidence."

2. Recommendation. The Criminal Jurisdiction Subcommittee recommends, in partial fulfillment of this task, that the following agreed view be adopted by the Joint Committee:

Agreed View No. 14 - Procedures for Obtaining Witnesses or Suspects for ROK Investigative Authorities.

3. Security Classification: None.

KIM, SUNG CHAE
Chairman, ROK Component
Criminal Jurisdiction Subcommittee

GERALD W. DAVIS
Colonel, JAGC
Chairman, US Component
Criminal Jurisdiction Subcommittee

APPROVED BY THE JOINT COMMITTEE ON
14 AUGUST 1968 AT TWENTY-NINTH MEETING

YOON HA JONG
Republic of Korea Representative

ROBERT J. FRIEDMAN
Lieutenant General
United States Air Force
United States Representative

29th JC
14 Aug 68 (Incl 12)

348

. These minutes are co[illegible]idered as official documents p[illegible]aining to both Governments and will not be released without mutual agreement.

CRIMINAL JURISDICTION

Agreed View No. 14

Procedures for Obtaining Witnesses or Suspects for ROK Investigative Authorities

한국 수사당국에 참고인이나 피의자를 출석케하는 절차

Pursuant to the provisions of paragraph 6(a), Article XXII, and paragraph 2
한미 행정협정 제 22 조 제 6 항 (가) 및 동조 제 3 항 (나) 에
of the Agreed Understanding to the Agreed Minute Re Paragraph 3(b),
관한 합의 의사록에 대한 합의 양해사항 제 2 항의 규정에
Article XXII, ROK-US Status of Forces Agreement, the following procedure
의하여 한국 당국이 미 합중국 군대의 구성원, 군속, 가족 및
will apply when the cooperation of US authorities is necessary to obtain
초청계약자를 수사상 참고인이나 피의자로 출석토록 하는데 미군
a member of the United States armed forces, civilian component, a dependent,
당국의 협력이 필요한 경우에는 다음 절차를 적용한다.
or an US invited contractor as a witness or as a suspect at an investigation

by ROK authorities:

1. The request for such witness or suspect will be in writing, if
동 참고인이나 피의자의 요청은 가능한한 서면으로 인근
possible, and delivered to the nearest area provost marshal/security police
헌병대장에게 하여야 하며, 동 요청서에는 한국당국이 필요로
officer. The request will contain the individual's name, organization,
하는 당사자의 성명, 소속과 출석장소 및 시간을 명시하여야 한다.
and the place and time that the ROK authorities desire the individual.

2. The area provost marshal/security police officer of his designee
요청서를 접수한 헌병대장이나 그 대리인은 당사자의 부대장,
will contact the commanding officer, supervisor, or employer of the
감독자나 고용인 또는 그 보호자에게 이를 통보한다.
individual, or the individual's sponsor.

349

29th JC
14 Aug 68 (Incl 1 to Incl 12)

3. The commanding officer, supervisor, or employer will make the necessary
부대장, 감독자 또는 고용인은 한국 당국의 요청에 응할 수

arrangements, including transportation, to comply with the ROK request.
있도록 교통편의를 포함한 필요한 조치를 한다.

4. If the individual is not available at the requested time because of
만일 당사자가 긴급한 군무나 질병, 기타 유사한 이유로

imperative military duties, illness, or other similar reason, the commanding
요청된 시간에 출석하지 못 할 때에는 부대장, 감독자 또는

officer, supervisor, or employer will propose to the ROK authorities, either
고용인은 직접 또는 헌병대장을 통하여 한국 당국에 참고인이나

directly or through the provost marshal/security police officer, a time
피의자가 출석할 수 있는 시간을 제시한다.

when the witness or suspect will be available.

Note: 주의

Procedures for obtaining witnesses and defendants at ROK trial proceedings
한국의 재판에 증인이나 피고인을 출석케 하는 절차는 한미

are set forth in unnumbered paragraph 2, 3, and 4 of paragraph 1 of the
행정협정 제 22 조 제 6 항에 관한 합의 의사록 제 1 항의

Agreed Minute Re Paragraph 6, Article XXII, US-ROK Status of Forces
제 2, 3 및 4 절에 규정되어 있다.

Agreement.

2

350

These minutes are considered as official documents pertaining to both Governments and will not be released without mutual agreement.

CRIMINAL JURISDICTION SUBCOMMITTEE
ROK/US SOFA JOINT COMMITTEE

16 July 1968

SUBJECT: Recommendation of Criminal Jurisdiction Subcommittee

ROK/US SOFA Joint Committee

1. Subject of recommendations. On 23 February 1967, the Joint Committee requested the Criminal Jurisdiction Subcommittee to recommend "mutually agreed procedures for cooperation in the conduct of investigations and in the collection and production of evidence."

2. Recommendation. The Criminal Jurisdiction Subcommittee recommends, in partial fulfillment of this task, that the following agreed view be adopted by the Joint Committee:

Agreed View No. 14 - Procedures for Obtaining Witnesses or Suspects for ROK Investigative Authorities.

3. Security Classification: None.

KIM, SUNG CHAE
Chairman, ROK Component
Criminal Jurisdiction Subcommittee

GERALD W. DAVIS
Colonel, JAGC
Chairman, US Component
Criminal Jurisdiction Subcommittee

APPROVED BY THE JOINT COMMITTEE ON
14 AUGUST 1968 AT TWENTY-NINTH MEETING

YOON HA JONG
Republic of Korea Representative

ROBERT J. FRIEDMAN
Lieutenant General
United States Air Force
United States Representative

29th JC
14 Aug 68 (Incl 13)

261

These minutes are considered as official documents pertaining to both Governments and will not be released without mutual agreement.

CRIMINAL JURISDICTION

Agreed View No. 14

Procedures for Obtaining Witnesses or Suspects for ROK Investigative Authorities

한국 수사당국에 참고인이나 피의자를 출석케하는 절차

Pursuant to the provisions of paragraph 6(a), Article XXII, and paragraph 2
한미 행정협정 제 22 조 제 6 항 (가) 및 동조 제 3 항 (나) 에
of the Agreed Understanding to the Agreed Minute Re Paragraph 3(b),
관한 합의 의사록에 대한 합의 양해사항 제 2 항의 규정에
Article XXII, ROK-US Status of Forces Agreement, the following procedure
의하여 한국 당국이 미 합중국 군대의 구성원, 군속, 가족 및
will apply when the cooperation of US authorities is necessary to obtain
초청계약자를 수사상 참고인이나 피의자로 출석토록 하는데 미군
a member of the United States armed forces, civilian component, a dependent,
당국의 협력이 필요한 경우에는 다음 절차를 적용한다.
or a US invited contractor as a witness or as a suspect at an investigation by ROK authorities:

1. The request for such witness or suspect will be in writing, if
동 참고인이나 피의자의 요청은 가능한한 서면으로 인근
possible, and delivered to the nearest area provost marshal/security police
헌병대장에게 하여야 하며, 동 요청서에는 한국당국이 필요로
officer. The request will contain the individual's name, organization,
하는 당사자의 성명, 소속과 출석장소 및 시간을 명시하여야 한다.
and the place and time that the ROK authorities desire the individual.

2. The area provost marshal/security police officer or his designee
요청서를 접수한 헌병대장이나 그 대리인은 당사자의 부대장,
will contact the commanding officer, supervisor, or employer of the
감독자나 고용인 또는 그 보호자에게 이를 통보한다.
individual, or the individual's sponsor.

29th JC
14 Aug 68, (Incl 1 to Incl 13)

352

3. The commanding officer, supervisor, or employer will make the necessary
부대장, 감독자 또는 고용인은 한국 당국의 요청에 응할 수

arrangements, including transportation, to comply with the ROK request.
있도록 교통편의를 포함한 필요한 조치를 한다.

4. If the individual is not available at the requested time because of
만일 당사자가 긴급한 군무나 질병, 기타 유사한 이유로

imperative military duties, illness, or other similar reason, the commanding
요청된 시간에 출석하지 못 할 때에는 부대장, 감독자 또는

officer, supervisor, or employer will propose to the ROK authorities, either
고용인은 직접 또는 헌병대장을 통하여 한국 당국에 참고인이나

directly or through the provost marshal/security police officer, a time
피의자가 출석할 수 있는 시간을 제시한다.

when the witness or suspect will be available.

Note: 주의

Procedures for obtaining witnesses and defendants at ROK trial proceedings
한국의 재판에 증인이나 피고인을 출석케 하는 절차는 한미

are set forth in unnumbered paragraph 2, 3, and 4 of paragraph 1 of the
행정협정 제 22 조 제 6 항에 관한 합의 의사록 제 1 항의

Agreed Minute Re Paragraph 6, Article XXII, US-ROK Status of Forces
제 2, 3 및 4 절에 규정되어 있다.

Agreement.

2

353

These minutes are considered as official documents pertaining to both Governments and will not be released without mutual agreement.

JOINT COMMITTEE
UNDER
THE REPUBLIC OF KOREA AND THE UNITED STATES
STATUS OF FORCES AGREEMENT

26 July 1968

MEMORANDUM FOR: The Joint Committee

SUBJECT: Designation of US Invited Contractor under Article XV, Status of Forces Agreement

1. References:

a. Paragraph 2, Article XV, Status of Forces Agreement.

b. US Commerce Subcommittee Memorandum of Consultation, dated 16 July 1968, subject as above (Inclosure 1).

c. ROK Commerce Subcommittee Memorandum of Consultation, dated 25 July 1968, subject as above (Inclosure 2).

2. The United States, after consultation with the ROK Commerce Subcommittee and after having duly considered their views, has designated Daniel, Mann, Johnson & Mendenhall as a US Invited Contractor for execution of Contract #F62087-69-C-0003 for Architect and Engineering services.

3. Pertinent data concerning US citizen employees will be provided to the Joint Secretariat in the established periodic arrival and departure format.

2 Incl
as

ROBERT J. FRIEDMAN
Lieutenant General
United States Air Force
United States Representative
Joint Committee

29th JC
14 Aug 68 (Incl [illegible])

354

These minutes are considered as official documents pertaining to both Governments and will not be released without mutual agreement.

REPUBLIC OF KOREA - UNITED STATES
COMMERCE SUBCOMMITTEE

16 July 1968

SUBJECT: Designation of US Invited Contractor under Article XV, Status of Forces Agreement

ROK Chairman, Commerce Subcommittee

1. Reference: Paragraph 2, Article XV of the Status of Forces Agreement.

2. The Government of the Republic of Korea is informed through this written consultive process that the United States Forces, Korea proposes to extend invited contractor status to the qualified US firm on the contract described in paragraph 3 below.

3. The following data is provided:

a. Company Name: Daniel, Mann, Johnson & Mendenhall.

b. Local Address: Bldg 1510, APO 96301.

c. Identification of US Citizen Employees: To be supplied after award of contract.

d. Number of US and ROK Employees:

US - 7
ROK - 12

e. Reasons for Designation of an Invited Contractor: Open Competitive bidding among local contractors is not practicable due to the following:

(1) Security considerations.

(2) Technical qualifications of the contractor involved.

f. Location of Contract: Kunsan Air Base and Osan Air Base, Korea.

355

29th JC
14 Aug 68 (Incl to Incl 14)

16 July 1968

SUBJECT: Designation of US Invited Contractor under Article XV, Status of Forces Agreement.

g. Type of Contract: Architect-Engineering services contract consisting of Type A service of field surveys and preliminary investigations and Type B service of preparations and production of designs, plans, drawings, estimates and specifications.

h. Length of Contract: 30 days from date of notice to proceed.

i. Sponsoring Component Command: Commander, Air Forces, Korea.

John T. Horrocks
JOHN T. HORROCKS
Colonel, US Air Force
US Alternate Chairman
Commerce Subcommittee

356

2

MINISTRY OF COMMERCE AND INDUSTRY
REPUBLIC OF KOREA
SEOUL, KOREA

25 July 1968

SUBJECT: Designation of US Invited Contractor under Article XV, Status of Forces Agreement.

TO : Chairman, US Commerce Subcommittee

1. References:

a. Paragraph 2, Article XV, Status of Forces Agreement.

b. US Commerce Subcommittee Memorandum of Consultation, Dated 16 July 1968, subject as above, pertaining to contract for Architect Engineering Services consisting of Type A and Type B.

2. The US memorandum, reference 1b above, has been reviewed and the Government of the Republic of Korea fully understands the requirement for an invited contractor in this instance.

For /signature/
Shim Ui Hwan
Chairman
ROK Commerce Subcommittee

357

29th JC
14 Aug 68 (Incl 2 to Incl 14)

These minutes are considered as official documents pertaining to both Governments and will not be released without mutual agreement.

**JOINT COMMITTEE
UNDER
THE REPUBLIC OF KOREA AND THE UNITED STATES
STATUS OF FORCES AGREEMENT**

16 July 1968

MEMORANDUM FOR: The Joint Committee

SUBJECT: Designation of US Invited Contractor under Article XV, Status of Forces Agreement

1. References:

a. Paragraph 2, Article XV, Status of Forces Agreement.

b. US Commerce Subcommittee Memorandum of Consultation, dated 11 July 1968, subject as above (Inclosure 1).

c. ROK Commerce Subcommittee Memorandum of Consultation, dated 15 July 1968, subject as above (Inclosure 2).

2. The United States, after consultation with the ROK Commerce Subcommittee and after having duly considered their views, has designated Daniel, Mann, Johnson & Mendenhall, as a US invited contractor for execution of Contract #DACA81-C-0075 for Architect and Engineering services.

3. Pertinent data concerning US citizen employees will be provided to the Joint Secretariat in the established periodic arrival and departure format.

2 Incl
as

ROBERT J. FRIEDMAN
Lieutenant General
United States Air Force
United States Representative
Joint Committee

358

29th JC
14 Aug 68 (Incl 15)

These minutes are c[illegible]sidered as official documents [illegible]taining to both Governments and will not be released without mutual agreement.

REPUBLIC OF KOREA - UNITED STATES
COMMERCE SUBCOMMITTEE

11 July 1968

SUBJECT: Designation of US Invited Contractor under Article XV, Status of Forces Agreement

ROK Chairman, Commerce Subcommittee

1. Reference: Paragraph 2, Article XV of the Status of Forces Agreement.

2. The Government of the Republic of Korea is informed through this written consultive process that the United States Forces, Korea proposes to extend invited contractor status to the qualified US firm on the contract described in paragraph 3 below.

3. The following data is provided:

a. Company Name: Daniel, Mann, Johnson & Mendenhall.

b. Local Address: Osan AB, APO 96570

c. Identification of US Citizen Employees: To be supplied after award of contract.

d. Number of US and ROK Employees:

US - 6
ROK - 0

e. Reasons for Designation of an Invited Contractor: Open competitive bidding among local contractors is not practicable due to the following:

(1) Security considerations.

(2) Technical qualifications of the contractor involved.

f. Location of Contract: Various locations in Korea.

359

29th JC
14 Aug 68 (Incl 1 to Incl 15)

11 July 1968

SUBJECT: Designation of US Invited Contractor under Article XV, Status of Forces Agreement

g. Type of Contract: Lump Sum Contract for Architect-Engineer Services for Preparation of Definitive Data and Budget Estimates for Supplemental FY 68 Projects, Various Locations, Korea.

h. Length of Contract: 1 Month.

i. Sponsoring Component Command: CGUSAEIGHT.

FLOYD R. WALTZ, JR.
Colonel, United States Army
Assistant Chief of Staff, J 4

2

2760

These minutes are considered as official documents pertaining to both Governments and will not be released without mutual agreement.

MINISTRY OF COMMERCE AND INDUSTRY
REPUBLIC OF KOREA
SEOUL, KOREA

15 July 1968

SUBJECT: Designation of US Invited Contractor under Article XV, Status of Forces Agreement.

TO : Chairman, US Commerce Subcommittee

1. References:

a. Paragraph 2, Article XV, Status of Forces Agreement.

b. US Commerce Subcommittee Memorandum of Consultation, dated 11 July 1968, subject as above, pertaining to contract for Architect-Engineer Services for Preparation of Definitive Data and Budget Estimates for Supplemental FY 68 Projects, Various Locations, Korea.

2. The US memorandum, reference 1b above, has been reviewed and the Government of the Republic of Korea fully understands the requirement for an invited contractor in this instance.

for Shin Ui Hwan
Chairman
ROK Commerce Subcommittee

361

29th JC
14 Aug 68 (Incl 2 to Incl 15)

These minutes are considered as official documents pertaining to both Governments and will not be released without mutual agreement.

JOINT COMMITTEE
UNDER
THE REPUBLIC OF KOREA AND THE UNITED STATES
STATUS OF FORCES AGREEMENT

5 July 1968

MEMORANDUM FOR: The Joint Committee

SUBJECT: Designation of US Invited Contractor under Article XV, Status of Forces Agreement

1. References:

a. Paragraph 2, Article XV, Status of Forces Agreement.

b. US Commerce Subcommittee Memorandum of Consultation, dated 12 June 1968, subject as above (Inclosure 1).

c. ROK Commerce Subcommittee Memorandum of Consultation, dated 3 July 1968, subject as above (Inclosure 2).

2. The United States, after consultation with the ROK Commerce Subcommittee and after having duly considered their views, has designated Daniel, Mann, Johnson & Mendenhall as a US invited contractor for execution of Contract #F62087-68-C-0130 for architect and engineering services.

3. Pertinent data concerning US citizen employees will be provided to the Joint Secretariat in the established periodic arrival and departure format.

2 Incl
as

ROBERT J. FRIEDMAN
Lieutenant General
United States Air Force
United States Representative
Joint Committee

362

29th JC
14 Aug 68 (Incl 16)

These minutes are considered as official documents pertaining to both Governments and will not be released without mutual agreement.

REPUBLIC OF KOREA - UNITED STATES
COMMERCE SUBCOMMITTEE

12 June 1968

SUBJECT: Designation of US Invited Contractor under Article XV, Status of Forces Agreement

ROK Chairman, Commerce Subcommittee

1. Reference: Paragraph 2, Article XV of the Status of Forces Agreement.

2. The Government of the Republic of Korea is informed through this written consultive process that the United States Forces, Korea, proposes to extend invited contractor status to the qualified US firm on the contract described in paragraph 3 below.

3. The following data is provided:

a. Company Name: Daniel, Mann, Johnson and Mendenhall.

b. Local Address: Box 11, APO 96570.

c. Identification of US Citizen Employees: To be supplied after award of contract.

d. Number of US and ROK Employees:

U.S. - 7
ROK - 10

e. Reasons for Designation of an Invited Contractor: Open competitive bidding among local contractors is not practicable due to the following:

(1) Security considerations.

(2) Technical qualifications of the contractor involved.

f. Location of Contract: Kunsan, Suwon and Osan Air Bases, Korea.

29th JC
14 Aug 68 (Incl 1 to Incl 16)

363

12 June 1968

SUBJECT: Designation of US Invited Contractor under Article XV, Status of Forces Agreement

g. Type of Contract: Architect-Engineering services.

h. Length of Contract: Approximately 30 days.

i. Sponsoring Component Command: Commander, Air Forces, Korea. (Headquarters, 6314th Support Wing (PACAF)).

John T. Horrocks

JOHN T. HORROCKS
Colonel, United States Air Force
US Alternate Chairman, Commerce
Subcommittee

364

MINISTRY OF COMMERCE AND INDUSTRY
REPUBLIC OF KOREA
SEOUL, KOREA

3 July 1968

SUBJECT: Designation of US Invited Contractor under Article XV, Status of Forces Agreement.

TO : Chairman, US Commerce Subcommittee.

1. References:

a. Paragraph 2, Article XV, Status of Forces Agreement.

b. US Commerce Subcommittee Memorandum of Consultation, Dated 12 June 1968, subject as above, pertaining to contract for architect-engineering service in the Kunsan, Suwon and Osan Air Bases construction projects.

2. The US memorandum, reference 1b above, has been reviewed and the Government of the Republic of Korea fully understands the requirement for an invited contractor in this instance.

For [signature]
Chairman
ROK Commerce Subcommittee

365

29th JC
14 Aug 68 (Incl 2 to Incl 16)

These minutes are considered as official documents pertaining to both Governments and will not be released without mutual agreement.

JOINT COMMITTEE
UNDER
THE REPUBLIC OF KOREA AND THE UNITED STATES
STATUS OF FORCES AGREEMENT

26 July 1968

MEMORANDUM FOR: The Joint Committee

SUBJECT: Designation of US Invited Contractor under Article XV, Status of Forces Agreement

1. References:

a. Paragraph 2, Article XV, Status of Forces Agreement.

b. US Commerce Subcommittee Memorandum of Consultation, dated 16 July 1968, subject as above (Inclosure 1).

c. ROK Commerce Subcommittee Memorandum of Consultation, dated 25 July 1968, subject as above (Inclosure 2).

2. The United States, after consultation with the ROK Commerce Subcommittee and after having duly considered their views, has designated Trans-Asia Engineering Associates, Inc. as a US invited contractor for execution of Contract #F62087-69-C-0004 for Architect and Engineering services.

3. Pertinent data concerning US citizen employees will be provided to the Joint Secretariat in the established periodic arrival and departure format.

2 Incl
as

ROBERT J. FRIEDMAN
Lieutenant General
United States Air Force
United States Representative
Joint Committee

366

29th JC
14 Aug 68 (Incl 17)

These minutes are considered as official documents pertaining to both Governments and will not be released without mutual agreement.

REPUBLIC OF KOREA - UNITED STATES
COMMERCE SUBCOMMITTEE

16 July 1968

SUBJECT: Designation of US Invited Contractor under Article XV, Status of Forces Agreement

ROK Chairman, Commerce Subcommittee

1. Reference: Paragraph 2, Article XV of the Status of Forces Agreement.

2. The Government of the Republic of Korea is informed through this written consultive process that the United States Forces, Korea proposes to extend invited contractor status to the qualified US firm on the contract described in paragraph 3 below.

3. The following data is provided:

a. Company Name: Trans-Asia Engineering Associates, Inc.

b. Local Address: Bldg 1510, APO 96301.

c. Identification of US Citizen Employees: To be supplied after award of contract.

d. Number of US and ROK Employees:

US - 7
ROK - 12

e. Reasons for Designation of an Invited Contractor: Open competitive bidding among local contractors is not practicable due to the following:

(1) Security considerations.

(2) Technical qualifications of the contractor involved.

f. Location of Contract: Kunsan Air Base and Osan Air Base, Korea.

367

29th JC
14 Aug 68 (Incl 1 to Incl 17)

16 July 1968

SUBJECT: Designation of US Invited Contractor under Article XV, Status of Forces Agreement

g. Type of Contract: Architect-Engineering services contract consisting of Type A service of field surveys and preliminary investigations and Type B service of preparations and production of designs, plans, drawings, estimates and specifications.

h. Length of Contract: 30 days from date of notice to proceed.

i. Sponsoring Component Command: Commander, Air Forces, Korea.

John T. Horrocks

JOHN T. HORROCKS
Colonel, US Air Force
US Alternate Chairman
Commerce Subcommittee

2

0369

These minutes are [redacted]dered as official documents [redacted]aining to both Governments and will not be released without mutual agreement.

MINISTRY OF COMMERCE AND INDUSTRY
REPUBLIC OF KOREA
SEOUL, KOREA

25 July 1968

SUBJECT: Designation of US Invited Contractor under Article XV, Status of Forces Agreement.

TO : Chairman, US Commerce Subcommittee

1. References:

a. Paragraph 2, Article XV, Status of Forces Agreement.

b. US Commerce Subcommittee Memorandum of Consultation, Dated 16 July 1968, subject as above, pertaining to contract for Architect Engineering Services consisting of Type A and Type B.

2. The US memorandum, reference 1b above, has been reviewed and the Government of the Republic of Korea fully understands the requirement for an invited contractor in this instance.

For [signature]
Shim Ui Hwan
Chairman
ROK Commerce Subcommittee

369

29th JC
14 Aug 68 (Incl 2 to Incl 17)

These minutes are considered as official documents pertaining to both Governments and will not be released without mutual agreement.

JOINT COMMITTEE
UNDER
THE REPUBLIC OF KOREA AND THE UNITED STATES
STATUS OF FORCES AGREEMENT

26 July 1968

MEMORANDUM FOR: The Joint Committee

SUBJECT: Designation of US Invited Contractor under Article XV, Status of Forces Agreement

1. References:

a. Paragraph 2, Article XV, Status of Forces Agreement.

b. US Commerce Subcommittee Memorandum of Consultation, dated 18 July 1968, subject as above (Inclosure 1).

c. ROK Commerce Subcommittee Memorandum of Consultation, dated 25 July 1968, subject as above (Inclosure 2).

2. The United States, after consultation with the ROK Commerce Subcommittee and after having duly considered their views, has designated Lyon Associates, Inc. as a US invited contractor for execution of Contract #DACA81-68-C-0067 for Architect and Engineering services.

3. Pertinent data concerning US citizen employees will be provided to the Joint Secretariat in the established periodic arrival and departure format.

2 Incl
as

ROBERT J. FRIEDMAN
Lieutenant General
United States Air Force
United States Representative
Joint Committee

370

29th JC
14 Aug 68 (Incl 18)

These minutes are considered as official documents pertaining to both Governments and will not be released without mutual agreement.

REPUBLIC OF KOREA - UNITED STATES
COMMERCE SUBCOMMITTEE

18 July 1968

SUBJECT: Designation of US Invited Contractor under Article XV, Status of Forces Agreement

ROK Chairman, Commerce Subcommittee

1. Reference: Paragraph 2, Article XV of the Status of Forces Agreement.

2. The Government of the Republic of Korea is informed through this written consultive process that the United States Forces, Korea proposes to extend invited contractor status to the qualified US firm on the contract described in paragraph 3 below.

3. The following data is provided:

a. Company Name: Lyon Associates, Inc.

b. Local Address: 6175 Air Base Group, BCEEE
Kunsan AB, APO 96264

c. Identification of US Citizen Employees: To be supplied after award of contract.

d. Number of US and ROK Employees:

US - 2
ROK - 0

e. Reasons for Designation of an Invited Contractor: Open competitive bidding among local contractors is not practicable due to the following:

(1) Security considerations.

(2) Technical qualifications of the contractor involved.

f. Location of Contract: Kunsan AB, Korea.

29th JC
14 Aug 68 (Incl 1 to Incl 18)

겨기

18 July 1968

SUBJECT: Designation of US Invited Contractor under Article XV, Status of Forces Agreement

g. Type of Contract: Lump Sum Contract for Architect-Engineer services for Hydro-Geologic Study and Water Treatment and Distribution Alterations, Kunsan Air Base, Korea.

h. Length of Contract: Approximately 9 months.

i. Sponsoring Component Command: CGUSAEIGHT.

JOHN T. HORROCKS
Colonel, US Air Force
US Alternate Chairman
Commerce Subcommittee

372

MINISTRY OF COMMERCE AND INDUSTRY
REPUBLIC OF KOREA
SEOUL, KOREA

25 July 1968

SUBJECT: Designation of US Invited Contractor under Article XV, Status of Forces Agreement.

TO : Chairman, US Commerce Subcommittee

1. References:

a. Paragraph 2, Article XV, Status of Forces Agreement.

b. US Commerce Subcommittee Memorandum of Consultation, Dated 18 July 1968, subject as above, pertaining to contract for architect-engineer services for Hydro-Geologic Study and Water Treatment and Distribution Alterations, Kunsan Air Base, Korea.

2. The US memorandum, reference 1b above, has been reviewed and the Government of the Republic of Korea fully understands the requirement for an invited contractor in this instance.

for [signature]
Shim Ui Hwan
Chairman
ROK Commerce Subcommittee

373

29th JC
14 Aug 68 (Incl 2 to Incl 18)

These minutes are considered as official documents pertaining to both Governments and will not be released without mutual agreement.

JOINT COMMITTEE
UNDER
THE REPUBLIC OF KOREA AND THE UNITED STATES
STATUS OF FORCES AGREEMENT

15 July 1968

MEMORANDUM FOR: The Joint Committee

SUBJECT: Designation of US Invited Contractor under Article XV, Status of Forces Agreement

1. References:

a. Paragraph 2, Article XV, Status of Forces Agreement.

b. US Commerce Subcommittee Memorandum of Consultation, dated 29 March 1968, subject as above (Inclosure 1).

c. ROK Commerce Subcommittee Memorandum of Consultation, dated 15 July 1968, subject as above (Inclosure 2).

2. The United States, after consultation with the ROK Commerce Subcommittee and after having duly considered their views, has designated Tectonics Asia, Incorporated as a US invited contractor for execution of Contract #DAJB03-68-C-0489 for repair and utilities in the I Corps area.

3. Pertinent data concerning US citizen employees will be provided to the Joint Secretariat in the established periodic arrival and departure format.

2 Incl
as

ROBERT J. FRIEDMAN
Lieutenant General
United States Air Force
United States Representative
Joint Committee

29th JC
14 Aug 68 (Incl 19)

374

REPUBLIC OF KOREA - UNITED STATES
COMMERCE SUBCOMMITTEE

29 March 1968

SUBJECT: Designation of US Invited Contractor under Article XV, Status of Forces Agreement

ROK Chairman, Commerce Subcommittee

1. Reference: Paragraph 2, Article XV of the Status of Forces Agreement.

2. The Government of the Republic of Korea is informed through this written consultive process that the United States Forces, Korea, proposes to extend invited contractor status to the successful negotiated bidder among qualified US firms on the contract described in paragraph 3 below.

3. The following data is provided:

a. Company Name:
1. Adrian Wilson Associates.
2. Associated American Engineers Overseas, Inc.
3. Barclay Overseas, Inc.
4. D. F. Fischer & Sons, Ltd.
5. Maintenance & Repair Services, Inc.
6. Pacific Architects & Engineers, Inc.
7. Universal American Enterprises, Inc.
8. Vinnel Corporation.
9. *Stolte-Korea Development Corporation.
10. *Huwin-Sam Whan.
11. *Cosmo Industry.
12. *Tetronics Asia Incorporated.

* Subject to approval of Accounting System by DCAA.

b. Local Address:
1. Eighth US Army/COMAFK, APO 96301.
2. Eighth US Army, APO 96301.
3. COMAFK, Sanryung Bldg., Room 302, Seoul.
4. Eighth US Army/COMAFK, APO 96301.
5. Eighth US Army, Bldg., 1510, Yongsan Mil Res, APO 96301.
6. Eighth US Army, APO 96302.
7. COMAFK, Osan AB, APO 96570.
8. Eighth US Army/COMAFK, CMR Box 521, APO 96570.

29th JC
14 Aug 68 (Incl 1 to Incl 19)

375

29 March 1968

SUBJECT: Designation of US Invited Contractor under Article XV, Status of Forces Agreement

9. #92 Kalwol Dong, Yongsan-Ku, Seoul.
10. #199-53, 2Ka, Ulchiro, Chung-Ku, Seoul.
11. #199-34, 2Ka, Ulchiro, Chung-Ku, Seoul.
12. Tongnam Bldg #97-2, Cho Dong, Chung-Ku, Seoul.

c. Identification of US Citizen Employees: To be supplied after award.

d. Number of US & ROK Employees (estimated):

(1) Camp Humphreys - US 25 ROK 925.

(2) I Corps - US 23 ROK 575.

e. Reasons for Designation of an Invited Contractor: Competitive bidding will be restricted to the above firms for the following reasons:

(1) Security considerations.

(2) Special management and technical skills are required.

(3) Experience in this type of operation is highly desirable.

(4) Limitations of US law regarding procurement.

f. Location of Contract: Camp Humphreys and I Corps.

g. Type of Contract: Cost-plus-fixed-fee.

h. Length of Contract: 1 July 68 thru 30 June 69 with 30 day transition period (13 months total).

i. Sponsoring Component Command: Commanding General, Eighth US Army.

4. The United States certifies that the successful bidder or named contractor is present in the Republic of Korea solely for the purpose of executing contracts with the United States, for the benefit of the United States Armed Forces or other armed forces under the Unified Command receiving logistical support from the United States Forces.

5. The views of the Government of the Republic of Korea are earnestly solicited prior to United States selection and designation of an invited

29 March 1968

SUBJECT: Designation of US Invited Contractor under Article XV, Status of Forces Agreement

contractor to perform the work outlined above. You may be assured that your views will be considered carefully.

6. Your early reply will be greatly appreciated.

FLOYD R. WALTZ, JR.
Colonel, United States Army
US Chairman, Commerce Subcommittee

29th JC
14 Aug 68 (Incl 1 to Incl 19)

2717

These minutes are considered as official documents pertaining to both Governments and will not be released without mutual agreement.

MINISTRY OF COMMERCE AND INDUSTRY
REPUBLIC OF KOREA
SEOUL, KOREA

15 July 1968

SUBJECT: Designation of US Invited Contractor under Article XV, Status of Forces Agreement.

TO : Chairman, US Commerce Subcommittee.

1. References:

a. Paragraph 2, Article XV, Status of Forces Agreement.

b. US Commerce Subcommittee Memorandum of Consultation, Dated 29 March 1968, subject as above, pertaining to contract for repair and utilities in Camp Humphreys and 1 Corps Area.

2. The US memorandum, reference 1b above, has been reviewed and the Government of the Republic of Korea fully understands the requirement for an invited contractor in this instance.

Shim Ui Hwan
Shim Ui Hwan
Chairman
ROK Commerce Subcommittee

29th JC
14 Aug 68 (Incl 2 to Incl 19)

378

These minutes are considered as official documents pertaining to both Governments and will not be released without mutual agreement.

JOINT COMMITTEE
UNDER
THE REPUBLIC OF KOREA AND THE UNITED STATES
STATUS OF FORCES AGREEMENT

23 July 1968

MEMORANDUM FOR: The Joint Committee

SUBJECT: Designation of US Invited Contractor under Article XV, Status of Forces Agreement

1. References:

a. Paragraph 2, Article XV, Status of Forces Agreement.

b. US Commerce Subcommittee Memorandum of Consultation, dated 6 July 1968, subject as above (Inclosure 1).

c. ROK Commerce Subcommittee Memorandum of Consultation, dated 11 July 1968, subject as above (Inclosure 2).

2. The United States, after consultation with the ROK Commerce Subcommittee and after having duly considered their views, has designated R. M. Towill Corporation as a US invited contractor for execution of Contract #DACA81-69-C-0001 for Architect and Engineering services for Aerial Photogrammetric Survey.

3. Pertinent data concerning US citizen employees will be provided to the Joint Secretariat in the established periodic arrival and departure format.

2 Incl
as

ROBERT J. FRIEDMAN
Lieutenant General
United States Air Force
United States Representative
Joint Committee

379

29th JC
14 Aug 68 (Incl 20)

These minutes are [illegible]nsidered as official documents [illegible]rtaining to both Governments and will not be released without mutual agreement.

REPUBLIC OF KOREA - UNITED STATES
COMMERCE SUBCOMMITTEE

6 July 1968

SUBJECT: Designation of US Invited Contractor under Article XV, Status of Forces Agreement

ROK Chairman, Commerce Subcommittee

1. Reference: Paragraph 2, Article XV of the Status of Forces Agreement.

2. The Government of the Republic of Korea is informed through this written consultive process that the United States Forces, Korea proposes to extend invited contractor status to the qualified US firm on the contract described in paragraph 3 below.

3. The following data is provided:

a. Company Name: 1. Pacific Architects & Engineers, Inc.
2. Towill Corporation

b. Local Address: 1. APO 96302
2. Honolulu, Hawaii

c. Identification of US Citizen Employees: To be supplied after award of contract.

d. Number of US and ROK Employees: To be supplied after award of contract.

e. Reasons for Designation of an Invited Contractor: Open competitive bidding among local contractors is not practicable due to the following:

(1) Security Considerations.

(2) Technical qualifications of the contractor involved.

f. Location of Contract: Various locations in Korea.

380

29th JC
14 Aug 68 (Incl 1 to Incl 20)

6 July 1968

SUBJECT: Designation of US Invited Contractor under Article XV, Status of Forces Agreement

g. Type of Contract: Lump Sum Contract for Architect-Engineer Services for Photogrammetric Surveys at various locations in Korea.

h. Length of Contract: To be supplied upon conclusion of negotiations.

i. Sponsoring Component Command: CGUSAEIGHT.

FLOYD R. WALTZ, JR.
Colonel, United States Army
Assistant Chief of Staff, J 4

381

These minutes are considered as official documents pertaining to both Governments and will not be released without mutual agreement.

MINISTRY OF COMMERCE AND INDUSTRY
REPUBLIC OF KOREA
SEOUL, KOREA

11 July 1968

SUBJECT: Designation of US Invited Contractor under Article XV, Status of Forces Agreement.

TO : Chairman, US Commerce Subcommittee

1. References:

a. Paragraph 2, Article XV, Status of Forces Agreement.

b. US Commerce Subcommittee Memorandum of Consultation, dated 6 July 1968, subject as above, pertaining to contract for Architect-Engineer Services for Photogrammetric Surveys at various locations in Korea.

2. The US memorandum, reference 1b above, has been reviewed and the Government of the Republic of Korea fully understands the requirement for an invited contractor in this instance.

For Shim Ui Hwan
Shim Ui Hwan
Chairman
ROK Commerce Subcommittee

382

29th JC
14 Aug 68 (Incl 2 to Incl 20)

These minutes are considered as official documents pertaining to both Governments and will not be released without mutual agreement.

JOINT COMMITTEE
UNDER
THE REPUBLIC OF KOREA AND THE UNITED STATES
STATUS OF FORCES AGREEMENT

13 July 1968

MEMORANDUM FOR: The Joint Committee

SUBJECT: Designation of US Invited Contractor under Article XV, Status of Forces Agreement

1. References:

a. Paragraph 2, Article XV, Status of Forces Agreement.

b. US Commerce Subcommittee Memorandum of Consultation, dated 6 July 1968, subject as above (Inclosure 1).

c. ROK Commerce Subcommittee Memorandum of Consultation, dated 11 July 1968, subject as above (Inclosure 2).

2. The United States, after consultation with the ROK Commerce Subcommittee and after having duly considered their views, has designated the Huwin Corporation as a US invited contractor for execution of Contract #DACA81-68-C-0065 for construction of access roads to AC&W sites.

3. Pertinent data concerning US citizen employees will be provided to the Joint Secretariat in the established periodic arrival and departure format.

2 Incl
as

ROBERT J. FRIEDMAN
Lieutenant General
United States Air Force
United States Representative
Joint Committee

383

29th JC
14 Aug 68 (Incl 21)

These minutes are considered as official documents pertaining to both Governments and will not be released without mutual agreement.

REPUBLIC OF KOREA - UNITED STATES
COMMERCE SUBCOMMITTEE

6 July 1968

SUBJECT: Designation of US Invited Contractor under Article XV, Status of Forces Agreement

ROK Chairman, Commerce Subcommittee

1. Reference: Paragraph 2, Article XV of the Status of Forces Agreement.

2. The Government of the Republic of Korea is informed through this written consultive process that the United States Forces, Korea proposes to extend invited contractor status to the qualified US firm on the contract described in paragraph 3 below.

3. The following data is provided:

a. Company Name: Huwin Corporation

b. Local Address: 130 Chong No, 3rd Street, Chongno-ku, Seoul, Korea.

c. Identification of US Citizen Employees: To be supplied after award of contract.

d. Number of US and ROK Employees:

U.S.	-	5
ROK	-	6

e. Reasons for Designation of an Invited Contractor: Open competitive bidding among local contractors is not practicable due to the following:

Restrictions imposed by United States law, specifically the Foreign Assistance Act of 1961. Further guidance is contained in the Armed Services Procurement Regulation, paragraph 6-703.2, which states, in part "...Procurement for the Military Assistance Program shall be restricted to domestic concerns and to United States end products..."

384

29th JC
14 Aug 68 (Incl 1 to Incl 21)

6 July 1968

SUBJECT: Designation of US Invited Contractor under Article XV, Status of Forces Agreement

f. Location of Contract: Yongmun-san and Palgong-san, Korea.

g. Type of Contract: Construction of access roads to AC&W Sites, Korea.

h. Length of Contract: To be supplied upon conclusion of negotiation.

i. Sponsoring Component Command: CGUSAEIGHT.

FLOYD R. WALTZ, JR.
Colonel, United States Army
Assistant Chief of Staff, J 4

385

These minutes are considered as official documents pertaining to both Governments and will not be released without mutual agreement.

MINISTRY OF COMMERCE AND INDUSTRY
REPUBLIC OF KOREA
SEOUL, KOREA

11 July 1968

SUBJECT: Designation of US Invited Contractor under Article XV, Status of Forces Agreement.

TO : Chairman, US Commerce Subcommittee

1. References:

a. Paragraph 2, Article XV, Status of Forces Agreement.

b. US Commerce Subcommittee Memorandum of Consultation, dated 6 July 1968, subject as above, pertaining to contract for construction of access roads to AC&W Sites, Korea.

2. The US memorandum, reference 1b above, has been reviewed and the Government of the Republic of Korea fully understands the requirement for an invited contractor in this instance.

Shim Ui Hwan
Chairman
ROK Commerce Subcommittee

386

29th JC
14 Aug 68 (Incl 2 to Incl 21)

These minutes are considered as official documents pertaining to both Governments and will not be released without mutual agreement.

JOINT COMMITTEE
UNDER
THE REPUBLIC OF KOREA AND THE UNITED STATES
STATUS OF FORCES AGREEMENT

15 July 1968

MEMORANDUM FOR: The Joint Committee

SUBJECT: Designation of US Invited Contractor under Article XV, Status of Forces Agreement

1. References:

a. Paragraph 2, Article XV, Status of Forces Agreement.

b. US Commerce Subcommittee Memorandum of Consultation, dated 29 March 1968, subject as above (Inclosure 1).

c. ROK Commerce Subcommittee Memorandum of Consultation, dated 15 July 1968, subject as above (Inclosure 2).

2. The United States, after consultation with the ROK Commerce Subcommittee and after having duly considered their views, has designated Maintenance & Repair Services, Inc. as a US invited contractor for execution of Contract #DAJB03-68-C-0490 for repair and utilities at Camp Humphreys.

3. Pertinent data concerning US citizen employees will be provided to the Joint Secretariat in the established periodic arrival and departure format.

2 Incl
as

ROBERT J. FRIEDMAN
Lieutenant General
United States Air Force
United States Representative
Joint Committee

29th JC
14 Aug 68 (Incl 22)

387

These minutes are [illegible]sidered as official documents [illegible]taining to both Governments and will not be released without mutual agreement.

REPUBLIC OF KOREA - UNITED STATES
COMMERCE SUBCOMMITTEE

29 March 1968

SUBJECT: Designation of US Invited Contractor under Article XV, Status of Forces Agreement

ROK Chairman, Commerce Subcommittee

1. Reference: Paragraph 2, Article XV of the Status of Forces Agreement.

2. The Government of the Republic of Korea is informed through this written consultive process that the United States Forces, Korea, proposes to extend invited contractor status to the successful negotiated bidder among qualified US firms on the contract described in paragraph 3 below.

3. The following data is provided:

a. Company Name:
1. Adrian Wilson Associates.
2. Associated American Engineers Overseas, Inc.
3. Barclay Overseas, Inc.
4. D. F. Fischer & Sons, Ltd.
5. Maintenance & Repair Services, Inc.
6. Pacific Architects & Engineers, Inc.
7. Universal American Enterprises, Inc.
8. Vinnel Corporation.
9. *Stolte-Korea Development Corporation.
10. *Huwin-Sam Whan.
11. *Cosmo Industry.
12. *Tetronics Asia Incorporated.

* Subject to approval of Accounting System by DCAA.

b. Local Address:
1. Eighth US Army/COMAFK, APO 96301.
2. Eighth US Army, APO 96301.
3. COMAFK, Sanryung Bldg., Room 301, Seoul.
4. Eighth US Army/COMAFK, APO 96301.
5. Eighth US Army, Bldg., 1510, Yongsan Mil Res, APO 96301.
6. Eighth US Army, APO 96302.
7. COMAFK, Osan AB, APO 96570.
8. Eighth US Army/COMAFK, CMR Box 521, APO 96570.

388

29th JC
14 Aug 68 (In[illegible] to Incl 22)

29 March 1968

SUBJECT: Designation of US Invited Contractor under Article XV, Status of Forces Agreement

9. #92 Kalwol Dong, Yongsan-Ku, Seoul.
10. #199-53, 2Ka, Ulchiro, Chung-Ku, Seoul.
11. #199-34, 2Ka, Ulchiro, Chung-Ku, Seoul.
12. Tongnam Bldg #97-2, Cho Dong, Chung-Ku, Seoul.

c. Identification of US Citizen Employees: To be supplied after award.

d. Number of US & ROK Employees (estimated):

(1) Camp Humphreys - US 25 ROK 925.

(2) I Corps - US 23 ROK 575.

e. Reasons for Designation of an Invited Contractor: Competitive bidding will be restricted to the above firms for the following reasons:

(1) Security considerations.

(2) Special management and technical skills are required.

(3) Experience in this type of operation is highly desirable.

(4) Limitations of US law regarding procurement.

f. Location of Contract: Camp Humphreys and I Corps.

g. Type of Contract: Cost-plus-fixed-fee.

h. Length of Contract: 1 July 68 thru 30 June 69 with 30 day transition period (13 months total).

i. Sponsoring Component Command: Commanding General, Eighth US Army.

4. The United States certifies that the successful bidder or named contractor is present in the Republic of Korea solely for the purpose of executing contracts with the United States, for the benefit of the United States Armed Forces or other armed forces under the Unified Command receiving logistical support from the United States Forces.

5. The views of the Government of the Republic of Korea are earnestly solicited prior to United States selection and designation of an invited

2

389

29 March 1968

SUBJECT: Designation of US Invited Contractor under Article XV, Status of Forces Agreement

contractor to perform the work outlined above. You may be assured that your views will be considered carefully.

6. Your early reply will be greatly appreciated.

FLOYD R. WALTZ, JR.
Colonel, United States Army
US Chairman, Commerce Subcommittee

29th JC
14 Aug 68 (Incl 1 to Incl 22)

390

3

These minutes are considered as official documents pertaining to both Governments and will not be released without mutual agreement.

MINISTRY OF COMMERCE AND INDUSTRY
REPUBLIC OF KOREA
SEOUL, KOREA

15 July 1968

SUBJECT: Designation of US Invited Contractor under Article XV, Status of Forces Agreement.

TO : Chairman, US Commerce Subcommittee.

1. References:

a. Paragraph 2, Article XV, Status of Forces Agreement.

b. US Commerce Subcommittee Memorandum of Consultation, Dated 29 March 1968, subject as above, pertaining to contract for repair and utilities in Camp Humphreys and 1 Corps Area.

2. The US memorandum, reference 1b above, has been reviewed and the Government of the Republic of Korea fully understands the requirement for an invited contractor in this instance.

Shim Ui Hwan
Chairman
ROK Commerce Subcommittee

29th JC
14 Aug 68 (Incl 2 to Incl 22)

391

These minutes are considered as official documents pertaining to both Governments and will not be released without mutual agreement.

JOINT COMMITTEE
UNDER
THE REPUBLIC OF KOREA AND THE UNITED STATES
STATUS OF FORCES AGREEMENT

23 July 1968

MEMORANDUM FOR: The Joint Committee

SUBJECT: Designation of US Invited Contractor under Article XV, Status of Forces Agreement

1. References:

a. Paragraph 2, Article XV, Status of Forces Agreement.

b. US Commerce Subcommittee Memorandum of Consultation, dated 14 May 1968, subject as above (Inclosure 1).

c. ROK Commerce Subcommittee Memorandum of Consultation, dated 16 May 1968, subject as above (Inclosure 2).

2. The United States, after consultation with the ROK Commerce Subcommittee and after having duly considered their views, has designated Adrian Wilson Associates as a US invited contractor for execution of Contract #DACA81-68-C-0076 for Architect and Engineering services.

3. Pertinent data concerning US citizen employees will be provided to the Joint Secretariat in the established periodic arrival and departure format.

2 Incl
as

ROBERT J. FRIEDMAN
Lieutenant General
United States Air Force
United States Representative
Joint Committee

29th JC
14 Aug 68 (Incl 23)

292

These minutes are [illegible]sidered as official document[illegible]rtaining to both Governments and will not be released without mutual agreement.

REPUBLIC OF KOREA - UNITED STATES
COMMERCE SUBCOMMITTEE

14 May 1968

SUBJECT: Designation of US Invited Contractor under Article XV, Status of Forces Agreement

ROK Chairman, Commerce Subcommittee

1. Reference: Paragraph 2, Article XV of the Status of Forces Agreement.

2. The Government of the Republic of Korea is informed through this written consultive process that the United States Forces, Korea, proposes to extend invited contractor status to the successful negotiated bidder among qualified US firms on the contract described in paragraph 3 below.

3. The following data is provided:

a. Company Name:
1. Lyon Associates, Inc.
2. Daniel, Mann, Johnson & Mendenhall
3. Adrian Wilson Associates
4. Sverdrup and Parcel
5. Quinton Engineers
6. Bechtel Corp.

b. Local Address:
1. APO 96331
2. Fuchu Air Station, Japan, APO 96525
3. JCA, 3-ka, 1 Yongsan-dong, Yongsan-ku, Seoul, APO 96301
4. 417 Montgomery St., San Francisco, Calif.
5. 812 W. Eighth St., Los Angeles, Calif.
6. 220 Bush St., San Francisco, Calif.

c. Identification of US Citizen Employees: To be supplied after award of contract.

d. Number of US and ROK Employees: Number of US citizens and Koreans is not known at this time and will be supplied upon conclusion of negotiations.

29th JC
14 Aug 68 (Incl 1 to Incl 23)

393

14 May 1968

SUBJECT: Designation of US Invited Contractor under Article XV, Status of Forces Agreement

e. Reasons for Designation of an Invited Contractor: Open competitive bidding among local contractors is not practicable due to the following:

(1) Security considerations.

(2) Technical qualifications of the contractors involved.

f. Location of Contract: Various locations in Korea.

g. Type of Contract: Lump Sum Contract for Architect-Engineer Services for Design of various airfields in Korea.

h. Length of Contract: Approximately 60 days.

i. Sponsoring Component Command: CGUSAEIGHT.

FLOYD R. WALTZ, JR.
Colonel, United States Army
Assistant Chief of Staff, J 4

394

These minutes are considered as official documents pertaining to both Governments and will not be released without mutual agreement.

MINISTRY OF COMMERCE AND INDUSTRY
REPUBLIC OF KOREA
SEOUL, KOREA

16 May 1968

SUBJECT: Designation of US Invited Contractor under Article XV, Status of Forces Agreement.

TO : Chairman, US Commerce Subcommittee

1. References:

a. Paragraph 2, Article XV, Status of Forces Agreement.

b. US Commerce Subcommittee Memorandum of Consultation, Dated 14 May 1968, subject as above, pertaining to contract for architect-engineer services for design of various airfields in Korea.

2. The US memorandum, reference 1b above, has been reviewed and the Government of the Republic of Korea fully understands the requirement for an invited contractor in this instance.

for Chairman
ROK Commerce Subcommittee

29th JC
14 Aug 68 (Incl 2 to Incl 23)

395

These minutes are considered as official documents pertaining to both Governments and will not be released without mutual agreement.

JOINT ROK - US PRESS RELEASE
TWENTY-NINTH ROK-US JOINT COMMITTEE MEETING
14 AUGUST 1968

The ROK-US Joint Committee adopted two recommendations of its Criminal Jurisdiction Subcommittee to facilitate implementation of the Criminal Jurisdiction procedures under the SOFA at its twenty-ninth meeting, held at the US SOFA Conference Room, on 14 August. The Joint Committee also assigned two new tasks to the Criminal Jurisdiction Subcommittee to clarify criminal jurisdiction procedures.

The Joint Committee also approved thirteen recommendations of its Facilities and Areas Subcommittee, relating to the acquisition and release of facilities and areas by the US armed forces in Korea. Five additional tasks were assigned to the Facilities and Areas Subcommittee.

The US Representative, Lieutenant General Robert J. Friedman, presided at this meeting and designated ten US invited contractors, as recommended by the Commerce Subcommittee.

The next meeting of the ROK-US Joint Committee is scheduled for Thursday, 12 September, at the ROK Capitol Building.

29th JC
14 Aug 68 (Incl 24)

396

대한민국 외무부
공보관실

보 도 자 료

一 호	이 기사는 제공처인 외무부를
년 월 일 시 분 발표	밝히고 보도할수 있음

한.미 합동위원회 제29차 회의 공동 발표문

1968. 8. 14. (수)

한.미 합동위원회는 8월 14일 미측 SOFA 회의실에서 열린 제29차 회의에서, 군대지위협정에 의거한 형사재판 절차의 운영을 원활하게 하기 위한 형사재판권 분과위원회의 건의 2건을 채택하였다. 또한 합동위원회는 형사재판권 분과위원회에 형사 재판 절차를 구체화 하기 위한 2개의 신규과제를 부여하였다.

합동위원회는 주한 미군에 의한 시설과 구역의 취득과 반환에 관한 시설구역 분과위원회의 건의 13건을 승인하고 동 분과위원회에 대하여 5건의 신규과제를 부여하였다.

미국대표 프리드만 중장이 동 회의를 사회하고 상무분과위원회가 건의한 미국 초청계약자 10명을 지명했다.

한.미 합동위원회 차기회의는 9월 12일 (목) 중앙청에서 개최될 예정이다.

2917

분류번호	729.41 1971 64차	등록번호	124	보존기간	영구
기능명칭	SOFA-한미 합동위원회 회의록, 제 64차. 1971				
생 산 과	안보담당관실		생산년도	1971	

주;

2. 제 64차. 1971. 7. 29

	M/F No.	

MINISTRY OF FOREIGN AFFAIRS
REPUBLIC OF KOREA

1. 사전준비

Introduction of New Joint Committee Members

US Presentation

1. The United States Alternate Representative would like to call the sixty-fourth United States-Republic of Korea Joint Committee meeting to order. Before taking up the first agenda item, I would like to take this opportunity to introduce two new members of the United States Component of the Joint Committee, as follows:

a. Colonel David P. Heekin, the new Deputy Chief of Staff, Eighth United States Army, who replaces Colonel Edward N. Hathaway.

b. Colonel Bruce T. Coggins, the new Staff Judge Advocate of the United States Forces, Korea, and the Eighth United States Army, who replaces Colonel Leonard Petkoff.

2. On behalf of the United States component of the Joint Committee, I wish to take this opportunity to welcome Colonel Heekin and Colonel Coggins to the Joint Committee.

(3. FOR YOUR INFORMATION: The ROK Alternate Representative will welcome these two new US members of the Joint Committee.)

2

AGENDA ITEM I   1. ROK Presentation

(1. FOR YOUR INFORMATION: The ROK Alternate Representative has no new tasks for assignment to the Facilities and Areas Subcommittee. He does, however, have three Facilities and Areas Subcommittee tasks assigned on an exigent basis since the last Joint Committee meeting, which he should be invited to present for recording in the minutes of this meeting.)

(2. FOR YOUR INFORMATION: The three above-referenced exigent tasks consist of two ROK requests for the relocation of facilities, and one ROK request for the temporary use of three warehouses on Seattle Installation in Inchon.)

3. The United States Alternate Representative is pleased to concur in the notation in the minutes of this meeting of the prior assignment to the Facilities and Areas Subcommittee of the three specified tasks.

3

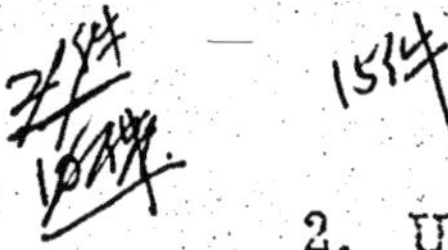

AGENDA ITEM I   2. US Presentation

1. The United States Alternate Representative would now like to present the remaining new tasks for assignment to the Facilities and Areas Subcommittee. Before doing so, however, I should like to propos that the assignment, on an exigent basis, of ten tasks to that Subcommitt in the interval since the last Joint Committee meeting be recorded in the minutes of this meeting. These ten prior assigned tasks comprise three requests for the acquisition of real estate on a permanent use basis, two requests for the acquisition of Temporary Use Permits, and five request for the release of parcels of real estate.

2. The United States Alternate Representative has, in addition, fifteen new tasks to present for assignment to the Facilities and Areas Subcommittee. These consist of two requests for easements, two requests for the acquisition of Temporary Use Permits, three requests for the extension of existing Temporary Use Permits, one request for authorization to dispose of a building, one request for the conversion of land from a temporary to a permanent use basis, and six requests for the release of parcels of real estate. All details concerning both these new tasks and the prior assigned tasks are contained in memoranda whic have been distributed to both sides.

3. It is proposed that the fifteen new tasks be assigned to the Facilities and Areas Subcommittee, and that the minutes of this meeting

4

reflect the prior assignment of ten additional tasks to that Subcommittee.

(4. FOR YOUR INFORMATION: The ROK SOFA Secretary has indicated that the ROK Alternate Representative will concur in this proposal.)

5

AGENDA ITEM II

1. ROK Presentation

(1. FOR YOUR INFORMATION: The US Alternate Representative should invite his ROK counterpart to present two recommendations of the Facilities and Areas Subcommittee. These recommendations relate to:

a. The relocation of a water supply line;

b. The release of 0.30 acre in Yongdongpo-Ku, Seoul City.)

2. The United States Alternate Representative is happy to concur in Joint Committee approval of the specified two recommendations of the Facilities and Areas Subcommittee.

6

AGENDA ITEM II

2. US Presentation

1. The United States Alternate Representative now wishes to present the remaining twenty-three recommendations of the Facilities and Areas Subcommittee. In summary, these comprise two recommendations for the acquisition of land for permanent use, two recommendations involving extension of Temporary Use Permits, two commendations for authorization to dispose of facilities, one recommendation for the withdrawal of a previous request for acquisition of land, and sixteen recommendations involving the release of parcels of real estate. All details concerning these recommendations will be found in memoranda which have been distributed to both sides.

2. It is proposed that the Joint Committee approve these twenty-three recommendations of the Facilities and Areas Subcommittee.

(3. FOR YOUR INFORMATION: The ROK SOFA Secretary has indicated that the ROK Alternate Representative will concur in this proposal.)

84.

AGENDA ITEM IV US Presentation

1. The United States Alternate Representative wishes to present memoranda to the Joint Committee informing the Government of the Republic of Korea of the designation of eight United States invited contractors under Article XV of the Status of Forces Agreement. These designations were made after consultations between Republic of Korea and United States Commerce Subcommittee personnel in accordance with Joint Committee procedures. The invited contractors so designated are Campbell Construction and Equipment Company, Incorporated; International Electronics Corporation; Fischer Engineering and Maintenance Company, Incorporated; Zurn Engineers; Huwin Corporation; Associated American Engineers Overseas, Incorporated; Daniel, Mann, Johnson, and Mendenhall; and Adrian Wilson Associates, Incorporated. These designations involve a total of eight contracts. Fischer Engineering and Maintenance Company, Incorporated has two contracts; Zurn Engineers and Huwin Corporation share one contract and the remaining contractors have one contract each. Four of these contracts are in joint venture with Korean firms.

2. Pertinent data concerning employees of these invited contractors will be provided to the Government of the Republic of Korea in accordance with mutually agreed procedures.

8

(3. FOR YOUR INFORMATION: The ROK SOFA Secretary has indicated that the ROK Alternate Representative will acknowledge the designation of these invited contractors.)

9

Proposed Reply by the US Alternate Representative
in Agenda Item V

"The United States Alternate Representative would like to take this opportunity to assure the Republic of Korea Alternate Representative of his equal and deep concern over the recent unfortunate incidents, involving some United States military personnel and Korean nationals. United States Forces, Korea PD 5-18 was designed to help to deal effectively with situations which may adversely affect Korean-American relations, and it is hoped that this new directive will assist in forestalling such unfortunate incidents as recently occurred.

"I fully concur in your statement that the appropriate authorities of our two Governments should cooperate closely in taking the necessary measures to forestall the reoccurrence of any incidents which may be detrimental to the traditional friendly relations between our two peoples."

10

AGENDA ITEM VI US Presentation

1. The United States Alternate Representative would like to note for the record that the United States Status of Forces Agreement Secretary has furnished the following information to his Korean counterpart, in accordance with the provisions of the Status of Forces Agreement and Joint Committee decisions:

a. Five copies of reports on the United States armed forces disposition of cases for the months of May and June.

b. One copy of pertinent information on cargo consigned to United States armed forces non-appropriated fund organizations in the Republic of Korea, for the month of June 1971.

c. Twenty copies of the report of United States armed forces personnel, the civilian component, invited contractors and the dependents of each, entering or departing the Republic of Korea during the month of June 1971.

(2. FOR YOUR INFORMATION: The ROK SOFA Secretary has indicated that the ROK Alternate Representative will acknowledge receipt of these reports).

11

AGENDA ITEM VII US Presentations

(1. FOR YOUR INFORMATION: The usual pattern of alternating Joint Committee meetings between US and ROK Conference Rooms will not be followed in August, in order to enable the US Representative to host a luncheon just before, and golf match just after, the next Joint Committee meeting.)

2. The Alternate United States Representative would like to propose that the sixty-fifth Joint Committee meeting be held on Thursday, 26 August 1971, in the United States Status of Forces Agreement Conference Room. Although this would be a deviation from the usual practice of alternating Joint Committee meetings between Republic of Korea and United States Conference Rooms, it is proposed to facilitate the United States Representative's plans to host a luncheon for Joint Committee members just before the next meeting and to enable the golfers on the Joint Committee to enjoy a round of golf together at the Eighth United States Army Golf Course just after the Joint Committee meeting.

(3. FOR YOUR INFORMATION: The ROK SOFA Secretary has indicated the ROK Representative will concur on this proposal.)

12

AGENDA ITEM VIII US Presentation

1. The United States Alternate Representative would like to propose approval of the press release for the sixty-fourth Joint Committee meeting, as prepared by our respective Secretaries and distributed in advance to both components of the Committee.

(2. FOR YOUR INFORMATION: The ROK SOFA Secretary has indicated that the ROK Alternate Representative will approve the proposed joint press release.)

13

AGENDA ITEM IX US Presentation

1. Do you have any further items to present at this meeting, Mr. LEE?

(2. FOR YOUR INFORMATION: The ROK Secretary has indicated that the ROK Alternate Representative will reply in the negative.)

3. If there is no other business to come before the Joint Committee, I declare the sixty-fourth meeting of the Joint Committee adjourned.

JOINT COMMITTEE
UNDER
THE REPUBLIC OF KOREA AND THE UNITED STATES
STATUS OF FORCES AGREEMENT

18 June 1971

MEMORANDUM FOR: Chairmen, Facilities and Areas Subcommittee

SUBJECT: Request for Relocation of POL Pipeline

1. SOFA provides, in Article II, paragraph 2, that the Governments of the Republic of Korea and the United States may agree that facilities and areas or portions thereof shall be returned to the Republic of Korea or that additional facilities and areas may be provided.

2. Pursuant to paragraph 1 above, it is requested that a recommendation be presented to the Joint Committee concerning a request for the relocation of a portion of POL pipeline between Pyongtaek and Anjung in Kyonggi-do, in connection with the widening of an existing road.

ROBERT N. SMITH
Lieutenant General
United States Air Force
United States Representative

KOO CHOONG WHAY
Republic of Korea
Representative

15

JOINT COMMITTEE
UNDER
THE REPUBLIC OF KOREA AND THE UNITED STATES
STATUS OF FORCES AGREEMENT

3 July 1971

MEMORANDUM FOR: Chairmen, Facilities and Areas Subcommittee

SUBJECT: Request for Relocation of Telegraph Poles

1. SOFA provides in Article II, paragraph 2, that the Governments of the Republic of Korea and the United States may agree that facilities and areas or portions thereof shall be returned to the Republic of Korea or that additional facilities and areas may be provided.

2. Pursuant to paragraph 1 above, it is requested that a recommendation be presented to the Joint Committee concerning a request for the relocation of telegraph poles located in Uijongbu City, Kyonggi-do.

KOO CHOONG WHAY
Republic of Korea
Representative

ROBERT N. SMITH
Lieutenant General
United States Air Force
United States Representative

16

JOINT COMMITTEE
UNDER
THE REPUBLIC OF KOREA AND THE UNITED STATES
STATUS OF FORCES AGREEMENT

15 July 1971

MEMORANDUM FOR: Chairmen, Facilities and Areas Subcommittee

SUBJECT: Request for Temporary Use of Three Warehouses at Docks in Camp Seattle

1. SOFA provides, in Article II, paragraph 2, that the Governments of the Republic of Korea and the United States may agree that facilities and areas or portions thereof shall be returned to the Republic of Korea or that additional facilities and areas may be provided.

2. Pursuant to paragraph 1 above, it is requested that a recommendation be presented to the Joint Committee concerning a Republic of Korea Government request for the temporary use of three warehouses in the vicinity of the tidal basin in Seattle Installation, Inchon City, Kyonggi-do, in connection with a massive import of grains.

KOO CHOONG WHAY
Republic of Korea
Representative

ROBERT N. SMITH
Lieutenant General
United States Air Force
United States Representative

17

JOINT COMMITTEE
UNDER
THE REPUBLIC OF KOREA AND THE UNITED STATES
STATUS OF FORCES AGREEMENT

24 June 1971

MEMORANDUM FOR: Chairmen, Facilities and Areas Subcommittee

SUBJECT: Request for Acquisition of Real Estate

1. SOFA provides, in Article II, paragraph 2, that the Governments of the Republic of Korea and the United States may agree that facilities and areas or portions thereof shall be returned to the Republic of Korea or that additional facilities and areas may be provided.

2. Pursuant to paragraph 1 above, it is requested that a recommendation be presented to the Joint Committee concerning a request for the acquisition, on a permanent use basis, of approximately 4.14 acres of land in three non-contiguous areas of 1.38 acres each, and located in Seoul City. The precise locations of these three sites are shown on a map, copies of which are in the possession of the ROK Ministry of National Defense and the Real Estate Division, USFK Engineer. This real estate is urgently required to establish facilities needed to measure the physical effects of disturbances in the atmosphere.

ROBERT N. SMITH
Lieutenant General
United States Air Force
United States Representative

KOO CHOONG WHAY
Republic of Korea
Representative

18

JOINT COMMITTEE
UNDER
THE REPUBLIC OF KOREA AND THE UNITED STATES
STATUS OF FORCES AGREEMENT

21 July 1971

MEMORANDUM FOR: Chairmen, Facilities and Areas Subcommittee

SUBJECT: Request for Acquisition of Temporary Use Permits

1. SOFA provides, in Article II, paragraph 2, that the Governments of the Republic of Korea and the United States may agree that facilities and areas or portions thereof shall be returned to the Republic of Korea or that additional facilities and areas may be provided.

2. Pursuant to paragraph 1 above, it is requested that recommendations be presented to the Joint Committee concerning requests for the acquisition of two Temporary Use Permits, and preliminary right-of-entry to the areas involved. These involve two separate areas at which navigational aid sites will be located, to be used for joint hydrographic surveys by the US Naval Oceanographic Office and the ROK Hydrographic Office, for the period 1 August 1971 through 31 January 1972. Specific locations involved are indicated on maps in the possession of the Republic of Korea Ministry of National Defense and the Real Estate Division of the Engineer, USFK. The names of the sites and general locations are as indicated below.

Name of Site	Location
a. KOGUM-DO	Island of Kogum, Kohung-gun, Chollanam-do
b. PYONGIL-DO	Island of Pyongil, Wando-gun, Chollanam-do

KOO CHOONG WHAY
Republic of Korea
Representative

for F M Romanick Capt USN
ROBERT N. SMITH
Lieutenant General
United States Air Force
United States Representative

JOINT COMMITTEE
UNDER
THE REPUBLIC OF KOREA AND THE UNITED STATES
STATUS OF FORCES AGREEMENT

30 June 1971

MEMORANDUM FOR: Chairmen, Facilities and Areas Subcommittee

SUBJECT: Requests for Release of Real Estate

1. SOFA provides, in Article II, paragraph 2, that the Governments of the Republic of Korea and the United States may agree that facilities and areas or portions thereof shall be returned to the Republic of Korea or that additional facilities and areas may be provided.

2. Pursuant to paragraph 1 above, it is requested that recommendations be presented to the Joint Committee concerning requests for the following actions:

a. Release of 209.50 acres of land with two Korean-constructed facilities, constituting Wolmido Installation, held under Acquisition Nos. ASCOM-363, ASCOM-375, AAC-381 and AAC-383, and located in Inchon City, Kyonggi-do. This request for release includes all USFK-constructed facilities located on the Installation to be released, with the exception of two water tank facilities (Nos. T-3421 and T-3422) and Building No. T-3343 with ingress and egress rights thereto, which will be retained under USFK control until 30 October 1971.

b. Release of 7.8 acres of land, constituting Area #3 portion of Camp Pililaau Installation, held under Acquisition No. IC-264 and located in Uijongbu-si, Kyonggi-do. This request for release includes a total of 50 USFK-constructed buildings and facilities located on the Installation.

c. Release of 20.942 acres of land, constituting Camp Nabors Installation, held under Acquisition Nos. SAC-705 and SAC-766, and located in Seoul City. This request for release includes a total of 108 USFK-constructed buildings and facilities located on the Installation.

d. Release of 23.86 acres of land, constituting the remaining portion of Camp Pililaau Installation, held under Acquisition No. IC-264 and located in Uijongbu-si, Kyonggi-do. This request for release includes a total of 78 USFK-constructed buildings and facilities located on the Installation.

e. Release of 21.27 acres of land containing two Korean-constructed buildings, constituting a portion of Market Installation held under Acquisition No. ACS-193, and located in Inchon City, Kyonggi-do, This request for release includes a total of 66 USFK- constructed buildings and facilities located on the Installation. Exempted from this release request are 0.659 acre of land containing an underground sanitary sewer line and an overhead electric power line, which will be retained together with unrestricted rights-of-entry for ingress and egress thereto.

ROBERT N. SMITH
Lieutenant General
United States Air Force
United States Representative

KOO CHOONG WHAY
Republic of Korea
Representative

21

JOINT COMMITTEE
UNDER
THE REPUBLIC OF KOREA AND THE UNITED STATES
STATUS OF FORCES AGREEMENT

29 July 1971

MEMORANDUM FOR: Chairmen, Facilities and Areas Subcommittee

SUBJECT: Requests for Acquisition of Easements

1. SOFA provides, in Article II, paragraph 2, that the Governments of the Republic of Korea and the United States may agree that facilities and areas or portions thereof shall be returned to the Republic of Korea or that additional facilities and areas may be provided.

2. Pursuant to paragraph 1 above, it is requested that recommendations be presented to the Joint Committee concerning requests for the following actions:

a. Acquisition, on a perpetual restrictive easement basis, of 3.84 acres of land located in Chilgok-gun, Kyongsangbuk-do. This real estate is required to widen an existing road.

b. Acquisition, on a perpetual restrictive easement basis, of approximately 5.48 acres of land located in Paju-gun, Kyonggi-do. This real estate is required to widen an existing road to reduce curves and to upgrade the road.

KOO CHOONG WHAY
Republic of Korea
Representative

ROBERT N. SMITH
Lieutenant General
United States Air Force
United States Representative

22

JOINT COMMITTEE
UNDER
THE REPUBLIC OF KOREA AND THE UNITED STATES
STATUS OF FORCES AGREEMENT

29 July 1971

MEMORANDUM FOR: Chairmen, Facilities and Areas Subcommittee

SUBJECT: Requests for Acquisition of Temporary Use Permits

1. SOFA provides, in Article II, paragraph 2, that the Governments of the Republic of Korea and the United States may agree that facilities and areas or portions thereof shall be returned to the Republic of Korea or that additional facilities and areas may be provided.

2. Pursuant to paragraph 1 above, it is requested that recommendations be presented to the Joint Committee concerning requests for the following actions:

a. Acquisition of a Temporary Use Permit, involving approximately 2.58 acres of land located in Worsung-gun, Kyongsangbuk-do, for the period 15 July 1971 through 14 August 1971. This acreage, comprising two non-contiguous areas, is required as a source of top soil for use as fill materials.

b. Acquisition of a Temporary Use Permit, involving a total of 0.08 acre of land in four non-contiguous areas of 0.02 acre each, located in the Mt. Halla area of Cheju-do, for the period 1 September 1971 through 28 February 1972. This real estate is required on a temporary exclusive use basis for the above-stated period in connection with a special DoD communications facilities project to be conducted on Cheju-do.

KOO CHOONG WHAY Republic of Korea Representative	ROBERT N. SMITH Lieutenant General United States Air Force United States Representative

23

JOINT COMMITTEE
UNDER
THE REPUBLIC OF KOREA AND THE UNITED STATES
STATUS OF FORCES AGREEMENT

29 July 1971

MEMORANDUM FOR: Chairmen, Facilities and Areas Subcommittee

SUBJECT: Requests for Extension of Temporary Use Permits

1. SOFA provides, in Article II, paragraph 2, that the Governments of the Republic of Korea and the United States may agree that facilities and areas, or portions thereof, shall be returned to the Republic of Korea or that additional facilities and areas may be provided.

2. Pursuant to paragraph 1 above, it is requested that recommendations be presented to the Joint Committee concerning requests for the following actions:

a. Extension of Temporary Use Permit K-E-T-105, involving approximately 100 acres of land located in Sokcho-si, Kangwon-do, from 1 April 1971 through 31 March 1972. This real estate is required for continued use for the purpose of topographic survey and exploratory drilling at R-407 airfield.

b. Extension of Temporary Use Permit K-E-T-106, involving approximately 193 acres of land located in Chechon-gun, Chungchongbuk-do, from 1 April 1971 through 31 March 1972. This real estate is required for continued use for the purpose of topographic survey and exploratory drilling at R-605 airfield.

c. Extension of Temporary Use Permit K-G-T-14, involving 25 acres of river bed soil located in Chilgok-gun, Kyongsangbuk-do, from 25 August 1971 through 24 February 1972. This real estate is required for continued use as a source of fill materials and to establish a temporary rock crusher site.

KOO CHOONG WHAY	ROBERT N. SMITH
Republic of Korea	Lieutenant General
Representative	United States Air Force
	United States Representative

24

JOINT COMMITTEE
UNDER
THE REPUBLIC OF KOREA AND THE UNITED STATES
STATUS OF FORCES AGREEMENT

29 July 1971

MEMORANDUM FOR: Chairmen, Facilities and Areas Subcommittee

SUBJECT: Request for Authorization to Dispose of Facility

1. SOFA provides, in Article II, paragraph 2, that the Governments of the Republic of Korea and the United States may agree that facilities and areas or portions thereof shall be returned to the Republic of Korea or that additional facilities and areas may be provided.

2. Pursuant to paragraph 1 above, it is requested that a recommendation be presented to the Joint Committee concerning a request for authorization to dispose of one Korean-constructed building (No. 1588) held under Acquisition No. SAC-526 and located on Yongsan Installation in Seoul. This building was partially destroyed by fire and the remaining portion has become excess to USFK requirements.

KOO CHOONG WHAY
Republic of Korea
Representative

ROBERT N. SMITH
Lieutenant General
United States Air Force
United States Representative

25

JOINT COMMITTEE
UNDER
THE REPUBLIC OF KOREA AND THE UNITED STATES
STATUS OF FORCES AGREEMENT

29 July 1971

MEMORANDUM FOR: Chairmen, Facilities and Areas Subcommittee

SUBJECT: Request for Conversion of Real Estate

1. SOFA provides, in Article 11, paragraph 2, that the Governments of the Republic of Korea and the United States may agree that facilities and areas or portions thereof shall be returned to the Republic of Korea or that additional facilities and areas may be provided.

2. Pursuant to paragraph 1 above, it is requested that a recommendation be presented to the Joint Committee concerning a request for the conversion, from a temporary use basis to a permanent use basis, of a total of approximately 14.967 acres of land in seven non-contiguous areas located throughout Heongsong-gun, Wonsong-gun, and Wonju-si, Kangwon-do. This acreage currently is held under Acquisition No. K-E-T-104. This conversion action is required for an access road, borehole operations, and the installation of support facilities.

KOO CHOONG WHAY	ROBERT N. SMITH
Republic of Korea	Lieutenant General
Representative	United States Air Force
	United States Representative

26

JOINT COMMITTEE
UNDER
THE REPUBLIC OF KOREA AND THE UNITED STATES
STATUS OF FORCES AGREEMENT

29 July 1971

MEMORANDUM FOR: Chairmen, Facilities and Areas Subcommittee

SUBJECT: Requests for Release of Real Estate

1. SOFA provides, in Article II, paragraph 2, that the Governments of the Republic of Korea and the United States may agree that facilities and areas or portions thereof shall be returned to the Republic of Korea or that additional facilities and areas may be provided.

2. Pursuant to paragraph 1 above, it is requested that recommendations be presented to the Joint Committee concerning requests for the following actions:

a. Release of 0.44 acre of land held on an easement basis, constituting a portion of the area held under Acquisition No. IC-168 and located in Uijongbu-si, Kyonggi-do. This request for release includes approximately 1,920 linear feet of USFK-installed power line. This real estate has become excess to USFK requirements.

b. Release of 1.24 acres of land held on an easement basis, constituting a portion of the area held under Acquisition No. IC-207, and located in Uijongbu-si, Kyonggi-do. This request for release includes approximately 4,030 linear feet of a USFK-installed water pipeline facility. This real estate has become excess to USFK requirements.

c. Release of 1.31 acres of land constituting a portion of the area held under Acquisition No. IC-97 and located in Uijongbu-si, Kyonggi-do. This real estate has become excess to USFK requirements.

d. Release of 0.227 acre of land constituting a portion of the area held under Acquisition No. CAV-64, and located in Paju-gun, Kyonggi-do. This real estate has become excess to USFK requirements.

27

e. Release of 0.024 acre of land constituting a portion of the area held under Acquisition No. CAV-97, and located in Paju-gun, Kyonggi-do. This real estate has become excess to USFK requirements.

KOO CHOONG WHAY	ROBERT N. SMITH
Republic of Korea	Lieutenant General
Representative	United States Air Force
	United States Representative

287.E

28

JOINT COMMITTEE
UNDER
THE REPUBLIC OF KOREA AND THE UNITED STATES
STATUS OF FORCES AGREEMENT

29 July 1971

MEMORANDUM FOR: Chairmen, Facilities and Areas Subcommittee

SUBJECT: Request for Release of Real Estate

1. SOFA provides, in Article II, paragraph 2, that the Governments of the Republic of Korea and the United States may agree that facilities and areas or portions thereof shall be returned to the Republic of Korea or that additional facilities and areas may be provided.

2. Pursuant to paragraph 1 above, it is requested that a recommendation be presented to the Joint Committee concerning the release of 3.591 acres of land, constituting a portion of Kimpo Peninsula Installation held under Acquisition No. AAC-398, and located in Kimpo-gun, Kyonggi-do. This request for release includes all USFK-constructed facilities located on the area to be released, except for an underground water line and an overhead electric power line.

KOO CHOONG WHAY Republic of Korea Representative	ROBERT N. SMITH Lieutenant General United States Air Force United States Representative

2P
1021

REPUBLIC OF KOREA -- UNITED STATES
FACILITIES AND AREAS SUBCOMMITTEE

21 June 1971

MEMORANDUM FOR: THE JOINT COMMITTEE

1. Subcommittee Members:

United States	Republic of Korea
BG Kenneth T. Sawyer, Chairman	BG PAK Woo Bum, Chairman
COL W. D. Lewis, Alt. Chairman	Mr. SONG Yong Tai, Secty
LTC E. W. Lingel, USAF	Mr. KANG Hong Suk, Asst Secty
LTC H. C. Goodson, J4, USFK	LTC SHIN Sang Pil
MAJ M. Jacobs, USAFCS, K	Mr. KIM Hyung Kun
Mr. Francis K. Cook, J5, USFK	Mr. PAK Bung Hun
Mr. S. F. O'Hop, EAEN-RE, Secty	Mr. KIM Moo Young
Mr. E. H. Brummett, EAEN-RE, Alt. Secty	Mr. PARK Byong Yong
	Mr. BAE Myong In
	Mr. KANG Dae Bin
	Mr. LEE Soung Woo
	Mr. PARK Dahl Young
	Mr. KIM Han Mo
	Mr. BAE Jeung Sun

2. Subject of Recommendation: Request for Partial Release of Real Estate, Joint Committee memorandum dated 22 April 1971.

3. Recommendation: Task 997 The request for release of 0.12 acre of land, which constitutes a portion of SP-51A held under Acq. No. SAC-103 (partial), and located in Majangdong, Sungbuk-ku, Seoul City, required for upgrading and widening of adjacent Seoul City street, has been accepted by the Ministry of National Defense and the Eighth US Army, subject to the conditions for release as stated in the attached mutual agreement. The Ministry of National Defense

30

Task 997

and the Eighth US Army Engineer will prepare the necessary documents. It is recommended that the Joint Committee, SOFA, approve this release request.

4. Security Classification: Unclassified.

Brigadier General PAK Woo Bum
Chairman, ROK Component
Facilities and Areas Subcommittee

Brigadier General Kenneth T. Sawyer
Chairman, US Component
Facilities and Areas Subcommittee

1 Incl
as

2

27 May 1971

SUBJECT: Memorandum of Agreement - Conditional Release of a Portion of Real Estate, SP 51A, Acquisition No. SAC-103, TASK No. 997

US-ROK Chairmen
Facilities and Areas Subcommittee
US-ROK Joint Committee, SOFA

1. Authority: Pursuant to Memorandum for: Chairmen, Facilities and Areas Subcommittee (FASC) from Joint Committee (JC), US-ROK Status of Forces Agreement (SOFA), Subject: Request for Partial Release of Real Estate, dated 22 April 1971 (Inclosure No. 1), the FASC ROK Chairman appointed Major LEE Yong Sang, MND, as the ROK Component Working Group Committee Chairman. The FASC US Chairman appointed Mr. Eugene H. BRUMMETT, DAC, as the US Component Working Group Committee Chairman. The above chairmen were charged with the responsibility for investigating subject matter and to conduct negotiations to reach a mutual agreement as basis for a proposed recommendations to the JC, SOFA in resolution of subject TASK No. 997.

2. Whereas, the Ministry of National Defense, Republic of Korea (MND/ROK) has requested the partial release of Acquisition No. SAC-103, SP 51A, for upgrading and widening of the adjacent Seoul City street as shown on inclosed

32

map (Inclosure No. 2), and has proposed that their request be processed in accordance with SOFA real estate procedures, and to relocate/construct existing facilities within the area to be released, at no cost to the US Government, and Whereas USFK agrees to the above proposed actions and has conducted a feasibility of release investigation to establish a USFK position contingent upon reaching a mutual agreement as follows: a. The USFK agrees to release the requested real estate consisting of 0.12 acre of land (Partial), Acquisition No. SAC-103 to MND/ROK in accordance with following conditions and provisions:

b. MND-ROK/Seoul City agrees: (1) To relocate/construct existing building, T-29 (1,242 SF), in same configuration, design and condition as the existing structure, to the location determined by the responsible Facilities Engineer, as shown on inclosed map (Inclosure No. 2).

(2) To earthfill the site (approximately 14,000 SF) to four feet in depth, properly compacted for the location of above building T-29.

(3) Construct a 250 LF long, four feet high stone or concrete block rip rap retaining wall around the above filled-in area, as shown on inclosed map (Inclosure No. 2).

2

(4) To relocate/construct 255 LF of security fence line to the same existing design and standard as shown on inclosed map (Inclosure No. 2).

(5) To acquire a satisfactory and acceptable alternate POL pipeline relocation/construction site, consisting of approximately 0.257 acre of land, on a perpetual restrictive easement acquisition basis for an indefinite period of time for USFK, as shown in orange on Inclosure No. 2.

(6) To relocate/construct existing four each steel 6" diameter POL pipelines, shown on Inclosure No. 2, to the above new 0.257 acre USFK acquired site, shown in orange on Inclosure No. 2, connecting SP 51A admin/operational area, Acquisition No. SAC-103 with the existing POL tank farm storage area, Acquisition No. SAC-24, as shown on Inclosure No. 2.

(7) All POL pipeline relocation/construction work will be accomplished by MND-ROK/Seoul City at no cost to the US Government and in close prior coordination between the using activity, responsible area Facilities Engineer and the authorized representatives of MND-ROK/Seoul City. All such work will be accomplished under the technical supervision and in accordance with

specifications of the using activity and the Facilities Engineer concerned.

(8) That relocation/construction work will be accomplished in accordance with existing applicable US Army standards, quality of existing materials used, and plans and drawings prepared by the responsible Area Command Facilities Engineer.

(9) That all relocation/construction work will be subject to inspection surveillance by the inspection personnel of the Facilities Engineer concerned, All noted inspection deficiencies will be immediately corrected by MND-ROK/ Seoul City.

c. USFK agrees: That upon completion of relocation/construction required and the acceptance thereof by the USFK of the said relocated/constructed facilities, 0.12 acre of land, a portion of SP 51A, held under Acquisition No. SAC-103, as shown on inclosed map in green (Inclosure No. 2), will be released to MND/ROK.

3. Normal ingress/egress by MND-ROK/Seoul City personnel concerned, within USFK controlled areas, for purpose of above relocation/construction activities, will be subject to security control and regulations imposed by the Commanding

SUBJECT: TASK No. 997 -- 27 May 1971

Officer of the SP 51A or his representative.

4. The US Government, its officers and assigns, will be held harmless and clear by MND/ROK for any claims for real property and personal damage incident to above relocation/construction work.

5. Direct coordination between the responsible Facilities Engineer; Installation Commander and the authorized representatives of MND-ROK/Seoul City, for purpose of accomplishing provisions of this agreement, is hereby authorized.

LEE YONG SANG, Major
Real Estate Division
Installation Bureau, MND/ROK

EUGENE H. BRUMMETT, DAC
Real Estate Division
Engineer Section, UNC/USFK

2 Incl
as

5

36

22 July 1971

SUBJECT: Amendment No. 1, Memorandum of Agreement, Conditional Release of a Portion of Real Estate, SP 51A, Acquisition No. SAC-103, TASK No. 997

US-ROK Chairmen
Facilities and Areas Subcommittee
US-ROK Joint Committee, SOFA

1. Reference is made to Basic Agreement, Subject: Memorandum of Agreement - Conditional Release of a Portion of Real Estate, SP 51A, Acquisition No. SAC-103, TASK No. 997, dated 27 May 1971.

2. It has been determined that the relocation of existing POL pipeline by the MND-ROK/Seoul City, specified in referenced basic agreement, is to be changed. Paragraph 2b(6) is amended to read: "To construct/install one each steel 8" diameter and one each steel 12" diameter POL pipelines. The new required 8" and 12" diameter POL steel pipelines will be furnished by USFK. Further the US Government reserves the right to remove the now existing pipeline."

3. All other conditions and provisions in referenced basic agreement, except as noted in above paragraph 2 of herein Amendment No. 1, remain the same and unchanged.

LEE YONG SANG, Major
Real Estate Division
Installation Bureau, MND/ROK

EUGENE H. BRUMMETT, DAC
Real Estate Division
Engineer Section, UNC/USFK

REPUBLIC OF KOREA -- UNITED STATES
FACILITIES AND AREAS SUBCOMMITTEE

20 July 1971

MEMORANDUM FOR: THE JOINT COMMITTEE

1. Subcommittee Members:

United States	Republic of Korea
BG Kenneth T. Sawyer, Chairman	BG PAK Woo Bum, Chairman
COL W. D. Lewis, Alt. Chairman	Mr. SONG Yong Tai, Secty
LTC E. W. Lingel, USAF	Mr. KANG Hong Suk, Asst Secty
LTC H. C. Goodwin, J4, USFK	LTC SHIN Sang Pil
Mr. Francis K. Cook, J5, USFK	Mr. KIM Hyoung Kun
Mr. S. F. O'Hop, EAEN-RE, Secty	Mr. PAK Bung Hun
Mr. E. H. Brummett, EAEN-RE Alt. Secty	Mr. KIM Moo Young
	Mr. PARK Byong Yong
	Mr. BAE Myong In
	Mr. KANG Dae Bin
	Mr. LEE Soung Woo
	Mr. PARK Dahl Young
	Mr. KIM Han Mo
	Mr. BAE Jeung Sun

2. Subject of Recommendation: Request for Relocation of Telegraph Poles, para 2, Joint Committee memorandum dated 3 July 1971.

3. Recommendation: Task 1045 The request for the relocation of three electric power distribution poles and lines, Acquisition No. IC-168 (Partial), located in Uijongbu City, Kyonggi-do, has been accepted by the Ministry of National Defense and the Eighth US Army subject to the conditions as stated in the attached mutual memorandum of agreement -- Conditional Release of Real Estate (Partial), 0.14 Acre, Acquisition No. IC-168.

38

Task 1045

The Ministry of National Defense and the Eighth US Army Engineer will prepare the necessary documents. It is recommended that the Joint Committee, SOFA, approve this request for relocation of telegraph poles.

4. Security Classification: Unclassified.

Brigadier General PAK Woo Bum
Chairman, ROK Component
Facilities and Areas Subcommittee

Brigadier General Kenneth T. Sawyer
Chairman, US Component
Facilities and Areas Subcommittee

1 Attch
as

2

20 July 1971

SUBJECT: Memorandum of Agreement - Conditional Release of Real Estate (Partial), 0.14 Acre, Acquisition No. IC-168 (TASK No. 1045)

US-ROK Chairmen
Facilities and Areas Subcommittee
US-ROK, Joint Committee, SOFA

1. Authority: Pursuant to Memorandum for: Chairmen, FASC, from Joint Committee (JC), US-ROK Status of Forces Agreement (SOFA), Subject: Request for Relocation of Telegraph Poles, dated 3 July 1971 (Inclosure No. 1), the FASC ROK Chairman appointed Captain KAL Jong Yong, MND/ROK, as the ROK Component Working Group Committee Chairman. The FASC US Chairman appointed Mr. Stanley F. O'HOP, DAC, as the US Component Working Group Committee Chairman. The above chairmen were charged with the responsibility for investigating subject matter and to conduct negotiations to reach a mutual agreement as basis for a proposed recommendation to the JC, SOFA in resolution of subject Task No. 1045.

2. Whereas, the Ministry of National Defense, Republic of Korea (MND/ROK) has requested the relocation of three electric power distribution poles and lines, Acquisition No. IC-168 (Partial), as shown on inclosed map (Inclosure No. 2), and

40

J

SUBJECT: TASK No. 1045 - - 20 July 1971

Whereas, USFK has conducted a feasibility investigation relative to the above MND-ROK/Korea Pulp Company's requirements and accordingly, has established a US position, that said requirements can be met provided: All USFK facilities affected by above requirements will be relocated/installed, at no cost to the US Government, in accordance with the following conditions and provisions:

a. MND-ROK/Korea Pulp Company agrees: (1) To provide USFK an acceptable alternate site for relocation/installation of the above electric poles and lines, comprising of approximately 0.16 acre (704' x 10') on a perpetual restrictive easement acquisition basis for USFK, as shown on Inclosure No. 2.

(2) To relocate/install three electric power distribution poles and lines, from Acquisition No. IC-168 to the above new 0.16 acre USFK acquired site, determined by the Area Facilities Engineer concerned.

(3) That all relocation/construction work will be accomplished by MND-ROK/Korea Pulp Company, in close prior coordination between the Using Activity, responsible Area Facilities Engineer and the Local MND/ROK Real Estate Representative.

2

SUBJECT: TASK No. 1045 - - 20 July 1971

b. USFK agrees: That upon the completion and acceptance of the new relocated/installed electric power distribution system, including acquisition of the new site location by USFK, subject 0.14 acre parcel of land, held on easement basis, by Acquisition No. IC-168, as shown on Inclosure No. 2 will be released to MND/ROK. The new relocated/installed electric power distribution system, upon acceptance will become the real property of USFK.

3. The US Government, its officers and assigns, will be held harmless and clear by MND/ROK for any claims for real property and/or personal damages incident to the above relocation/construction work.

4. Direct coordination between the responsible Installation Commander, Using Activity, Area Facilities Engineer concerned and MND-ROK/Korea Pulp Company authorized representative, for purposes of accomplishing provisions of this agreement, is hereby authorized.

KAL JONG YONG, Captain
Real Estate Division
Installation Bureau, MND/ROK

STANLEY F. OTTOF, DAC
Real Estate Division
Engineer Section, UNC/USFK

3

42

REPUBLIC OF KOREA -- UNITED STATES
FACILITIES AND AREAS SUBCOMMITTEE

28 June 1971

MEMORANDUM FOR: THE JOINT COMMITTEE

1. Subcommittee Members:

United States	Republic of Korea
BG Kenneth T. Sawyer, Chairman	BG PAK Woo Bum, Chairman
COL W. D. Lewis, Alt. Chairman	Mr. SONG Yong Tai, Secty
LTC E. W. Lingel, USAF	Mr. KANG Hong Suk, Asst Secty
LTC H. C. Goodson, J4, USFK	LTC SHIN Sang Pil
MAJ M. Jacobs, USAFCS, K	Mr. KIM Hyung Kun
Mr. Francis K. Cook, J5, USFK	Mr. PAK Bung Hun
Mr. S. F. O'Hop, EAEN-RE, Secty	Mr. KIM Moo Young
Mr. E. H. Brummett, EAEN-RE, Alt. Secty	Mr. PARK Byong Yong
	Mr. BAE Myong In
	Mr. KANG Dae Bin
	Mr. LEE Soung Woo
	Mr. PARK Dahl Young
	Mr. KIM Han Mo
	Mr. BAE Jeung Sun

2. Subject of Recommendation: Requests for Relocation of Facilities, para 2b, Joint Committee memorandum dated 26 May 1971.

3. Recommendation: Task 1018 The request for relocation of a water supply line located along the boundaries of the 36th Engineer Gp compound in connectio: with the construction of a highway between Seoul and Uijongbu City, has been accepted by the Ministry of National Defense and the Eighth US Army subject to the conditions as stated in the attached mutual memorandum of agreement - "Conditional Release of Real Estate (partial), 0.49 acre, Acq. No. IC-207.

43

Task 1018

The Ministry of National Defense and the Eighth US Army Engineer will prepare the necessary documents. It is recommended that the Joint Committee, SOFA, approve this request for relocation of facilities.

4. Security Classification: Unclassified.

Brigadier General PAK Woo Bum Chairman, ROK Component Facislities and Areas Subcommittee	Brigadier General Kenneth T. Sawyer Chairman, US Component Facilities and Areas Subcommittee

1 Attch
as

2

44

17 June 1971

SUBJECT: Memorandum of Agreement - Conditional Release of Real Estate (Partial), 0.49 Acre, Acquisition No. IC-207 (TASK No. 1018)

US-ROK Chairmen
Facilities and Areas Subcommittee
US-ROK Joint Committee, SOFA

1. Authority: Pursuant to Memorandum for: Chairmen, FASC, from Joint Committee (JC), US-ROK Status of Forces Agreement (SOFA), Subject: Requests for Relocation of Facilities, dated 26 May 1971 (Inclosure No. 1), the FASC ROK Chairman appointed Captain KAL Jong Yong, MND/ROK, as the ROK Component Working Group Committee Chairman. The FASC US Chairman appointed Mr. Roderick L. HARVEY, DAC, as the US Component Working Group Committee Chairman. The above chairmen were charged with the responsibility for investigating subject matter and to conduct negotiations to reach a mutual agreement as basis for a proposed recommendation to the JC, SOFA in resolution of subject Task No. 1018.

2. Whereas, the Ministry of National Defense, Republic of Korea (MND/ROK)/ Uijongbu City has requested the relocation of three (3) noncontiguous portions of water pipeline (Partial), Acquisition No. IC-207, as shown in red on

45

SUBJECT: TASK No. 1018 — 17 June 1971

inclosed map (Inclosure No. 2) for the purpose of upgrading and widening Seoul - Uijongbu City road, and

Whereas, USFK has conducted a feasibility investigation relative to the above MND-ROK/Uijongbu City's requirements and accordingly, has established a US position, that said requirement can be met provided: That all USFK facilities affected by above requirements will be relocated/constructed, at no cost to the US Government; that an adequate relocation/construction site will be furnished and placed under acquisition control of USFK, at no cost to the US Government.

3. Meetings were held, negotiations were conducted and a proposed mutual agreement reached based upon the following conditions and provisions:

a. MND-ROK/Uijongbu City agrees: (1) To provide USFK an acceptable alternate water pipeline relocation/construction site consisting of three (3) noncontiguous areas, comprising of approximately 0.49 acre of land (2,100' x 10') on a perpetual restrictive easement acquisition basis for USFK, as shown in red on Inclosure No. 2.

40

SUBJECT: TASK No. 1018 - - 17 June 1971

(2) To install 656 LF of 6" CAP and 1,444 LF of 4" CAP underground water pipelines on the three (3) acquired noncontiguous sites, as shown in red on Inclosure No. 2.

(3) That all water pipeline relocation/construction work will be accomplished by MND-ROK/Uijongbu City, in close prior coordination between the using activity, responsible Area Facilities Engineer and MND-ROK/Uijongbu City authorized representatives. All such work will be accomplished under technical supervision and in accordance with specifications of the using activity, and the Facilities Engineer concerned, at no cost to the US Government.

(4) That materials and component parts used in the relocation/construction work will be of same quality of existing pipeline and in accordance with applicable US Army standards and drawings prepared by the responsible Area Command Facilities Engineer.

(5) That all relocation/construction work will be subject to inspection surveillance by the inspection personnel of the Facilities Engineer concerned.

49

3

SUBJECT: TASK No. 1018 - - 17 June 1971

All noted inspection deficiencies will be immediately corrected by MND-ROK/ Uijongbu City.

b. USFK agrees: That upon the completion and acceptance of the new relocated/constructed water supply pipeline and required site locations by USFK, subject parcel of land, 0.49 acre of new water pipeline (Partial), Acquisition No. IC-207, as shown in red on Inclosure No. 2 will be released to MND/ROK. The new relocated/constructed water supply pipeline facility, upon acceptance will become the real property of USFK.

4. The US Government, its officers and assigns, will be held harmless and clear by MND/ROK for any claims for real property and/or personal damages incident to the above relocation/construction work.

5. Direct coordination between the responsible Facilities Engineer; Installation Commander and MND-ROK/Uijongbu City authorized representatives, for purpose of accomplishing provisions of this agreement, is hereby authorized.

KIL JONG YONG, Captain
Real Estate Division
Installation Bureau, MND/ROK

RODERICK L. HARVEY, DAC
Real Estate Division
Engineer Section, UNC/USFK

4

48

REPUBLIC OF KOREA -- UNITED STATES
FACILITIES AND AREAS SUBCOMMITTEE

15 July 1971

MEMORANDUM FOR: THE JOINT COMMITTEE

1. Subcommittee Members:

United States	Republic of Korea
BG Kenneth T. Sawyer, Chairman	BG PAK Woo Bum, Chairman
COL W. D. Lewis, Alt. Chairman	Mr. SONG Yong Tai, Secty
LTC E. W. Lingel, USAF	Mr. KANG Hong Suk, Asst Secty
LTC H. C. Goodson, J4, USFK	LTC SHIN Sang Pil
Mr. Francis K. Cook, J5, USFK	Mr. KIM Hyoung Kun
Mr. S. F. O'Hop, EAEN-RE, Secty	Mr. PAK Bung Hun
Mr. E. H. Brummett, EAEN-RE, Alt. Secty	Mr. KIM Moo Young
	Mr. PARK Byong Yong
	Mr. BAE Myong In
	Mr. KANG Dae Bin
	Mr. LEE Soung Woo
	Mr. PARK Dahl Young
	Mr. KIM Han Mo
	Mr. BAE Jeung Sun

2. Subject of Recommendation: Request for Partial Release of Real Estate, para 2, Joint Committee memorandum dated 17 June 1971.

3. Recommendation: Task 1031 The request for the release of approximately 0.[illegible] acre of land currently held as a portion of the area under Acq. No. SAC-715, and located in Yongdongpo-ku, Seoul City, in connection with the widening of an existing road, has been accepted by the Ministry of National Defense and the Eighth US Army subject to the conditions as stated in the attached mutual memorandum of agreement - Conditional Release of Real Estate (Partial), 0.244 Acre, Acquisition No. SAC-715, ASP 046.

49

Task 1031

The Ministry of National Defense and the Eighth US Army Engineer will prepare the necessary documents. It is recommended that the Joint Committee, SOFA, approve this request for partial release of real estate.

4. Security Classification: Unclassifed.

Brigadier General PAK Woo Bum	Brigadier General Kenneth T. Sawyer
Chairman, ROK Component	Chairman, US Component
Facilities and Areas Subcommittee	Facilities and Areas Subcommittee

1 Attch
as

2

50

13 July 1971

SUBJECT: Memorandum of Agreement - Conditional Release of Real Estate (Partial), 0.244 Acre, Acquisition No. SAC-715, ASP 046, TASK No. 1031

US-ROK Chairmen
Facilities and Areas Subcommittee
US-ROK Joint Committee, SOFA

1. Authority: Pursuant to Memorandum for: Chairmen, FASC, from Joint Committee (JC), US-ROK Status of Forces Agreement (SOFA), Subject: Request for Partial Release of Real Estate, dated 17 June 1971 (Inclosure No. 1), the FASC ROK Chairman appointed Major LEE Yong Sang, MND/ROK, as the ROK Component Working Group Committee Chairman. The FASC US Chairman appointed Mr. Stanley F. O'HOP, DAC, as the US Component Working Group Committee Chairman. The above chairmen were charged with the responsibility for investigating subject matter and to conduct negotiations to reach a mutual agreement as basis for a proposed recommendation to the JC, SOFA in resolution of subject Task No. 1031.

2. Whereas, the Ministry of National Defense, Republic of Korea (MND/ROK) has requested the relocation of a portion of the security fence and release of approximately 0.244 acre of land (Partial), Acquisition No. SAC-715, as

51

shown on inclosed map (Inclosure No. 2), for the purpose of upgrading and widening of an existing Seoul City road, and

Whereas, USFK has conducted a feasibility investigation relative to the above MND-ROK/Seoul City's requirements and accordingly, has established a US position, that said requirements can be met provided: That all USFK facilities affected by above requirements will be relocated/constructed, at no cost to the US Government, in accordance with the following conditions and provisions:

a. MND-ROK/Seoul City agrees: (1) To temporarily relocate the existing 390 feet of security fence to within 3 feet of Bldg T-1139 and T-1140 with concertina wire next to the buildings.

(2) That upon construction of retaining wall (420 LF in length), the security fence will be relocated to its original position.

(3) That at no time the fence be left open at night during construction.

(4) That relocation/construction of the security fence will be subject to inspection surveillance by the inspection personnel of the Facilities Engineer concerned.

52

SUBJECT: Task No. 1031 - - 13 July 1971

(5) That normal ingress/egress by MND-ROK/Seoul City personnel concerned, within USFK controlled areas, for purpose of above relocation/construction activities, will be subject to security control and regulations imposed by the Commanding Officer of the ASP 046 Installation.

b. USFK agrees: That upon completion of retaining wall construction and relocation of the security fence, 0.244 acre of land, a portion of ASP 046, Acquisition No. SAC-715, as shown on inclosed map (Inclosure No. 2), will be released to MND/ROK.

3. The US Government, its officers and assigns, will be held harmless and clear by MND/ROK for any claims for real property and/or personal damages incident to above relocation/construction work.

4. Direct coordination between the responsible Facilities Engineer; Installation Commander and MND-ROK/Seoul City authorized representatives, for purpose of accomplishing provisions of this agreement, is hereby authorized.

LEE YONG SANG, Major
Real Estate Division
Installation Bureau, MND/ROK

STANLEY F. O'HOP, DAC
Real Estate Division
Engineer Section, UNC/USFK

53

3

REPUBLIC OF KOREA -- UNITED STATES
FACILITIES AND AREAS SUBCOMMITTEE

15 July 1971

MEMORANDUM FOR: THE JOINT COMMITTEE

1. Subcommittee Members:

United States	Republic of Korea
BG Kenneth T. Sawyer, Chairman	BG PAK Woo Bum, Chairman
COL W. D. Lewis, Alt. Chairman	Mr. SONG Yong Tai, Secty
LTC E. W. Lingel, USAF	Mr. KANG Hong Suk, Asst Secty
LTC H. C. Goodson, J4, USFK	LTC SHIN Sang Pil
Mr. Francis K. Cook, J5, USFK	Mr. KIM Hyoung Kun
Mr. S. F. O'Hop, EAEN-RE, Secty	Mr. PAK Bung Hun
Mr. E. H. Brummett, EAEN-RE, Alt. Secty	Mr. KIM Moo Young
	Mr. PARK Byong Yong
	Mr. BAE Myong In
	Mr. KANG Dae Bin
	Mr. LEE Soung Woo
	Mr. PARK Dahl Young
	Mr. KIM Han Mo
	Mr. BAE Jeung Sun

2. Subject of Recommendation: Requests for Acquisition of Real Estate, para 2b, Joint Committee memorandum dated 28 January 1971.

3. Recommendation: Task 867 The request for acquisition on a permanent use basis of 4.178 acres of land located in Pyongtaek-gun, Kyonggi-do, adjacent to Camp Humphreys Installation, required for construction of quarters and a mess hall, has been accepted by the Ministry of National Defense. The Ministry of National Defense and the Eighth US Army Engineer will prepare the necessary documents. It is recommended that the Joint Committee, SOFA, approve this acquisition request.

54

Task 867

4. Security Classification: Unclassified.

Brigadier General PAK Woo Bum
Chairman, ROK Component
Facilities and Areas Subcommittee

Brigadier General Kenneth T. Sawyer
Chairman, US Component
Facilities and Areas Subcommittee

55

REPUBLIC OF KOREA -- UNITED STATES
FACILITIES AND AREAS SUBCOMMITTEE

15 July 1971

MEMORANDUM FOR: THE JOINT COMMITTEE

1. Subcommittee Members:

United States	Republic of Korea
BG Kenneth T. Sawyer, Chairman	BG PAK Woo Bum, Chairman
COL W. D. Lewis, Alt. Chairman	Mr. SONG Yong Tai, Secty
LTC E. W. Lingel, USAF	Mr. KANG Hong Suk, Asst Secty
LTC H. C. Goodson, J4, USFK	LTC SHIN Sang Pil
Mr. Francis K. Cook, J5, USFK	Mr. KIM Hyoung Kun
Mr. S. F. O'Hop, EAEN-RE, Secty	Mr. PAK Bung Hun
Mr. E. H. Brummett, EAEN-RE, Alt. Secty	Mr. KIM Moo Young
	Mr. PARK Byong Yong
	Mr. BAE Myong In
	Mr. KANG Dae Bin
	Mr. LEE Soung Woo
	Mr. PARK Dahl Young
	Mr. KIM Han Mo
	Mr. BAE Jeung Sun

2. Subject of Recommendation: Requests for Acquisition of Real Estate, para 2a, Joint Committee memorandum dated 25 February 1971.

3. Recommendation: Task 922 The request for acquisition on a permanent exclusive use basis of 25.6 acres of land located at Pyongtaek, Kyonggi-do, required for the construction of buildings and facilities for Camp Humphreys Installation has been accepted by the Ministry of National Defense. The Ministry of National Defense and the Eighth US Army Engineer will prepare the necessary documents. It is recommended that the Joint Committee, SOFA, approve this acquisition request.

56

Task 922

4. Security Classification: Unclassified.

Brigadier General PAK Woo Bum
Chairman, ROK Component
Facilities and Areas Subcommittee

Brigadier General Kenneth T. Sawyer
Chairman, US Component
Facilities and Areas Subcommittee

REPUBLIC OF KOREA -- UNITED STATES
FACILITIES AND AREAS SUBCOMMITTEE

15 July 1971

MEMORANDUM FOR: THE JOINT COMMITTEE

1. Subcommittee Members:

United States

BG Kenneth T. Sawyer, Chairman
COL W. D. Lewis, Alt. Chairman
LTC E. W. Lingel, USAF
Mr. Francis K. Cook, J5, USFK
LTC H. C. Goodson, J4, USFK
Mr. S. F. O'Hop, EAEN-RE, Secty
Mr. E. H. Brummett, EAEN-RE, Alt. Secty

Republic of Korea

BG PAK Woo Bum, Chairman
Mr. SONG Yong Tai, Secty
Mr. KANG Hong Suk, Asst Secty
LTC SHIN Sang Pil
Mr. KIM Hyung Kun
Mr. PAK Bung Hun
Mr. KIM Moo Young
Mr. PARK Byong Yong
Mr. BAE Myong In
Mr. KANG Dae Bin
Mr. LEE Soung Woo
Mr. PARK Dahl Young
Mr. KIM Han Mo
Mr. BAE Jeung Sun

2. Subject of Recommendation: Requests for Extension of Temporary Use Permits, Joint Committee memorandum dated 17 June 1971.

3. Recommendation: Tasks 1034-1035 The following requests for extension of temporary use permits have been accepted by the Ministry of National Defense:

a. Task 1034 Extension of Temporary Use Permit K-H-T-2, involving 9.65 acres of land including 600 linear feet of railroad spur, located in Pusan City, from 16 July 1971 through 15 July 1972. This real estate has been used since 1969 as a temporary property disposal holding area and there is a continuing requirement for its use for that purpose.

58

Tasks 1034-1035

b. Task 1035 Extension of Temporary Use Permit K-G-T-12, involving 10 acres of riverbed area located in Kwangsan-gun, Chollanam-do, from 10 September 1971 through 9 September 1972. This real estate has been used since 1969 as a source of fill material for land reclamation and there is a continuing need for its use for that purpose.

The Ministry of National Defense and the Eighth US Army Engineer will prepare the necessary documents. It is recommended that the Joint Committee, SOFA, approve these two requests for extensions.

4. Security Classification: Unclassified.

Brigadier General PAK Woo Bum
Chairman, ROK Component
Facilities and Areas Subcommittee

Brigadier General Kenneth T. Sawyer
Chairman, US Component
Facilities and Areas Subcommittee

2

59

REPUBLIC OF KOREA -- UNITED STATES
FACILITIES AND AREAS SUBCOMMITTEE

15 July 1971

MEMORANDUM FOR: THE JOINT COMMITTEE

1. Subcommittee Members:

United States	Republic of Korea
BG Kenneth T. Sawyer, Chairman	BG PAK Woo Bum, Chairman
COL W. D. Lewis, Alt. Chairman	Mr. SONG Yong Tai, Secty
LTC E. W. Lingel, USAF	Mr. KANG Hong Suk, Asst Secty
LTC H. C. Goodson, J4, USFK	LTC SHIN Sang Pil
Mr. Francis K. Cook, J5, USFK	Mr. KIM Hyoung Kun
Mr. S. F. O'Hop, EAEN-RE, Secty	Mr. PAK Bung Hun
Mr. E. H. Brummett, EAEN-RE, Alt. Secty	Mr. KIM Moo Young
	Mr. PARK Byong Yong
	Mr. BAE Myong In
	Mr. KANG Dae Bin
	Mr. LEE Soung Woo
	Mr. PARK Dahl Young
	Mr. KIM Han Mo
	Mr. BAE Jeung Sun

2. Subject of Recommendation: Request for Authorization to Dispose of Facility, Joint Committee memorandum dated 17 June 1971.

3. Recommendation: Task 1032 The request for authorization to dispose of one facility, consisting of one Korean-constructed smoke stack, currently held as a portion of Camp Randall E. Coiner Installation in Seoul City, under Acq. No. SAC-526, has been accepted by the Ministry of National Defense with the request that prior coordination be made with the local MND real estate representative. This facility has become excess to USFK requirements. The Ministry of National Defense and the Eighth US Army Engineer will prepare the necessary documents. It is recommended that the Joint Committee, SOFA, approve this request.

60

Task 1032

4. Security Classification: Unclassified.

Brigadier General PAK Woo Bum	Brigadier General Kenneth T. Sawyer
Chairman, ROK Component	Chairman, US Component
Facilities and Areas Subcommittee	Facilities and Areas Subcommittee

2

REPUBLIC OF KOREA -- UNITED STATES
FACILITIES AND AREAS SUBCOMMITTEE

15 July 1971

MEMORANDUM FOR: THE JOINT COMMITTEE

1. Subcommittee Members:

United States	Republic of Korea
BG Kenneth T. Sawyer, Chairman	BG PAK Woo Bum, Chairman
COL W. D. Lewis, Alt. Chairman	Mr. SONG Yong Tai, Secty
LTC E. W. Lingel, USAF	Mr. KANG Hong Suk, Asst Secty
LTC H. C. Goodson, J4, USFK	LTC SHIN Sang Pil
Mr. Francis K. Cook, J5, USFK	Mr. KIM Hyoung Kun
Mr. S. F. O'Hop, EAEN-RE, Secty	Mr. PAK Bung Hun
Mr. E. H. Brummett, EAEN-RE, Alt. Secty	Mr. KIM Moo Young
	Mr. PARK Byong Yong
	Mr. BAE Myong In
	Mr. KANG Dae Bin
	Mr. LEE Soung Woo
	Mr. PARK Dahl Young
	Mr. KIM Han Mo
	Mr. BAE Jeung Sun

2. Subject of Recommendation: Request for Authorization to Dispose of Facility, Joint Committee memorandum dated 17 June 1971.

3. Recommendation: Task 1033 The request for authorization to dispose of one facility, consisting of one Korean-constructed building (S-1124), currently held as a portion of Camp Randall E. Coiner Installation in Seoul City, under Acq. No. SAC-526, has been accepted by the Ministry of National Defense with the request that prior coordination be made with the local MND real estate representative. This facility has become excess to USFK requirements. The Ministry of National Defense and the Eighth US Army Engineer will prepare the necessary documents. It is recommended that the Joint Committee, SOFA, approve this request.

62

Task 1033

4. Security Classification: Unclassified.

Brigadier General PAK Woo Bum
Chairman, ROK Component
Facilities and Areas Subcommittee

Brigadier General Kenneth T. Sawyer
Chairman, US Component
Facilities and Areas Subcommittee

2

63

REPUBLIC OF KOREA -- UNITED STATES
FACILITIES AND AREAS SUBCOMMITTEE

15 July 1971

MEMORANDUM FOR: THE JOINT COMMITTEE

1. Subcommittee Members:

United States	Republic of Korea
BG Kenneth T. Sawyer, Chairman	BG PAK Woo Bum, Chairman
COL W. D. Lewis, Alt. Chairman	Mr. SONG Yong Tai, Secty
LTC E. W. Lingel, USAF	Mr. KANG Hong Suk, Asst Secty
LTC H. C. Goodson, J4, USFK	LTC SHIN Sang Pil
Mr. Francis K. Cook, J5, USFK	Mr. KIM Hyoung Kun
Mr. S. F. O'Hop, EAEN-RE, Secty	Mr. PAK Bung Hun
Mr. E. H. Brummett, EAEN-RE, Alt. Secty	Mr. KIM Moo Young
	Mr. PARK Byong Yong
	Mr. BAE Myong In
	Mr. KANG Dae Bin
	Mr. LEE Soung Woo
	Mr. PARK Dahl Young
	Mr. KIM Han Mo
	Mr. BAE Jeung Sun

2. Subject of Recommendation: Requests for Acquisition of Real Estate, para 2b, Joint Committee memorandum dated 25 February 1971.

3. Recommendation: Task 923 The request for acquisition of a total of 52.41 acres of land located at Chilgok-gun, Kyongsangbuk-do (19.71 acres on a permanent exclusive use basis and the remaining 32.7 acres on a perpetual restrictive easement basis) required for a permanent rock quarry to provide construction materials for Camp Carroll Depot and ALOC Airfield projects, has been withdrawn by the US requesting agency in lieu of reacquisition of existing old rock quarry (Acq. No. PAC-152). Therefore, it is recommended that no further action be taken on this task.

64

1093

Task 923

The Ministry of National Defense and the Eighth US Army Engineer will prepare the necessary documents. It is recommended that the Joint Committee, SOFA, approve this request.

4. Security Classification: Unclassified.

Brigadier General PAK Woo Bum	Brigadier General Kenneth T. Sawyer
Chairman, ROK Component	Chairman, US Component
Facilities and Areas Subcommittee	Facilities and Areas Subcommittee

2

65

REPUBLIC OF KOREA -- UNITED STATES
FACILITIES AND AREAS SUBCOMMITTEE

15 July 1971

MEMORANDUM FOR: THE JOINT COMMITTEE

1. Subcommittee Members:

United States	Republic of Korea
BG Kenneth T. Sawyer, Chairman	BG PAK Woo Bum, Chairman
COL W. D. Lewis, Alt. Chairman	Mr. SONG Yong Tai, Secty
LTC E. W. Lingel, USAF	Mr. KANG Hong Suk, Asst Secty
LTC H. C. Goodson, J4, USFK	LTC SHIN Sang Pil
Mr. Francis K. Cook, J5, USFK	Mr. KIM Hyung Kun
Mr. S. F. O'Hop, EAEN-RE, Secty	Mr. PAK Bung Hun
Mr. E. H. Brummett, EAEN-RE, Alt. Secty	Mr. KIM Moo Young
	Mr. PARK Byong Yong
	Mr. BAE Myong In
	Mr. KANG Dae Bin
	Mr. LEE Soung Woo
	Mr. PARK Dahl Young
	Mr. KIM Han Mo
	Mr. BAE Jeung Sun

2. Subject of Recommendation: Requests for Release of Real Estate, Joint Committee memorandum dated 17 June 1971.

3. Recommendations: Tasks 1020-1030 The following requests for release of real estat have been accepted by the Ministry of National Defense and the Eighth US Army:

a. Task 1020 Release of a total of 0.75 acre of land, comprising 0.043 acre held under Acq. No. I-41, 0.025 acre held under Acq. No. I-42, and 0.682 acre held under Acq. No. AAC-395, and located on Seattle Installation in Inchon City, Kyonggi-do

66

Tasks 1020-1030 contd

b. Task 1021 Release of 52.47 acres of land, constituting Tac 4, Site 40 Installation, located in Chunsong-gun, Kangwon-do, and currently held under Acq. Nos. SAC-729 and SAC-780, including a total of 53 buildings and facilities existing at the time of release.

c. Task 1022 Release of 23.18 acres of land, constituting Tac 2, Site 31 Installation, located in Pochon-gun, Kyonggi-do, and currently held under Acq. No. 7X-136, including a total of 14 buildings and facilities existing at the time of release.

d. Task 1023 Release of 68.3626 acres of land, constituting Tac 4, Site 35 Installation, located in Kapyong-gun, Kyonggi-do, and currently held under Acq. Nos. SAC-737, SAC-750, SAC-751, and SAC-784. This request for release includes a total of 53 buildings and facilities existing at the time of release.

e. Task 1024 Release of approximately 0.91 acre of land held on an easement basis as a portion of the area held under Acq. No. IC-168 and located in Uijongbu-si, Kyonggi-do, including 3,965 LF of USFK-installed electric power line currently held under Facility No. F-115.

f. Task 1025 Release of 2.17 acres of land, constituting a portion of Camp Albany Installation, located within and in the vicinity of Uijongbu-si, Kyonggi-do, and currently held as a portion of the area under Acq. No. IC-164. This request for release includes a total of 11 buildings and facilities existing at the time of release.

g. Task 1026 Release of 2,722.68 acres of land, constituting the remaining portion of Camp Saint Barbara Installation, located in Pochon-gun, Kyonggi-do, and currently held under Acq. Nos. 7X-100, 7X-101, and K-C-201, including a total of 247 buildings and facilities existing at the time of release.

h. Task 1027 Release of 22.208 acres of land held on an easement basis under Acq. No. K-B-319 and used in support of an overhead electric power line, located in Paju-gun, Kyonggi-do.

i. Task 1028 Release of 0.80 acre of land held on an easement basis under Acq. No. CAV-269 and used in support of an overhead electric power line, located in Paju-gun, Kyonggi-do.

2

67

Tasks 1020-1030 contd

j. Task 1029 Release of 0.60 acre of land held on an easement basis under Acq. No. CAV-268 and used in support of an overhead electric power line, located in Paju-gun, Kyonggi-do.

k. Task 1030 Release of 14.61 acres of land, constituting the remaining portion of Love Installation, located in Paju-gun, Kyonggi-do, and currently held under Acq. No. CAV-208, including a total of 27 buildings and facilities existing at the time of release.

The Ministry of National Defense and the Eighth US Army Engineer will prepare the necessary documents. It is recommended that the Joint Committee, SOFA, approve these 11 requests for release of real estate.

4. Security Classification: Unclassified.

Pak Woo Bum

Brigadier General PAK Woo Bum
Chairman, ROK Component
Facilities and Areas Subcommittee

K T Sawyer

Brigadier General Kenneth T. Sawyer
Chairman, US Component
Facilities and Areas Subcommittee

REPUBLIC OF KOREA -- UNITED STATES
FACILITIES AND AREAS SUBCOMMITTEE

15 July 1971

MEMORANDUM FOR: THE JOINT COMMITTEE

1. Subcommittee Members:

United States	Republic of Korea
BG Kenneth T. Sawyer, Chairman	BG PAK Woo Bum, Chairman
COL W. D. Lewis, Alt. Chairman	Mr. SONG Yong Tai, Secty
LTC E. W. Lingel, USAF	Mr. KANG Hong Suk, Asst Secty
LTC H. C. Goodson, J4, USFK	LTC SHIN Sang Pil
Mr. Francis K. Cook, J5, USFK	Mr. KIM Hyung Kun
Mr. S. F. O'Hop, EAEN-RE, Secty	Mr. PAK Bung Hun
Mr. E. H. Brummett, EAEN-RE, Alt. Secty	Mr. KIM Moo Young
	Mr. PARK Byong Yong
	Mr. BAE Myong In
	Mr. KANG Dae Bin
	Mr. LEE Soung Woo
	Mr. PARK Dahl Young
	Mr. KIM Han Mo
	Mr. BAE Jeung Sun

2. Subject of Recommendation: Requests for Release of Real Estate.

3. Recommendations: Tasks 1039-1043 The following requests for release of real estate have been accepted by the Ministry of National Defense and the Eighth US Army:

a. Task 1039 Release of 209.50 acres of land with two Korean-constructed facilities, constituting Wolmido Installation, held under Acq. Nos. ASCOM-363, ASCOM-375, AAC-381 and AAC-383, and located in Inchon City, Kyonggi-do. This release includes all USFK-constructed facilities located on the Installation

69

3. Tasks 1039-1043

a. Task 1039 contd

to be released, with the exception of two water tank facilities (Nos T-3421 and T-3422) and Building No. T-3343 with ingress and egress rights thereto, which will be retained under USFK control until 30 October 1971.

b. Task 1040 Release of 7.8 acres of land, constituting Area #3 portion of Camp Pililaau Installation, held under Acq. No. IC-264 and located in Uijongbu-si, Kyonggi-do, including a total of 50 USFK-constructed buildings and facilities located on the Installation.

c. Task 1041 Release of 20.942 acres of land, constituting Camp Nabors Installation, held under Acq. Nos. SAC-705 and SAC-766, and located in Seoul City, including a total of 108 USFK-constructed buildings and facilities located on the Installation.

d. Task 1042 Release of 23.86 acres of land, constituting the remaining portion of Camp Pililaau Installation, held under Acq. No. IC-264 and located in Uijongbu-si, Kyonggi-do. This request for release includes a total of 78 USFK-constructed buildings and facilities located on the Installation.

e. Task 1043 Release of 21.27 acres of land containing two Korean-constructed buildings, constituting a portion of Market Installation held under Acq. No. ACS-193, and located in Inchon City, Kyonggi-do. This request for release includes a total of 66 USFK-constructed buildings and facilities located on the Installation. Exempted from this release request are 0.659 acre of land containing an underground sanitary sewer line and an overhead electric power line, which will be retained together with unrestricted rights-of-entry for ingress and egress thereto. (Tyler)

The Ministry of National Defense and the Eighth US Army Engineer will prepare the necessary documents. It is recommended that the Joint Committee, SOFA, approve these five release requests.

2

170

Tasks 1039-1043

4. Security Classification: Unclassified.

Brigadier General PAK Woo Bum
Chairman, ROK Component
Facilities and Areas Subcommittee

Brigadier General Kenneth T. Sawyer
Chairman, US Component
Facilities and Areas Subcommittee

3

71

REPUBLIC OF KOREA - UNITED STATES
FINANCE (PERSONNEL AFFAIRS) SUBCOMMITTEE

20 July 1971

MEMORANDUM FOR: THE JOINT COMMITTEE

1. Subcommittee Members:

United States	Republic of Korea
COL Dana F. McFall, Chairman	Mr. PARK Dong Hee, Chairman
COL Thomas F. Henderson, USAF	Mr. KWON Tai Won
COL D. J. Helterbran, USA	Mr. SHIN Myoung Ho
COL Robert J. Kriwanek, USA	Mr. LEE Jin Moo
CDR George E. Thibault, USN	Mr. KANG Yung Joo
LTC Ronald S. McCaul, USA	Mr. LEE Chul Hee
LTC William T. Tinsley, USA	Mr. CHOO Byung Guk
LTC Fred L. Bowden, USAF	Mr. KIM Kyung Tai
MAJ Allen D. Adams, USA	Mr. SHIN Yung Su
Mr. Francis K. Cook	Mr. KIM Kee Joe

2. Subject to Recommendation: Review of procedures established by the Joint Committee at its ninth meeting on 5 June 1967, relating to the examination by Republic of Korea Customs Inspectors of parcel post packages delivered through United States military post office channels, contained as Inclosure (6) to the minutes of the ninth Joint Committee meeting.

3. Recommendation: Paragraph 3c and d of the above referenced Inclosures be revised to read:

a. "3c. It is mutually agreed that, in the interest of full compliance with the Agreed Understandings of Article IX, Republic of Korea-United States Status of Forces Agreement, whereby delay of mail and increased administrative burden on postal authorities will be held to a minimum, sufficient Republic of Korea customs inspectors and repackers will be present to conduct inspections.

72

(1) The "sample" inspection will consist of no more than 10% of the incoming bags/containers of nonofficial parcel mail. The sample will be selected jointly by United States postal personnel and Republic of Korea customs inspectors.

(2) At Inchon inspections will be completed sufficiently before the scheduled loading time to permit onward transportation to depart on schedule. At Kimpo Air Base the inspection will be completed within six hours after the arrival of the airline flight. When customs officials are not present to designate mail for examination, it will be forwarded to its final destination without delay.

d. A "customs inspection area" will be designated by the respective commander in charge and all examinations will be conducted in this designated area. United States military postal personnel will be present in the inspection area during the conduct of all such customs inspections."

b. It is further recommended that paragraph 5c of the above-referenced Inclosure be revised to read:

"5c. Parcels containing items which, per se, appear to be unreasonable in quantity will be retained under the control of the United States military postal authorities until their disposition is mutually determined by appropriate Republic of Korea and United States authorities. It is mutually agreed that the determination as to what constitutes a reasonable/unreasonable quantity of any given item rests with United States officials based upon the addressee's mission, family requirements, stated purpose for importation, and any other considerations deemed appropriate by the United States. A guide as to what represents reasonable quantities of specified items is attached as Inclosure 2."

c. Questions concerning increased personnel and space for the conduct of customs examination continue under review by the Finance/ Personnel Affairs Subcommittee.

d. It is further recommended that the effective date of this recommendation be the date upon which it is approved by the Joint Committee.

4. Security Classification: Unclassified.

Mr. PARK Dong Hee Chairman, ROK Component Finance (Personnel Affairs)Subcommittee	COL Dana F. McFall, USAF Chairman, US Component Finance (Personnel Affairs) Subcommittee

Reasonable Quantities of Specified Items Delivered through US Military Post Office During an Individual's tour of duty in Korea.

	Item	Quantity
1.	Air Conditioner	1 per individual (See Note 1) 2 per family
2.	Dryer	1 per family
3.	Electric Fan	1 per individual
4.	Freezer	1 per family
5.	Water Heater	1 per family
6.	Movie Camera	1 per individual
7.	Gramophone	1 per individual
8.	Turntable	1 per individual
9.	Radio	1 per individual
10.	Gas Range	1 per family
11.	Refrigerator	1 per family
12.	Speaker System	1 per individual
13.	Camera (still)	1 per individual
14.	Tape Deck	1 per individual
15.	Tape Recorder	1 per individual
16.	Television	1 per individual
17.	Amplifier Tuner	1 per individual
18.	Typewriter	1 per individual
19.	Washing Machine	1 per family
20.	Binoculars	1 per individual
21.	Stereo Music System	1 per individual
22.	Mixer	1 per family
23.	Rice Cooker	1 per family
24.	Toaster	1 per family
25.	Coffee Maker	1 per individual
26.	Cleaner (Vacuum)	1 per family
27.	Golf Set	1 per individual
28.	Car Cooler	1 per car
29.	Car Radio	1 per car
30.	Receiver	1 per individual
31.	Mink (coat, shawl, collar)	1 each per individual
32.	Handbag (alligator)	not authorized
33.	Ring (US value over $100 US)	1 per individual
34.	Watch (US value over $100 US)	1 per individual
35.	Textiles	Maximum of 25 yds per shipment, to include no more than 5 yds same color/design.

Note 1: If an individual is authorized to live off-post he will be considered as a "family" for the purposes of this list.

Mr. PARK Dong Hee [signature] COL Dana F. McFall, USAF [signature]

75

JOINT COMMITTEE
UNDER
THE REPUBLIC OF KOREA AND THE UNITED STATES
STATUS OF FORCES AGREEMENT

15 JUL 1971

MEMORANDUM FOR: The Joint Committee

SUBJECT: Designation of U.S. Invited Contractor Under Article XV, Status of Forces Agreement

1. References:

a. Paragraph 2, Article XV, Status of Forces Agreement.

b. U.S. Chairman, Commerce Subcommittee, letter dated 27 April 1971, subject as above (Inclosure 1).

c. ROK Chairman, Commerce Subcommittee, letter dated 4 May 1971, subject as above (Inclosure 2).

2. The United States, after consultation with the ROK Commerce Subcommittee and having duly considered their views, has designated Daniel, Mann, Johnson, and Mendenhall as a US Invited Contractor for design of integrated communications system for USFK/EUSA - Underground Command Post, Seoul, Korea, contract #DACA79-71-C-0082.

3. Pertinent data concerning U.S. citizen employees will be provided to the Joint Secretariat in the established format.

2 Incl
as

ROBERT N. SMITH
Lieutenant General, USAF
United States Representative
Joint Committee

76

REPUBLIC OF KOREA - UNITED STATES
COMMERCE SUBCOMMITTEE

27 April 1971

SUBJECT: Designation of US Invited Contractor Under Article XV, Status of Forces Agreement

ROK Chairman, Commerce Subcommittee

1. Reference: Paragraph 2, Article XV, Status of Forces Agreement.

2. The Government of the Republic of Korea is informed through this written consultative process that the United States Forces, Korea, proposes to extend invited contractor status to the US firm awarded the contract for design of Integrated Communications System for USFK/EUSA Underground Command Post, Korea.

3. The following data are provided:

a. Company Name:

(1) Lyon Associates

(2) Daniel, Mann, Johnson and Mendenhall

(3) Adrian Wilson Associates

b. Local Address: APO 96301

c. Identification of US Citizen Employees: Information will be provided as soon as received from the contractor.

d. Number of US and ROK Employees: Information will be provided as soon as received from the contractor.

e. Reason for Designation of an Invited Contractor:

(1) Security Considerations.

(2) Technical Qualifications of the contractors involved.

f. Location of Contract: Underground Command Post, Korea.

-27

27 April 1971

SUBJECT: Designation of US Invited Contractor Under Article XV, Status of Forces Agreement

g. Type of Contract: Fixed Price, Type B.

h. Length of Contract: To be supplied upon award award of contract.

i. Sponsoring Component Commander: USAEDFE

RICHARD T. CANN
Colonel, U.S. Army
United States Chairman
Commerce Subcommittee

MINISTRY OF COMMERCE AND INDUSTRY
REPUBLIC OF KOREA
SEOUL, KOREA

4 May 1971

Subject: Designation of US Invited Contractor under Article XV Status of Forces Agreement

US Chairman, Commerce Subcommittee

1. Reference:

a. Paragraph 2, Article XV, Status of Forces Agreement

b. US Commerce Subcommittee Memorandum of Consultation, dated 27 April 1971, subject as above, pertaining to contract for design of Integrated Communications System for USFK/EUSA Underground Command Post, Korea.

2. The US memorandum reference 1b above, has been reviewed and the Government of the Republic of Korea understands the requirement for an invited contractor in this instance.

Chung Min Kil
Chairman
Commerce Subcommittee, ROK

기

JOINT COMMITTEE
UNDER
THE REPUBLIC OF KOREA AND THE UNITED STATES
STATUS OF FORCES AGREEMENT

15 JUL 1971

MEMORANDUM FOR: The Joint Committee

SUBJECT: Designation of U.S. Invited Contractor Under Article XV, Status of Forces Agreement

1. References:

a. Paragraph 2, Article XV, Status of Forces Agreement.

b. U.S. Chairman, Commerce Subcommittee, letter dated 2 June 1971, subject as above (Inclosure 1).

c. ROK Chairman, Commerce Subcommittee, letter dated 25 June 1971, subject as above (Inclosure 2).

2. The United States, after consultation with the ROK Commerce Subcommittee and having duly considered their views, has designated Adrian Wilson Associates, Incorporated as a US Invited Contractor for design of ordnance storage facilities, Taegu and Kwang-Ju Air Bases, Korea, contract #DACA79-71-C-0076.

3. Pertinent data concerning U.S. citizen employees will be provided to the Joint Secretariat in the established format.

2 Incl
as

ROBERT N. SMITH
Lieutenant General, USAF
United States Representative
Joint Committee

80

REPUBLIC OF KOREA - UNITED STATES
COMMERCE SUBCOMMITTEE

2 June 1971

SUBJECT: Designation of US Invited Contractor Under Article XV, Status of Forces Agreement

ROK Chairman, Commerce Subcommittee

1. Reference: Paragraph 2, Article XV, of the Status of Forces Agreement.

2. The Government of the Republic of Korea is informed through this written consultative process that the United States Forces, Korea, proposes to extend invited contractor status to the US firm awarded the contract for the Design of Ordance Storage Facility, Taegu and Kwang-Ju Air Bases, Korea.

3. The following data are provided:

a. Company Name:

(1) Adrian Wilson Associates

(2) Daniel, Mann, Johnson & Mendenhall

(3) Pacific Architects and Engineers, Inc.

b. Local Address: APO 96301

c. Identification of US Citizen Employees: Information will be provided as soon as received from the contractor.

d. Number of US and ROK Employees: Information will be provided as soon as received from the contractor.

e. Reason for Designation of an Invited Contractor: Open competitive bidding among local contractors is not practicable due to technical qualifications of the contractors involved.

f. Location of Contract: Taegu and Kwang-Ju, Korea.

81

2 June 1971

SUBJECT: Designation of US Invited Contractor Under Article XV, Status of Forces Agreement

g. Type of Contract: Fixed Price, Type B.

h. Length of Contract: To be supplied upon conclusion of negotiations.

i. Sponsoring Component Commander: USAEDFE

Norman W. Hammer, COL
for
RICHARD T. CANN
Colonel, U.S. Army
United States Chairman
Commerce Subcommittee

82

MINISTRY OF COMMERCE AND INDUSTRY
REPUBLIC OF KOREA
SEOUL, KOREA

25 June 1971

Subject : Designation of US Invited Contractor under Article XV, Status of Forces Agreement

US Chairman, Commerce Subcommittee

1. Reference :

a. Paragraph 2, Article XV, Status of Forces Agreement

b. US Commerce Subcommittee Memorandum of Consultation, dated 2 June 1971 subject as above, pertaining to contract for Design of Ordnance Storage Facility, Taegu and Kwang-Ju, Air Bases, Korea.

2. The US memorandum, reference 1b above, has been reviewed and the government of the Republic of Korea understands the requirement for an invited contractor in this instance.

Chung Min Kil
Chairman
Commerce Subcommittee, ROK

83

JOINT COMMITTEE
UNDER
THE REPUBLIC OF KOREA AND THE UNITED STATES
STATUS OF FORCES AGREEMENT

3 0 JUN 1971

MEMORANDUM FOR: The Joint Committee

SUBJECT: Designation of U.S. Invited Contractor Under Article XV, Status of Forces Agreement

1. References:

a. Paragraph 2, Article XV, Status of Forces Agreement.

b. U.S. Chairman, Commerce Subcommittee, letter dated 11 September 1970, subject as above (Inclosure 1).

c. ROK Chairman, Commerce Subcommittee, letter dated 29 September 1970, subject as above (Inclosure 2).

2. The United States, after consultation with the ROK Commerce Subcommittee and having duly considered their views, has designated Associated American Engineers Overseas, Incorporated as a U.S. Invited Contractor for Repair of Intrusion Detection Alarm System and Installation of Intrusion Detection Alarm System, Kunsan AB, Korea, contract #F62087-71-C-0046.

3. Pertinent data concerning U.S. citizen employees will be provided to the Joint Secretariat in the established format.

2 Incl
as

ROBERT N. SMITH
Lieutenant General, USAF
United States Representative
Joint Committee

84

REPUBLIC OF KOREA - UNITED STATES
COMMERCE SUBCOMMITTEE

11 September 1970

SUBJECT: Designation of US Invited Contractor under Article XV, Status of Forces Agreement

ROK Chairman, Commerce Subcommittee

1. Reference: Paragraph 2, Article XV, Status of Forces Agreement.

2. The Government of the Republic of Korea is informed through this written consultative process that the United States Forces, Korea, proposes to extend invited contractor status to the qualified US firm on the contract described in paragraph 3 below for installation, inspection, maintenance and repair of an Intrusion Detection System at Kunsan Air Base, Korea.

3. The following data are provided:

a. Company Name: The following qualified US firms are to be considered for performance of this contract.

(1) Associated American Engineers Overseas, Inc., APO 96301

(2) International Electronics Corp., APO 96301

(3) Tectonics Inc., APO 96301

b. Local Address: To be supplied upon designation.

c. Identification of US Citizen Employees: To be supplied upon designation.

d. Number of US and ROK Employees: To be supplied upon designation.

e. Reasons for Designation of an Invited Contractor: Open competitive bidding is not practicable due to the following:

(1) Unavailability of materials and services required from local sources.

(2) The work includes classified items and requires utilization of a contractor who has a Security Clearance. All operation, maintenance and spare parts manuals required in this procurement are marked SECRET

85

11 September 1970

SUBJECT: Designation of US Invited Contractor under Article XV, Status of Forces Agreement

in accordance with AFR 205-1.

(3) Local contractors do not possess the required technical qualifications or security clearances.

f. Location of Contract: Kunsan Air Base, Korea.

g. Type of Contract: Firm Fixed Price.

h. Length of Contract: Thru January 30, 1971.

i. Sponsoring Component Command: Commander, Air Forces, Korea.

GERALD L. HAYMAKER
Colonel, U.S. Army
United States Chairman
Commerce Subcommittee

2

MINISTRY OF COMMERCE AND INDUSTRY
REPUBLIC OF KOREA
SEOUL, KOREA

29 September 1970

SUBJECT: Designation of US Invited Contractor under Article XV Status of Forces Agreement.

US Chairman, Commerce Subcommittee.

1. Reference:

a. Paragraph 2, Article XV, Status of Forces Agreement.

b. US Commerce Subcommittee Memorandum of Consultation, dated 11 September 1970, subject as above, pertaining to fixed price contract for installation, inspection, maintenance and repair of an Intrusion Detection System at Kunsan Air Base, Korea.

2. The US memorandum, reference 1b above, has been reviewed and the Government of the Republic of Korea understand the requirement for an invited contractor in this instance.

Chung Min Kil
Chairman
Commerce Subcommittee, ROK

87

JOINT COMMITTEE
UNDER
THE REPUBLIC OF KOREA AND THE UNITED STATES
STATUS OF FORCES AGREEMENT

22 JUL 1971

MEMORANDUM FOR: The Joint Committee

SUBJECT: Designation of US Invited Contractor Under Article XV, Status of Forces Agreement

1. References:

a. Paragraph 2, Article XV, Status of Forces Agreement.

b. US Chairman, Commerce Subcommittee, letter dated 30 March 1971, subject as above (Inclosure 1).

c. US Chairman, Commerce Subcommittee, letter dated 6 April 1971, subject as above (Inclosure 2).

d. ROK Chairman, Commerce Subcommittee, letter dated 8 April 1971, subject as above (Inclosure 3).

2. The United States, after consultation with the ROK Commerce Subcommittee and having duly considered their views, has designated the Fischer Engineering and Maintenance Company, Inc., as a US invited contractor, in joint venture with a Korean firm, for execution of contract DAJB03-72-6001 for facilities engineering services for the Northern Sector Comprehensive Facilities Engineering area.

3. Pertinent data concerning US citizen employees will be provided to the Joint Secretariat in the established format.

3 Incl
as

ROBERT N. SMITH
Lieutenant General, USAF
United States Representative
Joint Committee

88

REPUBLIC OF KOREA - UNITED STATES
COMMERCE SUBCOMMITTEE

30 March 1971

SUBJECT: Designation of US Invited Contractor Under Article XV, Status of Forces Agreement

ROK Chairman, Commerce Subcommittee

1. Reference: Paragraph 2, Article XV of the Status of Forces Agreement.

2. The Government of the Republic of Korea is informed through this written consultative process that the United States Forces, Korea, proposes to extend invited contractor status to the US firm awarded the contract for the Northern Sector Comprehensive Facilities Engineering Area or to the US member firm of the US-ROK Joint Venture contractor awarded this contract. This new contract will encompass the existing Forward Area facilities engineering contract and the Camp Page portion of the present Camp Page-Sihung facilities engineering contract.

3. The following data are provided:

a. Company Name: The names of the US firms to be considered are attached as Inclosure 1.

b. Local Address: As shown in Inclosure 1.

c. Identification of US Citizen Employees: To be supplied after the contract has been awarded.

d. Number of US and ROK Employees: To be supplied after the contract has been awarded.

e. Reasons for Designation of an Invited Contractor:

(1) Security considerations. A contract utilizing a Korean contract only is not feasible due to the extensive security requirements demanded by the US Army. The contractor will be involved in the operations and maintenance of critical support facilities which directly affect the mission capabilities of the US Army. He will also be involved in programming actions which may be classified and releasable only to US personnel holding valid security clearances.

8P

30 March 1971

SUBJECT: Designation of US Invited Contractor Under Article XV, Status of Forces Agreement

(2) Technical qualifications of the contractor personnel. Fully qualified and trained managers and supervisors are essential to meet facility engineering requirements.

(3) Materials and services required by US standards. The management of government resources such as supplies, equipment, tools and vehicles require the contractor to be responsible for and responsive to US Army policies and requirements. The contractor is required to comply with various Army manuals and regulations and other applicable publications which are technical in nature. The facilities and technical equipment are US design and manufacture and must be maintained to US standards.

f. Location of Contract: Northern Sector Comprehensive Facilities Engineering area.

g. Type of Contract: A cost-plus-fixed-fee type contract for the management, operations, maintenance and repair of real property facilities.

h. Length of Contract: 1 July 1971 thru 30 June 1972. Additionally, the contract would have a 30-day transition period at the end of the contract as determined above.

i. Sponsoring Component Commander: Commanding General, Eighth United States Army.

1 Incl
as

RICHARD T. CANN
Colonel, US Army
United States Chairman
Commerce Subcommittee

2

90

REPUBLIC OF KOREA - UNITED STATES
COMMERCE SUBCOMMITTEE

6 April 1971

SUBJECT: Designation of US Invited Contractor Under Article XV, Status of Forces Agreement

ROK Chairman, Commerce Subcommittee

1. Reference: a.. Paragraph 2, Article XV, Status of Forces Agreement.

b. US Chairman, Commerce Subcommittee, letter of consultation, dated 30 March 1971, subject as above.

c. Verbal discussion on 2 April 1971 between members of the US and ROK Commerce Subcommittees.

2. Based on the verbal request of the ROK Commerce Subcommittee, paragraph 2 of reference 1b above is amended to read as follows: The Government of the Republic of Korea is informed through this written consultative process that the United States Forces, Korea, proposes to extend invited contractor status to the US member firm of the US-ROK joint venture contractor awarded the contract for the Northern Sector Comprehensive Facilities Engineering area. This new contract will encompass the existing forward area facilities engineering contract and the Camp Page portion of the present Camp Page-Sihung facilities engineering contract.

Richard T. Cann
RICHARD T. CANN
Colonel, US Army
United States Chairman
Commerce Subcommittee

91

MINISTRY OF COMMERCE AND INDUSTRY
REPUBLIC OF KOREA
SEOUL, KOREA

8 April 1971

Subject: Designation of US Invited Contractor under Article XV Status of Forces Agreement

US Chairman, Commerce Subcommittee

1. Reference:

a. Paragraph 2, Article XV, Status of Forces Agreement

b. US Commerce Subcommittee Memorandum of Consultation, dated 30 March 1971, subject as above, pertaining to joint venture contract for Facilities Engineering Services for the Forward Area and Camp Page-Sihung-ri, Korea.

2. The US memorandum reference 1b above, has been reviewed and the Government of the Republic of Korea understands the requirement for invited contractor status to the US member firm of the ROK/US joint venture contract in this instance.

3. The list of qualified Korean contractors to be considered for joint venture with US firms for the above contract is attached herewith.

Chung Min Kil
Chairman
Commerce Subcommittee, ROK

92

JOINT COMMITTEE
UNDER
THE REPUBLIC OF KOREA AND THE UNITED STATES
STATUS OF FORCES AGREEMENT

22 JUL 1971

MEMORANDUM FOR: The Joint Committee

SUBJECT: Designation of US Invited Contractor Under Article XV, Status of Forces Agreement

1. References:

a. Paragraph 2, Article XV, Status of Forces Agreement.

b. US Chairman, Commerce Subcommittee letter, dated 28 April 1971, subject as above (Inclosure 1).

c. ROK Chairman, Commerce Subcommittee letter, dated 15 May 1971, subject as above (Inclosure 2).

2. The United States, after consultation with the ROK Commerce Subcommittee and having duly considered their views, has designated Campbell Construction and Equipment Company, Inc., as a US invited contractor, in joint venture with a Korean firm, for execution of contract DACA79-72-C-0006 for upgrading of utilities, Yongsan.

3. Pertinent data concerning US citizen employees will be provided to the Joint Secretariat in the established format.

2 Incl
as

ROBERT N. SMITH
Lieutenant General, USAF
United States Representative
Joint Committee

93

REPUBLIC OF KOREA - UNITED STATES
COMMERCE SUBCOMMITTEE

28 April 1971

SUBJECT: Designation of US Invited Contractor Under Article XV, Status of Forces Agreement

ROK Chairman, Commerce Subcommittee

1. Reference: Paragraph 2, Article XV, of the Status of Forces Agreement.

2. The Government of the Republic of Korea is informed through this written consultative process that the United States Forces, Korea, proposes to extend invited contractor status to the US member firm of the US-ROK joint venture contractor awarded the contract for the Upgrading of Utilities Yongsan, Korea, construction project.

3. The following data are provided:

a. Company Name:

A list of qualified US Firms is attached as Inclosure 1.

b. Local Address: To be supplied when designation is made.

c. Identification of US Citizen Employees: To be supplied on on conclusion of negotiations.

d. Number of US and ROK Employees: Number of US Citizen and Koreans is not known at this time and will be supplied upon conclusion of negotiations.

e. Reasons for Designation of an Invited Contractor: Open competitive bidding among local contractors is not practical due to the following.

(1) Limited technical qualifications of the contractors involved.

(2) Unavailability of services required by US Standards.

f. Location of contracts: Yongsan, Seoul, Korea.

94

SUBJECT: Designation of US Invited Contractor Under Article XV, Status of Forces Agreement

g. Type of Contracts: Fixed Price

h. Length of Contracts: To be supplied on conclusion of negotiations.

i. Sponsoring Component Commander: USAEDFE.

1 Incl
as

RICHARD T. CANN
Colonel, U.S. Army
United States Chairman
Commerce Subcommittee

MINISTRY OF COMMERCE AND INDUSTRY
REPUBLIC OF KOREA
SEOUL, KOREA

15 May 1971

Subject: Designation of US Invited Contractor under Article XV Status of Forces Agreement

US Chairman, Commerce Subcommittee

1. Reference:

a. Paragraph 2, Article XV, Status of Forces Agreement

b. US Commerce Subcommittee Memorandum of Consultation, dated 28 April 1971, subject as above, pertaining to contract for the Upgrading of Utilities at Yongsan, Korea, construction project.

2. The US memorandum reference 1b above, has been reviewed and the Government of the Republic of Korea understands the requirement for an invited contractor status to the US member firm of the ROK-US joint venture contract in this instance.

Chung Min Kil
Chairman
Commerce Subcommittee, ROK

96

JOINT COMMITTEE
UNDER
THE REPUBLIC OF KOREA AND THE UNITED STATES
STATUS OF FORCES AGREEMENT

22 JUL 1971

MEMORANDUM FOR: The Joint Committee

SUBJECT: Designation of US Invited Contractor Under Article XV, Status of Forces Agreement

1. References:

a. Paragraph 2, Article XV, Status of Forces Agreement.

b. US Chairman, Commerce Subcommittee, letter dated 14 May 1971, subject as above (Inclosure 1).

c. ROK Chairman, Commerce Subcommittee, letter dated 24 May 1971, subject as above (Inclosure 2).

2. The United States, after consultation with the ROK Commerce Subcommittee and having duly considered their views, has designated the Fischer Engineering and Maintenance Company, Inc., as a US invited contractor, in joint venture with a Korean firm, for execution of contract DACA79-71-C-0070 for construction of troop housing, KORSCOM, Camp Walker, Taegu, Korea.

3. Pertinent data concerning US citizen employees will be provided to the Joint Secretariat in the established format.

2 Incls
as

ROBERT N. SMITH
Lieutenant General, USAF
United States Representative
Joint Committee

97

REPUBLIC OF KOREA - UNITED STATES
COMMERCE SUBCOMMITTEE

14 May 1971

SUBJECT: Designation of US Invited Contractor Under Article XV, Status of Forces Agreement

ROK Chairman, Commerce Subcommittee

1. Reference: Paragraph 2, Article XV, of the Status of Forces Agreement.

2. The Government of the Republic of Korea is informed through this written consultative process that the United States Forces, Korea, proposes to extend invited contractor status to the US member firm of the US-ROK joint venture contractor awarded the contract for the FY-70 MCA, Troop Housing, KORSCOM, Camp Walker, Taegu, Korea.

3. The following data are provided:

a. Company Name: A list of qualified US Firms is attached as Inclosure 1.

b. Local Address: To be supplied when designation is made.

c. Identification of US Citizen Employees: To be supplied on conclusion of negotiations.

d. Number of US and ROK Employees: Number of US Citizen and Koreans is not known at this time and will be supplied upon conclusion of negotiations.

e. Reasons for Designation of an Invited Contractor: Open competitive bidding among local contractors is not practical due to the following:

(1) Limited technical qualifications of the contractors involved.

(2) Unavailability of services required by US standards.

f. Location of Contract: Taegu, Korea.

g. Type of Contract: Fixed price.

SUBJECT: Designation of US Invited Contractor Under Article XV, Status of Forces Agreement

h. Length of Contract: To be supplied upon award of contract.

i. Sponsoring Component Commander: USAEDFE.

1 Incl
as

RICHARD T. CANN
Colonel, U.S. Army
United States Chairman
Commerce Subcommittee

99

MINISTRY OF COMMERCE AND INDUSTRY
REPUBLIC OF KOREA
SEOUL, KOREA

24 May 1971

Subject: Designation of US Invited Contractor under Article XV Status of Forces Agreement

US Chairman, Commerce Subcommittee

1. Reference:

a. Paragraph 2, Article XV, Status of Forces Agreement

b. US Commerce Subcommittee Memorandum of Consultation, dated 14 May 1971, subject as above, pertaining to contract for the construction of FY-70 MCA, Troop Housing, KORSCOM, Camp Walker, Taegu, Korea.

2. The US memorandum reference 1b above, has been reviewed and the Government of the Republic of Korea understands the requirement for an invited contractor status to the US member firm of the ROK-US joint venture contract in this instance.

Sgd Chung Min Kil
Chairman
Commerce Subcommittee, ROK

0160

JOINT COMMITTEE
UNDER
THE REPUBLIC OF KOREA AND THE UNITED STATES
STATUS OF FORCES AGREEMENT

2 2 JUL 1971

MEMORANDUM FOR: The Joint Committee

SUBJECT: Designation of US Invited Contractor Under Article XV, Status of Forces Agreement

1. References:

a. Paragraph 2, Article XV, Status of Forces Agreement.

b. US Chairman, Commerce Subcommittee, letter dated 14 May 1971, subject as above (Inclosure 1).

c. ROK Chairman, Commerce Subcommittee, letter dated 24 May 1971, subject as above (Inclosure 2).

2. The United States, after consultation with the ROK Commerce Subcommittee and having duly considered their views, has designated the Fischer Engineering and Maintenance Company, Inc., as a US invited contractor, in joint venture with a Korean firm, for execution of contract DACA79-71-C-0070 for construction of troop housing, KORSCOM, Camp Walker, Taegu, Korea.

3. Pertinent data concerning US citizen employees will be provided to the Joint Secretariat in the established format.

2 Incls
as

ROBERT N. SMITH
Lieutenant General, USAF
United States Representative
Joint Committee

101

REPUBLIC OF KOREA - UNITED STATES
COMMERCE SUBCOMMITTEE

14 May 1971

SUBJECT: Designation of US Invited Contractor Under Article XV, Status of Forces Agreement

ROK Chairman, Commerce Subcommittee

1. Reference: Paragraph 2, Article XV, of the Status of Forces Agreement.

2. The Government of the Republic of Korea is informed through this written consultative process that the United States Forces, Korea, proposes to extend invited contractor status to the US member firm of the US-ROK joint venture contractor awarded the contract for the FY-70 MCA, Troop Housing, KORSCOM, Camp Walker, Taegu, Korea.

3. The following data are provided:

a. Company Name: A list of qualified US Firms is attached as Inclosure 1.

b. Local Address: To be supplied when designation is made.

c. Identification of US Citizen Employees: To be supplied on conclusion of negotiations.

d. Number of US and ROK Employees: Number of US Citizen and Koreans is not known at this time and will be supplied upon conclusion of negotiations.

e. Reasons for Designation of an Invited Contractor: Open competitive bidding among local contractors is not practical due to the following:

(1) Limited technical qualifications of the contractors involved.

(2) Unavailability of services required by US standards.

f. Location of Contract: Taegu, Korea.

g. Type of Contract: Fixed price.

102

SUBJECT: Designation of US Invited Contractor Under Article XV, Status of Forces Agreement

h. Length of Contract: To be supplied upon award of contract.

i. Sponsoring Component Commander: USAEDFE.

1 Incl
as

RICHARD T. CANN
Colonel, U.S. Army
United States Chairman
Commerce Subcommittee

103

MINISTRY OF COMMERCE AND INDUSTRY
REPUBLIC OF KOREA
SEOUL, KOREA

24 May 1971

Subject: Designation of US Invited Contractor under Article XV Status of Forces Agreement

US Chairman, Commerce Subcommittee

1. Reference:

a. Paragraph 2, Article XV, Status of Forces Agreement

b. US Commerce Subcommittee Memorandum of Consultation, dated 14 May 1971, subject as above, pertaining to contract for the construction of FY-70 MCA, Troop Housing, KORSCOM, Camp Walker, Taegu, Korea.

2. The US memorandum reference 1b above, has been reviewed and the Government of the Republic of Korea understands the requirement for an invited contractor status to the US member firm of the ROK-US joint venture contract in this instance.

Sgd/ Chung Min Kil
Chairman
Commerce Subcommittee, ROK

104

JOINT COMMITTEE
UNDER
THE REPUBLIC OF KOREA AND THE UNITED STATES
STATUS OF FORCES AGREEMENT

22 JUL 1971

MEMORANDUM FOR: The Joint Committee

SUBJECT: Designation of US Invited Contractor Under Article XV, Status of Forces Agreement

1. References:

a. Paragraph 2, Article XV, Status of Forces Agreement.

b. US Chairman, Commerce Subcommittee, letter dated 1 February 1971, subject as above (Inclosure 1).

c. ROK Chairman, Commerce Subcommittee, letter dated 24 February 1971, subject as above (Inclosure 2).

2. The United States, after consultation with the ROK Commerce Subcommittee and having duly considered their views, has designated International Electronics Corporation as an invited contractor to install microwave equipment at 21 sites throughout the Republic of Korea, contract DAJB03-71-C-6385.

3. Pertinent data concerning US citizen employees will be provided to the Joint Secretariat in the established format.

ROBERT N. SMITH
Lieutenant General, USAF
United States Representative
Joint Committee

2 Incl
as

105

REPUBLIC OF KOREA - UNITED STATES
COMMERCE SUBCOMMITTEE

1 February 1971

SUBJECT: Designation of US Invited Contractor Under Article XV, Status of Forces Agreement

ROK Chairman, Commerce Subcommittee

1. References: Paragraph 2, Article XV of the Status of Forces Agreement.

2. The Government of the Republic of Korea is informed through this written consultative process that the United States Forces, Korea, proposes to extend invited contractor status to the qualified US firm on the contract described in paragraph 3 below for the installation of US Government furnished microwave and ancilliary equipment at 21 sites throughout the Republic of Korea.

3. The following data are provided:

a. Company Name: The list of contractors being considered is attached at inclosure 1.

b. Local Address: To be supplied upon designation.

c. Identification of US Citizen Employees: To be supplied upon designation.

d. Number of US and ROK Employees: To be supplied upon designation.

e. Reason for Designation of an Invited Contractor: Open competitive bidding is not practicable due to the following:

(1) Limited "State of the Art" qualifications of local contractors.

(2) Unavailability of services required by US standards.

f. Location of Contract: Various locations throughout the Republic of Korea.

g. Type of Contract: Fixed price contract.

106

1 February 1971

SUBJECT: Designation of US Invited Contractor Under Article XV, Status of Forces Agreement

h. <u>Length of Contract</u>: To be supplied upon conclusion of negotiations.

i. <u>Sponsoring Component Command</u>: Assistant Chief of Staff, Communications-Electronics, Eighth United States Army, APO San Francisco 96301.

1 Incl
Contractor list

RICHARD T. CANN
Colonel, U.S. Army
ACofS, J4

2

107

LIST OF US FIRMS TO BE CONSIDERED FOR INSTALLATION OF MICROWAVE AND ANCILLIARY EQUIPMENT

1. Collins Radio Corporation

2. International Electronics Corporation

3. Kentron Hawaii Ltd.

4. Lenkurt Electric Company

5. Nippon Electric Company, New York

6. Page Communications Engineers, Inc.

7. Philco-Ford Coproration

8. Raytheon Service Corporation

9. Tectonics, Inc.

108

MINISTRY OF COMMERCE AND INDUSTRY
REPUBLIC OF KOREA
SEOUL, KOREA

24 February 1971

Subject: Designation of US Invited Contractor under Article XV Status of Forces Agreement

US Chairman, Commerce Subcommittee

1. Reference:

a. Paragraph 2, Article XV, Status of Forces Agreement.

b. US Commerce Subcommittee Memorandum of Consultation, dated 1 February 1971, subject as above, pertaining to contract for the installation of US Government furnished microwave and ancilliary equipment at 21 sites throughout Korea.

2. The US memorandum reference 1b above, has been reviewed and the Government of the Republic of Korea understands the requirement for an invited contractor in this instance.

Chung Min Kil
Chairman
Commerce Subcommittee, ROK

109

JOINT ROK-US PRESS RELEASE
SIXTY-FOURTH ROK-US JOINT COMMITTEE MEETING
29 JULY 1971

The ROK-US Joint Committee approved 27 recommendations of its Facilities and Areas Subcommittee and assigned 28 new tasks to the same Subcommittee at its sixty-fourth meeting, held on 29 July 1971 in the US SOFA Conference Room.

The Joint Committee approved the recommendation of its Finance (Personnel Affairs) Subcommittee, concerning revised procedures for examination of incoming APO parcel post packages by ROK customs inspectors. The Joint Committee also discussed the recent incidents involving US military personnel and Korean nationals which have taken place in the vicinity of some US military installations, with a view to forestalling recurrence of such incidents.

The next meeting of the ROK-US Joint Committee is scheduled to be held on Thursday, 26 August 1971.

110

기 안 용 지

분류기호 문서번호	미이 720 -	(전화번호)	전결규정 조 항 국장 전결사항
처리기간			
시행일자	71. 8. 12.		
보존년한		국 장	
보조기관	북미 2과장		협
기안책임자	박 양 천	북미 2과 (71. 8. 12.)	
경유 수신 참조	배부처 참조	발신	통제
제 목	한.미 합동위원회 회의록 송부		

1971. 8. 17. 외무부 16213 10956

1971. 8. 17. 통제관 검열

1. 한.미간 군대지위협정에 의하여 1971. 7. 29. 에 개최된 한.미 합동위원회 제 64차 회의의 회의록을 별첨 송부하오니 참고하시기 바랍니다.

2. 본 회의록은 한.미 양측의 합의에 의하여서만 공개할수 있는 문서이오니 유념하시기 바랍니다.

첨부 : 합동위원회 64차 회의록 부. 끝

(배부처) : 법무부장관 (법무실장, 검찰국장, 출입국관리국장), 국방부장관 (기획국장, 시설국장), 재무부장관 (세관국장, 세제국장), 상공부장관 (상역국장), 노동청장 (노정국장), 교통부장관 (종합수송관), 내무부장관 (치안국장), 경제기획원장관 (물가정책관), 주미, 주일, 주중, 주비대사.

정서 관인 발송

공통서식 1—2 (갑) 1967. 4. 4 승인

190mm×268mm 중질지 7 g/m² 조달청 1,000,000매 인쇄)

These minutes are considered as official documents pertaining to both Governments and will not be released without mutual agreement.

JOINT COMMITTEE
UNDER
THE REPUBLIC OF KOREA AND THE UNITED STATES
STATUS OF FORCES AGREEMENT

MINUTES OF THE SIXTY-FOURTH MEETING

29 July 1971
Headquarters
U.S. Forces, Korea
Seoul, Korea

1. The meeting was convened at 1530 hours by Captain Frank M. Romanick, USN, the U.S. Alternate Representative, who presided at the meeting. A copy of the agenda is attached as Inclosure 1.

2. The following were in attendance:

ROK	U.S.
Mr. LEE Sun Jung	CAPT Frank M. Romanick, USN
Mr. PARK Dong Hee	COL David P. Heekin, USA
Mr. PARK Won Ho	COL Robert G. Eklund, USAF
MAJ GEN CHO Jae Joon	COL Bruce T. Coggins, USA
BRIG GEN PAK Woo Bum	Mr. John P. Leonard, U.S. Embassy
Mr. KIM Hyung Kun	Mr. Robert A. Kinney, USFK
Mr. LEE Kyung Ku	MAJ Dick J. Petersen, USAF
Mr. KWON Chan	Mr. Francis K. Cook, USFK
Mr. LEE Seung Kon	

3. The U.S. Alternate Representative stated that before taking up the first agenda item, he would like to take the opportunity to introduce two new members of the U.S. component of the Joint Committee, as follows:

a. Colonel David P. Heekin, the new Deputy Chief of Staff, Eighth U.S. Army, who replaces Colonel Edward N. Hathaway.

b. Colonel Bruce T. Coggins, the new Staff Judge Advocate of the USFK and the Eighth U.S. Army, who replaces Colonel Leonard Petkoff.

4. Captain Romanick stated that, on behalf of the U.S. component of the Joint Committee, he wished to welcome Colonel Heekin and Colonel Coggins to the Joint Committee.

64th JC
29 July 1971

112

These minutes are considered as official documents pertaining to both Governments and will not be released without mutual agreement.

5. The ROK Alternate Representative, Mr. LEE Sun Jung, stated t on behalf of the ROK component of the Joint Committee, he wished to welcome Colonel David P. Heekin and Colonel Bruce T. Coggins to the ROK-US Joint Committee.

6. The ROK Alternate Representative introduced two new members of the ROK component of the Joint Committee, as follows:

a. Mr. PARK Dong Hee, Director, Bureau of Customs, Ministry of Finance, who had recently replaced Mr. LEE Kun Choong as a member of Joint Committee as well as ROK Chairman of the Finance Subcommittee.

b. Mr. LEE Seung Kon, staff member of North America Second Section, Ministry of Foreign Affairs, who has rejoined the Joint Committee again as an Assistant Secretary after a five-month TDY assignment to the Blue House.

7. On behalf of the ROK component of the Joint Committee, the ROK Alternate Representative welcomed Mr. Park and Mr. Lee to the ROK-US SOFA Joint Committee.

8. On behalf of the United States component of the Joint Committee, the U.S. Alternate Representative welcomed Mr. PARK Dong Hee as a new member of the Joint Committee, and Mr. LEE Seung Kon who is rejoining the Joint Committee after his temporary absence.

9. The ROK Alternate Representative stated that he had no new tasks for assignment to the Facilities and Areas Subcommittee, but he did have three Facilities and Areas Subcommittee tasks assigned on an exigent basis since the last Joint Committee meeting. These exigent tasks consisted of two requests for the relocation of facilities (Inclosures 2 and 3) and one request for the temporary use of three warehouses on Seattle Installation in Inchon (Inclosure 4).

10. Mr. Lee proposed that the Joint Committee approve the inclusion in the minutes of this meeting of the prior assignment of these three exigent tasks to the Facilities and Areas Subcommittee. The U.S. Alternate Representative concurred.

11. The U.S. Alternate Representative presented the remaining new tasks for assignment to the Facilities and Areas Subcommittee. Before doing so, however, he said he would like to propose that the assignment, on an exigent basis, of ten tasks to that Subcommittee in the interval since the last Joint Committee meeting, be recorded in the minutes of this meeting. He said that these ten prior assigned tasks comprised three requests for the acquisition of real estate on a permanent use basis (Inclosure 5), two requests for the acquisition of Temporary Use Permits (Inclosure 6), and five requests for the release of parcels of real estate (Inclosure 7).

12. The U.S. Alternate Representative stated that, in addition, he had fifteen new tasks to present for assignment to the Facilities and Areas Subcommittee. These consisted of two requests for easements (Inclosure 8), two requests for the acquisition of Temporary Use Permits (Inclosure 9), three requests for the extension of existing Temporary Use Permits (Inclosure 10), one request for authorization to dispose of a building (Inclosure 11), one request for the conversion of land from a temporary to a permanent basis (Inclosure 12), and six requests for the release of parcels of real estate (Inclosures 13 and 14). He stated that details concerning both these new tasks and the prior assigned tasks were contained in memoranda which had been distributed to both sides.

13. Captain Romanick proposed that the fifteen new tasks be assigned to the Facilities and Areas Subcommittee, and that the minutes of this meeting reflect the prior assignment of ten additional tasks to that Subcommittee. The ROK Alternate Representative concurred.

14. The ROK Alternate Representative presented four recommendations of Facilities and Areas Subcommittee. These consist of two recommendations for the relocation of a water supply line and of telegraph poles (Inclosures 15 and 16) and two recommendations for the release of real estate located in Seoul (Inclosures 17 and 18).

15. The ROK Alternate Representative proposed that the Joint Committee approve these four recommendations of the Facilities and Areas Subcommittee. The U.S. Alternate Representative concurred.

16. The U.S. Alternate Representative presented the remaining 23 recommendations of the Facilities and Areas Subcommittee. He

stated that, in summary, these comprised two recommendations for the acquisition of land for permanent use (Inclosures 19 and 20), two recommendations involving extension of Temporary Use Permits (Inclosure 21), two recommendations for authorization to dispose of facilities (Inclosures 22 and 23), one recommendation for the withdrawal of a previous request for acquisition of land (Inclosure 24), and sixteen recommendations involving the release of parcels of real estate (Inclosures 25 and 26). He indicated that details concerning these recommendations were included in memoranda which have been distributed to both sides.

17. Captain Romanick proposed that the Joint Committee approve these twenty-three recommendations of the Facilities and Areas Subcommittee, and Mr. Lee concurred.

18. The ROK Alternate Representative stated that at the Sixty-First Joint Committee meeting, the Finance (Personnel Affairs) Subcommittee was assigned a task requesting a review of existing procedures of the customs examinations of APO non-official parcel post packages (Inclosure 27). He said that the ROK-US Finance (Personnel Affairs) Subcommittee, through mutual consultations, had reached agreement on revised procedures for ROK customs examination of non-official APO parcel mail. This agreement provided for an increase of the sample check of such parcels to 10 percent of the total incoming parcels, without reference to geographic areas of origin. This agreement also provided for a guide list as to what represents reasonable quantities of specified items.

19. The ROK Alternate Representative proposed that the Joint Committee approve the recommendations of the Finance (Personnel Affairs) Subcommittee relating to ROK customs examination of non-official APO parcels.

20. The U.S. Alternate Representative concurred in Joint Committee approval of the recommendation of the Finance (Personnel Affairs) Subcommittee relative to the review of and revision in procedures governing ROK customs examination of parcel post packages delivered through U.S. military post office channels.

21. The U.S. Alternate Representative presented memoranda to the Joint Committee informing the Government of the ROK of the designation of eight U.S. invited contractors under Article XV of the SOFA.

These designations were made after consultations between ROK and U.S. Commerce Subcommittee personnel in accordance with Joint Committee procedures. Captain Romanick stated that the invited contractors so designated were Campbell Construction and Equipment Company, Incorporated (Inclosure 28); International Electronics Corporation (Inclosure 29); Fischer Engineering and Maintenance Company, Incorporated (Inclosures 30 and 31); Zurn Engineers (Inclosure 32); Huwin Corporation (Inclosure 32); Associated American Engineers Overseas, Incorporated (Inclosure 33); Daniel, Mann, Johnson, and Mendenhall (Inclosure 34); and Adrian Wilson Associates, Incorporated (Inclosure 35). These designations involved a total of eight contracts. Fischer Engineering and Maintenance Company, Incorporated had two contracts; Zurn Engineers and Huwin Corporation shared one contract and the remaining contractors had one contract each. Four of these contracts were in joint venture with Korean firms.

22. The U.S. Alternate Representative stated that pertinent data concerning employees of these invited contractors would be provided to the Government of the ROK in accordance with mutually agreed procedures.

23. The ROK Alternate Representative acknowledged the designation of eight U.S. invited contractors involving eight contracts.

24. The ROK Alternate Representative made the following statement:

"The ROK Alternate Representative would like to express his concern over the unfortunate incidents involving U.S. military personnel in Korea and Korean nationals which have taken place in the vicinity of some U.S. military installations.

"However, the Republic of Korea Alternate Representative takes note with satisfaction the appropriate and timely action taken in this connection by the United States Forces, Korea, namely, the issuance of USFK PD 5-18, of 15 July 1971, 'Standards of Conduct, U.S. Forces Personnel.'

"Since such incidents are detrimental to the friendly relationship between the ROK and the United States, the authorities concerned of both Governments need to cooperate closely in taking effective measures, preventive and corrective, to forestall their recurrence."

25. The U.S. Alternate Representative responded as follows:

"The United States Alternate Representative would like to take this opportunity to assure the Republic of Korea Alternate Representative of his equal and deep concern over the recent unfortunate incidents, involving some United States military personnel and Korean nationals. United States Forces, Korea Policy Directive 5-18 of 15 July 1971 was designed to help to deal effectively with situations which may adversely affect Korean-American relations, and it is hoped that in the future this new directive will assist in forestalling such unfortunate incidents as recently occurred.

"The United States Alternate Representative fully concurs in the statement of the Republic of Korea Alternate Representative that the appropriate authorities of our two Governments should cooperate closely in taking the necessary measures to forestall the reoccurrence of any incidents which may be detrimental to the traditional friendly relations between our two peoples."

26. The U.S. Alternate Representative noted for the record that the U.S. SOFA Secretary had furnished the following information to his Korean counterpart, in accordance with the provisions of the SOFA and Joint Committee agreements:

a. Five copies of reports on the U.S. armed forces disposition of cases for the months of May and June.

b. One copy of pertinent information on cargo consigned to U.S. armed forces non-appropriated fund organizations in the ROK for the month of June 1971.

c. Twenty copies of the report of U.S. armed forces personnel, the civilian component, invited contractors and the dependents of each, entering or departing the ROK during the month of June 1971.

27. The ROK Alternate Representative acknowledged the receipt of these reports as enumerated by the U.S. Alternate Representative.

These minutes are considered as official documents pertaining to both Governments and will not be released without mutual agreement.

28. The U.S. Alternate Representative proposed that the sixty-fifth Joint Committee meeting be held on Thursday, 26 August 1971, in the U.S. SOFA Conference Room. The ROK Alternate Representative concurred.

29. The U.S. Alternate Representative proposed approval of the press release for the sixty-fourth Joint Committee meeting (Inclosure 36) as prepared by the respective Secretaries and distributed in advance to both components of the Committee. The ROK Alternate Representative concurred.

30. The meeting adjourned at 1605 hours.

KOO CHOONG WHAY
Republic of Korea
Representative

for ROBERT N. SMITH
Lieutenant General
United States Air Force
United States Representative

7

64th JC
29 July 1971

118

These minutes are considered as official documents pertaining to both Governments and will not be released without mutual agreement.

AGENDA FOR THE SIXTY-FOURTH MEETING
OF THE ROK-US JOINT COMMITTEE
1530 HOURS, 29 JULY 1971, US SOFA CONFERENCE ROOM

I. Assignment of Tasks to Facilities and Areas Subcommittee

1. Three tasks - ROK Presentation

2. Twenty-five tasks - US Presentation

II. Recommendations of Facilities and Areas Subcommittee

1. Four Recommendations - ROK Presentation

2. Twenty-three Recommendations - US Presentation

III. Recommendation of Finance/Personnel Affairs Subcommittee on Revision of Procedures for Examination of Parcels Received Through the APO - ROK Presentation

IV. Memoranda on the Designation of US Invited Contractors - US Presentation

V. Statement Regarding Prevention of Incidents Between US and Korean Personnel - ROK Presentation

VI. Memoranda Presented to the ROK Government by the US in the Implementation of the SOFA - US Presentation

VII. Proposed Time of Next Meeting - Thursday, 26 August 1971, in the US SOFA Conference Room

VIII. Agreement on Joint Press Release

IX. Adjourn

8

64th JC (Incl 1)
29 July 71

119

These minutes are considered as official documents pertaining to both Governments and will not be released without mutual agreement.

JOINT COMMITTEE
UNDER
THE REPUBLIC OF KOREA AND THE UNITED STATES
STATUS OF FORCES AGREEMENT

18 June 1971

MEMORANDUM FOR: Chairmen, Facilities and Areas Subcommittee

SUBJECT: Request for Relocation of POL Pipeline

1. SOFA provides, in Article II, paragraph 2, that the Governments of the Republic of Korea and the United States may agree that facilities and areas or portions thereof shall be returned to the Republic of Korea or that additional facilities and areas may be provided.

2. Pursuant to paragraph 1 above, it is requested that a recommendation be presented to the Joint Committee concerning a request for the relocation of a portion of POL pipeline between Pyongtaek and Anjung in Kyonggi-do, in connection with the widening of an existing road.

KOO CHOONG WHAY
Republic of Korea
Representative

ROBERT N. SMITH
Lieutenant General
United States Air Force
United States Representative

9

64 JC (Incl 2)
29 July 71

120

These minutes are considered as official documents pertaining to both Governments and will not be released without mutual agreement.

JOINT COMMITTEE
UNDER
THE REPUBLIC OF KOREA AND THE UNITED STATES
STATUS OF FORCES AGREEMENT

3 July 1971

MEMORANDUM FOR: Chairmen, Facilities and Areas Subcommittee

SUBJECT: Request for Relocation of Telegraph Poles

1. SOFA provides in Article II, paragraph 2, that the Governments of the Republic of Korea and the United States may agree that facilities and areas or portions thereof shall be returned to the Republic of Korea or that additional facilities and areas may be provided.

2. Pursuant to paragraph 1 above, it is requested that a recommendation be presented to the Joint Committee concerning a request for the relocation of telegraph poles located in Uijongbu City, Kyonggi-do.

KOO CHOONG WHAY	ROBERT N. SMITH
Republic of Korea	Lieutenant General
Representative	United States Air Force
	United States Representative

64th JC (Incl 3)
29 July 71

(2)

These minutes are considered as official documents pertaining to both Governments and will not be released without mutual agreement.

JOINT COMMITTEE
UNDER
THE REPUBLIC OF KOREA AND THE UNITED STATES
STATUS OF FORCES AGREEMENT

15 July 1971

MEMORANDUM FOR: Chairmen, Facilities and Areas Subcommittee

SUBJECT: Request for Temporary Use of Three Warehouses at Docks in Camp Seattle

1. SOFA provides, in Article II, paragraph 2, that the Governments of the Republic of Korea and the United States may agree that facilities and areas or portions thereof shall be returned to the Republic of Korea or that additional facilities and areas may be provided.

2. Pursuant to paragraph 1 above, it is requested that a recommendation be presented to the Joint Committee concerning a Republic of Korea Government request for the temporary use of three warehouses in the vicinity of the tidal basin in Seattle Installation, Inchon City, Kyonggi-do, in connection with a massive import of grains.

KOO CHOONG WHAY
Republic of Korea
Representative

ROBERT N. SMITH
Lieutenant General
United States Air Force
United States Representative

64th JC (Incl 4)
29 July 71

122

These minutes are considered as official documents pertaining to both Governments and will not be released without mutual agreement.

JOINT COMMITTEE
UNDER
THE REPUBLIC OF KOREA AND THE UNITED STATES
STATUS OF FORCES AGREEMENT

24 June 1971

MEMORANDUM FOR: Chairmen, Facilities and Areas Subcommittee

SUBJECT: Request for Acquisition of Real Estate

1. SOFA provides, in Article II, paragraph 2, that the Governments of the Republic of Korea and the United States may agree that facilities and areas or portions thereof shall be returned to the Republic of Korea or that additional facilities and areas may be provided.

2. Pursuant to paragraph 1 above, it is requested that a recommendation be presented to the Joint Committee concerning a request for the acquisition, on a permanent use basis, of approximately 4.14 acres of land in three non-contiguous areas of 1.38 acres each, and located in Seoul City. The precise locations of these three sites are shown on a map, copies of which are in the possession of the ROK Ministry of National Defense and the Real Estate Division, USFK Engineer. This real estate is urgently required to establish facilities needed to measure the physical effects of disturbances in the atmosphere.

KOO CHOONG WHAY Republic of Korea Representative	ROBERT N. SMITH Lieutenant General United States Air Force United States Representative

64th JC (Incl 5)
29 July 71

123

These minutes are considered as official documents pertaining to both Governments and will not be released without mutual agreement.

JOINT COMMITTEE
UNDER
THE REPUBLIC OF KOREA AND THE UNITED STATES
STATUS OF FORCES AGREEMENT

21 July 1971

MEMORANDUM FOR: Chairmen, Facilities and Areas Subcommittee

SUBJECT: Request for Acquisition of Temporary Use Permits

1. SOFA provides, in Article II, paragraph 2, that the Governments of the Republic of Korea and the United States may agree that facilities and areas or portions thereof shall be returned to the Republic of Korea or that additional facilities and areas may be provided.

2. Pursuant to paragraph 1 above, it is requested that recommendations be presented to the Joint Committee concerning requests for the acquisition of two Temporary Use Permits, and preliminary right-of-entry to the areas involved. These involve two separate areas at which navigational aid sites will be located, to be used for joint hydrographic surveys by the US Naval Oceanographic Office and the ROK Hydrographic Office, for the period 1 August 1971 through 31 January 1972. Specific locations involved are indicated on maps in the possession of the Republic of Korea Ministry of National Defense and the Real Estate Division of the Engineer, USFK. The names of the sites and general locations are as indicated below.

Name of Site	Location
a. KOGUM-DO	Island of Kogum, Kohung-gun, Chollanam-do
b. PYONGIL-DO	Island of Pyongil, Wando-gun, Chollanam-do

KOO CHOONG WHAY
Republic of Korea
Representative

F M Romanick Capt USN for

ROBERT N. SMITH
Lieutenant General
United States Air Force
United States Representative

64th JC (Incl 6)
29 July 71

124

These minutes are considered as official documents pertaining to both Governments and will not be released without mutual agreement.

JOINT COMMITTEE
UNDER
THE REPUBLIC OF KOREA AND THE UNITED STATES
STATUS OF FORCES AGREEMENT

30 June 1971

MEMORANDUM FOR: Chairmen, Facilities and Areas Subcommittee

SUBJECT: Requests for Release of Real Estate

1. SOFA provides, in Article II, paragraph 2, that the Governments of the Republic of Korea and the United States may agree that facilities and areas or portions thereof shall be returned to the Republic of Korea or that additional facilities and areas may be provided.

2. Pursuant to paragraph 1 above, it is requested that recommendations be presented to the Joint Committee concerning requests for the following actions:

a. Release of 209.50 acres of land with two Korean-constructed facilities, constituting Wolmido Installation, held under Acquisition Nos. ASCOM-363, ASCOM-375, AAC-381 and AAC-383, and located in Inchon City, Kyonggi-do. This request for release includes all USFK-constructed facilities located on the Installation to be released, with the exception of two water tank facilities (Nos. T-3421 and T-3422) and Building No. T-3343 with ingress and egress rights thereto, which will be retained under USFK control until 30 October 1971.

b. Release of 7.8 acres of land, constituting Area #3 portion of Camp Pililaau Installation, held under Acquisition No. IC-264 and located in Uijongbu-si, Kyonggi-do. This request for release includes a total of 50 USFK-constructed buildings and facilities located on the Installation.

c. Release of 20.942 acres of land, constituting Camp Nabors Installation, held under Acquisition Nos. SAC-705 and SAC-766, and located in Seoul City. This request for release includes a total of 108 USFK-constructed buildings and facilities located on the Installation.

64th JC (Incl 7)
29 July 71

125

These minutes are considered as official documents pertaining to both Governments and will not be released without mutual agreement.

d. Release of 23.86 acres of land, constituting the remaining portion of Camp Pililaau Installation, held under Acquisition No. IC-264 and located in Uijongbu-si, Kyonggi-do. This request for release includes a total of 78 USFK-constructed buildings and facilities located on the Installation.

e. Release of 21.27 acres of land containing two Korean-constructed buildings, constituting a portion of Market Installation held under Acquisition No. ACS-193, and located in Inchon City, Kyonggi-do. This request for release includes a total of 66 USFK-constructed buildings and facilities located on the Installation. Exempted from this release request are 0.659 acre of land containing an underground sanitary sewer line and an overhead electric power line, which will be retained together with unrestricted rights-of-entry for ingress and egress thereto.

KOO CHOONG WHAY	ROBERT N. SMITH
Republic of Korea	Lieutenant General
Representative	United States Air Force
	United States Representative

These minutes are considered as official documents pertaining to both Governments and will not be released without mutual agreement.

JOINT COMMITTEE
UNDER
THE REPUBLIC OF KOREA AND THE UNITED STATES
STATUS OF FORCES AGREEMENT

29 July 1971

MEMORANDUM FOR: Chairmen, Facilities and Areas Subcommittee

SUBJECT: Requests for Acquisition of Easements

1. SOFA provides, in Article II, paragraph 2, that the Governments of the Republic of Korea and the United States may agree that facilities and areas or portions thereof shall be returned to the Republic of Korea or that additional facilities and areas may be provided.

2. Pursuant to paragraph 1 above, it is requested that recommendations be presented to the Joint Committee concerning requests for the following actions:

a. Acquisition, on a perpetual restrictive easement basis, of 3.84 acres of land located in Chilgok-gun, Kyongsangbuk-do. This real estate is required to widen an existing road.

b. Acquisition, on a perpetual restrictive easement basis, of approximately 5.48 acres of land located in Paju-gun, Kyonggi-do. This real estate is required to widen an existing road to reduce curves and to upgrade the road.

Choong Whay Koo
KOO CHOONG WHAY
Republic of Korea
Representative

F M Romanick Capt USN
for ROBERT N. SMITH
Lieutenant General
United States Air Force
United States Representative

16

64th JC (Incl 8)
29 July 71

(27)

These minutes are considered as official documents pertaining to both Governments and will not be released without mutual agreement.

JOINT COMMITTEE
UNDER
THE REPUBLIC OF KOREA AND THE UNITED STATES
STATUS OF FORCES AGREEMENT

29 July 1971

MEMORANDUM FOR: Chairmen, Facilities and Areas Subcommittee

SUBJECT: Requests for Acquisition of Temporary Use Permits

1. SOFA provides, in Article II, paragraph 2, that the Governments of the Republic of Korea and the United States may agree that facilities and areas or portions thereof shall be returned to the Republic of Korea or that additional facilities and areas may be provided.

2. Pursuant to paragraph 1 above, it is requested that recommendations be presented to the Joint Committee concerning requests for the following actions:

a. Acquisition of a Temporary Use Permit, involving approximately 2.58 acres of land located in Worsung-gun, Kyongsangbuk-do, for the period 15 July 1971 through 14 August 1971. This acreage, comprising two non-contiguous areas, is required as a source of top soil for use as fill materials.

b. Acquisition of a Temporary Use Permit, involving a total of 0.08 acre of land in four non-contiguous areas of 0.02 acre each, located in the Mt. Halla area of Cheju-do, for the period 1 September 1971 through 28 February 1972. This real estate is required on a temporary exclusive use basis for the above-stated period in connection with a special DoD communications facilities project to be conducted on Cheju-do.

KOO CHOONG WHAY
Republic of Korea
Representative

for ROBERT N. SMITH
Lieutenant General
United States Air Force
United States Representative

64th JC (Incl 9)
29 July 71

17

128

These minutes are considered as official documents pertaining to both Governments and will not be released without mutual agreement.

JOINT COMMITTEE
UNDER
THE REPUBLIC OF KOREA AND THE UNITED STATES
STATUS OF FORCES AGREEMENT

29 July 1971

MEMORANDUM FOR: Chairmen, Facilities and Areas Subcommittee

SUBJECT: Requests for Extension of Temporary Use Permits

1. SOFA provides, in Article II, paragraph 2, that the Governments of the Republic of Korea and the United States may agree that facilities and areas, or portions thereof, shall be returned to the Republic of Korea or that additional facilities and areas may be provided.

2. Pursuant to paragraph 1 above, it is requested that recommendations be presented to the Joint Committee concerning requests for the following actions:

a. Extension of Temporary Use Permit K-E-T-105, involving approximately 100 acres of land located in Sokcho-si, Kangwon-do, from 1 April 1971 through 31 March 1972. This real estate is required for continued use for the purpose of topographic survey and exploratory drilling at R-407 airfield.

b. Extension of Temporary Use Permit K-E-T-106, involving approximately 193 acres of land located in Chechon-gun, Chungchongbuk-do, from 1 April 1971 through 31 March 1972. This real estate is required for continued use for the purpose of topographic survey and exploratory drilling at R-605 airfield.

c. Extension of Temporary Use Permit K-G-T-14, involving 25 acres of river bed soil located in Chilgok-gun, Kyongsangbuk-do, from 25 August 1971 through 24 February 1972. This real estate is required for continued use as a source of fill materials and to establish a temporary rock crusher site.

Choong Whay Koo
KOO CHOONG WHAY
Republic of Korea
Representative

F M Romanick Capt USN
for
ROBERT N. SMITH
Lieutenant General
United States Air Force
United States Representative

18

64th JC (Incl 10)
29 July 71

129

These minutes are considered as official documents pertaining to both Governments and will not be released without mutual agreement.

JOINT COMMITTEE
UNDER
THE REPUBLIC OF KOREA AND THE UNITED STATES
STATUS OF FORCES AGREEMENT

29 July 1971

MEMORANDUM FOR: Chairmen, Facilities and Areas Subcommittee

SUBJECT: Request for Authorization to Dispose of Facility

1. SOFA provides, in Article 11, paragraph 2, that the Governments of the Republic of Korea and the United States may agree that facilities and areas or portions thereof shall be returned to the Republic of Korea or that additional facilities and areas may be provided.

2. Pursuant to paragraph 1 above, it is requested that a recommendation be presented to the Joint Committee concerning a request for authorization to dispose of one Korean-constructed building (No. 1588) held under Acquisition No. SAC-526 and located on Yongsan Installation in Seoul. This building was partially destroyed by fire and the remaining portion has become excess to USFK requirements.

F M Romanick Capt USN
for ROBERT N. SMITH
Lieutenant General
United States Air Force
United States Representative

Choong Whay Koo
KOO CHOONG WHAY
Republic of Korea
Representative

64th JC (Incl 11)
29 July 71

130

These minutes are considered as official documents pertaining to both Governments and will not be released without mutual agreement.

JOINT COMMITTEE
UNDER
THE REPUBLIC OF KOREA AND THE UNITED STATES
STATUS OF FORCES AGREEMENT

29 July 1971

MEMORANDUM FOR: Chairmen, Facilities and Areas Subcommittee

SUBJECT: Request for Conversion of Real Estate

1. SOFA provides, in Article II, paragraph 2, that the Governments of the Republic of Korea and the United States may agree that facilities and areas or portions thereof shall be returned to the Republic of Korea or that additional facilities and areas may be provided.

2. Pursuant to paragraph 1 above, it is requested that a recommendation be presented to the Joint Committee concerning a request for the conversion, from a temporary use basis to a permanent use basis, of a total of approximately 14.967 acres of land in seven non-contiguous areas located throughout Heongsong-gun, Wonsong-gun, and Wonju-si, Kangwon-do. This acreage currently is held under Acquisition No. K-E-T-104. This conversion action is required for an access road, borehole operations, and the installation of support facilities.

KOO CHOONG WHAY
Republic of Korea
Representative

for ROBERT N. SMITH
Lieutenant General
United States Air Force
United States Representative

20

64th JC (Incl 12)
29 July 71

131

These minutes are considered as official documents pertaining to both Governments and will not be released without mutual agreement.

JOINT COMMITTEE
UNDER
THE REPUBLIC OF KOREA AND THE UNITED STATES
STATUS OF FORCES AGREEMENT

29 July 1971

MEMORANDUM FOR: Chairmen, Facilities and Areas Subcommittee

SUBJECT: Requests for Release of Real Estate

1. SOFA provides, in Article II, paragraph 2, that the Governments of the Republic of Korea and the United States may agree that facilities and areas or portions thereof shall be returned to the Republic of Korea or that additional facilities and areas may be provided.

2. Pursuant to paragraph 1 above, it is requested that recommendations be presented to the Joint Committee concerning requests for the following actions:

a. Release of 0.44 acre of land held on an easement basis, constituting a portion of the area held under Acquisition No. IC-168 and located in Uijongbu-si, Kyonggi-do. This request for release includes approximately 1,920 linear feet of USFK-installed power line. This real estate has become excess to USFK requirements.

b. Release of 1.24 acres of land held on an easement basis, constituting a portion of the area held under Acquisition No. IC-207, and located in Uijongbu-si, Kyonggi-do. This request for release includes approximately 4,030 linear feet of a USFK-installed water pipeline facility. This real estate has become excess to USFK requirements.

c. Release of 1.31 acres of land constituting a portion of the area held under Acquisition No. IC-97 and located in Uijongbu-si, Kyonggi-do. This real estate has become excess to USFK requirements.

d. Release of 0.227 acre of land constituting a portion of the area held under Acquisition No. CAV-64, and located in Paju-gun, Kyonggi-do. This real estate has become excess to USFK requirements.

64th JC (Incl 13)
29 July 71

These minutes are considered as official documents pertaining to both Governments and will not be released without mutual agreement.

e. Release of 0.024 acre of land constituting a portion of the area held under Acquisition No. CAV-97, and located in Paju-gun, Kyonggi-do. This real estate has become excess to USFK requirements.

KOO CHOONG WHAY	for ROBERT N. SMITH
Republic of Korea	Lieutenant General
Representative	United States Air Force
	United States Representative

22

64th JC (Incl 13)
29 July 71

133

These minutes are considered as official documents pertaining to both Governments and will not be released without mutual agreement.

JOINT COMMITTEE
UNDER
THE REPUBLIC OF KOREA AND THE UNITED STATES
STATUS OF FORCES AGREEMENT

29 July 1971

MEMORANDUM FOR: Chairmen, Facilities and Areas Subcommittee

SUBJECT: Request for Release of Real Estate

1. SOFA provides, in Article 11, paragraph 2, that the Governments of the Republic of Korea and the United States may agree that facilities and areas or portions thereof shall be returned to the Republic of Korea or that additional facilities and areas may be provided.

2. Pursuant to paragraph 1 above, it is requested that a recommendation be presented to the Joint Committee concerning the release of 3.591 acres of land, constituting a portion of Kimpo Peninsula Installation held under Acquisition No. AAC-398, and located in Kimpo-gun, Kyonggi-do. This request for release includes all USFK-constructed facilities located on the area to be released, except for an underground water line and an overhead electric power line.

KOO CHOONG WHAY
Republic of Korea
Representative

for ROBERT N. SMITH
Lieutenant General
United States Air Force
United States Representative

64th JC (Incl 14)
29 July 71

134

These minutes are considered as official documents pertaining to both Governments and will not be released without mutual agreement.

REPUBLIC OF KOREA -- UNITED STATES
FACILITIES AND AREAS SUBCOMMITTEE

28 June 1971

MEMORANDUM FOR: THE JOINT COMMITTEE

1. Subcommittee Members:

United States	Republic of Korea
BG Kenneth T. Sawyer, Chairman	BG PAK Woo Bum, Chairman
COL W. D. Lewis, Alt. Chairman	Mr. SONG Yong Tai, Secty
LTC E. W. Lingel, USAF	Mr. KANG Hong Suk, Asst Secty
LTC H. C. Goodson, J4, USFK	LTC SHIN Sang Pil
MAJ M. Jacobs, USAFCS,K	Mr. KIM Hyung Kun
Mr. Francis K. Cook, J5, USFK	Mr. PAK Bung Hun
Mr. S. F. O'Hop, EAEN-RE, Secty	Mr. KIM Moo Young
Mr. E. H. Brummett, EAEN-RE, Alt. Secty	Mr. PARK Byong Yong
	Mr. BAE Myong In
	Mr. KANG Dae Bin
	Mr. LEE Soung Woo
	Mr. PARK Dahl Young
	Mr. KIM Han Mo
	Mr. BAE Jeung Sun

2. Subject of Recommendation: Requests for Relocation of Facilities, para 2b, Joint Committee memorandum dated 26 May 1971.

3. Recommendation: Task 1018 The request for relocation of a water supply line located along the boundaries of the 36th Engineer Gp compound in connection with the construction of a highway between Seoul and Uijongbu City, has been accepted by the Ministry of National Defense and the Eighth US Army subject to the conditions as stated in the attached mutual memorandum of agreement - "Conditional Release of Real Estate (partial), 0.49 acre, Acq. No. IC-207.

24

64th JC (Incl 15)
29 July 71

135

Task 1018

The Ministry of National Defense and the Eighth US Army Engineer will prepare the necessary documents. It is recommended that the Joint Committee, SOFA, approve this request for relocation of facilities.

4. Security Classification: Unclassified.

for Brigadier General PAK Woo Bum
Chairman, ROK Component
Facislities and Areas Subcommittee

Brigadier General Kenneth T. Sawyer
Chairman, US Component
Facilities and Areas Subcommittee

1 Attch
as

APPROVED BY THE JOINT COMMITTEE ON
29 JULY 1971 AT THE SIXTY-FOURTH MEETING

KOO CHOONG WHAY
Republic of Korea
Representative

ROBERT N. SMITH
for Lieutenant General
United States Air Force
United States Representative

These minutes are considered as official documents pertaining to both Governments and will not be released without mutual agreement.

17 June 1971

SUBJECT: Memorandum of Agreement - Conditional Release of Real Estate (Partial), 0.49 Acre, Acquisition No. IC-207 (TASK No. 1018)

US-ROK Chairmen
Facilities and Areas Subcommittee
US-ROK Joint Committee, SOFA

1. Authority: Pursuant to Memorandum for: Chairmen, FASC, from Joint Committee (JC), US-ROK Status of Forces Agreement (SOFA), Subject: Requests for Relocation of Facilities, dated 26 May 1971 (Inclosure No. 1), the FASC ROK Chairman appointed Captain KAL Jong Yong, MND/ROK, as the ROK Component Working Group Committee Chairman. The FASC US Chairman appointed Mr. Roderick L. HARVEY, DAC, as the US Component Working Group Committee Chairman. The above chairmen were charged with the responsibility for investigating subject matter and to conduct negotiations to reach a mutual agreement as basis for a proposed recommendation to the JC, SOFA in resolution of subject Task No. 1018.

2. Whereas, the Ministry of National Defense, Republic of Korea (MND/ROK)/ Uijongbu City has requested the relocation of three (3) noncontiguous portions of water pipeline (Partial), Acquisition No. IC-207, as shown in red on

64th JC (Incl 15)
29 July 71

26

SUBJECT: TASK No. 1018 -- 17 June 1971

inclosed map (Inclosure No. 2) for the purpose of upgrading and widening Seoul - Uijongbu City road, and

Whereas, USFK has conducted a feasibility investigation relative to the above MND-ROK/Uijongbu City's requirements and accordingly, has established a US position, that said requirement can be met provided: That all USFK facilities affected by above requirements will be relocated/constructed, at no cost to the US Government; that an adequate relocation/construction site will be furnished and placed under acquisition control of USFK, at no cost to the US Government.

3. Meetings were held, negotiations were conducted and a proposed mutual agreement reached based upon the following conditions and provisions:

a. MND-ROK/Uijongbu City agrees: (1) To provide USFK an acceptable alternate water pipeline relocation/construction site consisting of three (3) noncontiguous areas, comprising of approximately 0.49 acre of land (2,100' x 10') on a perpetual restrictive easement acquisition basis for USFK, as shown in red on Inclosure No. 2.

SUBJECT: TASK No. 1018 - - 17 June 1971

(2) To install 656 LF of 6" CAP and 1,444 LF of 4" CAP underground water pipelines on the three (3) acquired noncontiguous sites, as shown in red on Inclosure No. 2.

(3) That all water pipeline relocation/construction work will be accomplished by MND-ROK/Uijongbu City, in close prior coordination between the using activity, responsible Area Facilities Engineer and MND-ROK/Uijongbu City authorized representatives. All such work will be accomplished under technical supervision and in accordance with specifications of the using activity, and the Facilities Engineer concerned, at no cost to the US Government.

(4) That materials and component parts used in the relocation/construction work will be of same quality of existing pipeline and in accordance with applicable US Army standards and drawings prepared by the responsible Area Command Facilities Engineer.

(5) That all relocation/construction work will be subject to inspection surveillance by the inspection personnel of the Facilities Engineer concerned.

64th JC (Incl 15)
29 July 71

These minutes are considered as official documents pertaining to both Governments and will not be released without mutual agreement.

SUBJECT: TASK No. 1018 - - 17 June 1971

All noted inspection deficiencies will be immediately corrected by MND-ROK/ Uijongbu City.

b. USFK agrees: That upon the completion and acceptance of the new relocated/constructed water supply pipeline and required site locations by USFK, subject parcel of land, 0.49 acre of new water pipeline (Partial), Acquisition No. IC-207, as shown in red on Inclosure No. 2 will be released to MND/ROK. The new relocated/constructed water supply pipeline facility, upon acceptance will become the real property of USFK.

4. The US Government, its officers and assigns, will be held harmless and clear by MND/ROK for any claims for real property and/or personal damages incident to the above relocation/construction work.

5. Direct coordination between the responsible Facilities Engineer; Installation Commander and MND-ROK/Uijongbu City authorized representatives, for purpose of accomplishing provisions of this agreement, is hereby authorized.

KAL JONG YONG, Captain
Real Estate Division
Installation Bureau, MND/ROK

RODERICK L. HARVEY, DAC
Real Estate Division
Engineer Section, UNC/USFK

64th JC (Incl 15)
29 29 July 71

140

REPUBLIC OF KOREA -- UNITED STATES
FACILITIES AND AREAS SUBCOMMITTEE

20 July 1971

MEMORANDUM FOR: THE JOINT COMMITTEE

1. Subcommittee Members:

United States	Republic of Korea
BG Kenneth T. Sawyer, Chairman	BG PAK Woo Bum, Chairman
COL W. D. Lewis, Alt. Chairman	Mr. SONG Yong Tai, Secty
LTC E. W. Lingel, USAF	Mr. KANG Hong Suk, Asst Secty
LTC H. C. Goodwin, J4, USFK	LTC SHIN Sang Pil
Mr. Francis K. Cook, J5, USFK	Mr. KIM Hyoung Kun
Mr. S. F. O'Hop, EAEN-RE, Secty	Mr. PAK Bung Hun
Mr. E. H. Brummett, EAEN-RE Alt. Secty	Mr. KIM Moo Young
	Mr. PARK Byong Yong
	Mr. BAE Myong In
	Mr. KANG Dae Bin
	Mr. LEE Soung Woo
	Mr. PARK Dahl Young
	Mr. KIM Han Mo
	Mr. BAE Jeung Sun

2. Subject of Recommendation: Request for Relocation of Telegraph Poles, para 2, Joint Committee memorandum dated 3 July 1971.

3. Recommendation: Task 1045 The request for the relocation of three electric power distribution poles and lines, Acquisition No. IC-168 (Partial), located in Uijongbu City, Kyonggi-do, has been accepted by the Ministry of National Defense and the Eighth US Army subject to the conditions as stated in the attached mutual memorandum of agreement -- Conditional Release of Real Estate (Partial), 0.14 Acre, Acquisition No. IC-168.

64th JC (Incl 16)
30 29 July 71

141

Task 1045

The Ministry of National Defense and the Eighth US Army Engineer will prepare the necessary documents. It is recommended that the Joint Committee, SOFA, approve this request for relocation of telegraph poles.

4. Security Classification: Unclassified.

Brigadier General PAK Woo Bum
Chairman, ROK Component
Facilities and Areas Subcommittee

Brigadier General Kenneth T. Sawyer
Chairman, US Component
Facilities and Areas Subcommittee

1 Attch
as

APPROVED BY THE JOINT COMMITTEE ON
29 JULY 1971 AT THE SIXTY-FOURTH MEETING

KOO CHOONG WHAY
Republic of Korea
Representative

for ROBERT N. SMITH
Lieutenant General
United States Air Force
United States Representative

64th JC (Incl 16)
29 July 1971

142

20 July 1971

SUBJECT: Memorandum of Agreement - Conditional Release of Real Estate (Partial), 0.14 Acre, Acquisition No. IC-168 (TASK No. 1045)

US-ROK Chairmen
Facilities and Areas Subcommittee
US-ROK, Joint Committee, SOFA

1. Authority: Pursuant to Memorandum for: Chairmen, FASC, from Joint Committee (JC), US-ROK Status of Forces Agreement (SOFA), Subject: Request for Relocation of Telegraph Poles, dated 3 July 1971 (Inclosure No. 1), the FASC ROK Chairman appointed Captain KAL Jong Yong, MND/ROK, as the ROK Component Working Group Committee Chairman. The FASC US Chairman appointed Mr. Stanley F. O'HOP, DAC, as the US Component Working Group Committee Chairman. The above chairmen were charged with the responsibility for investigating subject matter and to conduct negotiations to reach a mutual agreement as basis for a proposed recommendation to the JC, SOFA in resolution of subject Task No. 1045.

2. Whereas, the Ministry of National Defense, Republic of Korea (MND/ROK) has requested the relocation of three electric power distribution poles and lines, Acquisition No. IC-168 (Partial), as shown on inclosed map (Inclosure No. 2), and

64th JC (Incl 16)
29 July 71

143

SUBJECT: TASK No. 1045 - -   20 July 1971

Whereas, USFK has conducted a feasibility investigation relative to the above MND-ROK/Korea Pulp Company's requirements and accordingly, has established a US position, that said requirements can be met provided: All USFK facilities affected by above requirements will be relocated/installed, at no cost to the US Government, in accordance with the following conditions and provisions:

a. MND-ROK/Korea Pulp Company agrees: (1) To provide USFK an acceptable alternate site for relocation/installation of the above electric poles and lines, comprising of approximately 0.16 acre (704' x 10') on a perpetual restrictive easement acquisition basis for USFK, as shown on Inclosure No. 2.

(2) To relocate/install three electric power distribution poles and lines, from Acquisition No. IC-168 to the above new 0.16 acre USFK acquired site, determined by the Area Facilities Engineer concerned.

(3) That all relocation/construction work will be accomplished by MND-ROK/Korea Pulp Company, in close prior coordination between the Using Activity, responsible Area Facilities Engineer and the Local MND/ROK Real Estate Representative.

64th JC (Incl 16)
29 July 71

SUBJECT: TASK No. 1045 - - 20 July 1971

b. USFK agrees: That upon the completion and acceptance of the new relocated/installed electric power distribution system, including acquisition of the new site location by USFK, subject 0.14 acre parcel of land, held on easement basis, by Acquisition No. IC-168, as shown on Inclosure No. 2 will be released to MND/ROK. The new relocated/installed electric power distribution system, upon acceptance will become the real property of USFK.

3. The US Government, its officers and assigns, will be held harmless and clear by MND/ROK for any claims for real property and/or personal damages incident to the above relocation/construction work.

4. Direct coordination between the responsible Installation Commander, Using Activity, Area Facilities Engineer concerned and MND-ROK/Korea Pulp Company authorized representative, for purposes of accomplishing provisions of this agreement, is hereby authorized.

KAL JONG YONG, Captain
Real Estate Division
Installation Bureau, MND/ROK

STANLEY F. O'HOP, DAC
Real Estate Division
Engineer Section, UNC/USFK

64th JC (Incl 16)
29 July 71

34

145

These minutes are considered as official documents pertaining to both Governments and will not be released without mutual agreement.

REPUBLIC OF KOREA -- UNITED STATES
FACILITIES AND AREAS SUBCOMMITTEE

15 July 1971

MEMORANDUM FOR: THE JOINT COMMITTEE

1. Subcommittee Members:

United States	Republic of Korea
BG Kenneth T. Sawyer, Chairman	BG PAK Woo Bum, Chairman
COL W. D. Lewis, Alt. Chairman	Mr. SONG Yong Tai, Secty
LTC E. W. Lingel, USAF	Mr. KANG Hong Suk, Asst Secty
LTC H. C. Goodson, J4, USFK	LTC SHIN Sang Pil
Mr. Francis K. Cook, J5, USFK	Mr. KIM Hyoung Kun
Mr. S. F. O'Hop, EAEN-RE, Secty	Mr. PAK Bung Hun
Mr. E. H. Brummett, EAEN-RE, Alt. Secty	Mr. KIM Moo Young
	Mr. PARK Byong Yong
	Mr. BAE Myong In
	Mr. KANG Dae Bin
	Mr. LEE Soung Woo
	Mr. PARK Dahl Young
	Mr. KIM Han Mo
	Mr. BAE Jeung Sun

2. Subject of Recommendation: Request for Partial Release of Real Estate, para 2, Joint Committee memorandum dated 17 June 1971.

3. Recommendation: Task 1031 The request for the release of approximately 0.30 acre of land currently held as a portion of the area under Acq. No. SAC-715, and located in Yongdongpo-ku, Seoul City, in connection with the widening of an existing road, has been accepted by the Ministry of National Defense and the Eighth US Army subject to the conditions as stated in the attached mutual memorandum of agreement - Conditional Release of Real Estate (Partial), 0.244 Acre, Acquisition No. SAC-715, ASP 046.

These minutes are considered as official documents pertaining to both Governments and will not be released without mutual agreement.

Task 1031

The Ministry of National Defense and the Eighth US Army Engineer will prepare the necessary documents. It is recommended that the Joint Committee, SOFA, approve this request for partial release of real estate.

4. Security Classification: Unclassifed.

Brigadier General PAK Woo Bum
Chairman, ROK Component
Facilities and Areas Subcommittee

Brigadier General Kenneth T. Sawyer
Chairman, US Component
Facilities and Areas Subcommittee

1 Attch
as

APPROVED BY THE JOINT COMMITTEE ON
29 JULY 1971 AT THE SIXTY-FOURTH MEETING

KOO CHOONG WHAY
Republic of Korea
Representative

ROBERT N. SMITH
Lieutenant General
United States Air Force
United States Representative

64th JC (Incl 17)
29 July 1971

147

13 July 1971

SUBJECT: Memorandum of Agreement - Conditional Release of Real Estate (Partial), 0.244 Acre, Acquisition No. SAC-715, ASP 046, TASK No. 1031

US-ROK Chairmen
Facilities and Areas Subcommittee
US-ROK Joint Committee, SOFA

1. Authority: Pursuant to Memorandum for: Chairmen, FASC, from Joint Committee (JC), US-ROK Status of Forces Agreement (SOFA), Subject: Request for Partial Release of Real Estate, dated 17 June 1971 (Inclosure No. 1), the FASC ROK Chairman appointed Major LEE Yong Sang, MND/ROK, as the ROK Component Working Group Committee Chairman. The FASC US Chairman appointed Mr. Stanley F. O'HOP, DAC, as the US Component Working Group Committee Chairman. The above chairmen were charged with the responsibility for investigating subject matter and to conduct negotiations to reach a mutual agreement as basis for a proposed recommendation to the JC, SOFA in resolution of subject Task No. 1031.

2. Whereas, the Ministry of National Defense, Republic of Korea (MND/ROK) has requested the relocation of a portion of the security fence and release of approximately 0.244 acre of land (Partial), Acquisition No. SAC-715, as

64th JC (Incl 17)
29 July 71

148

SUBJECT: Task No. 1031, 13 July 1971

shown on inclosed map (Inclosure No. 2), for the purpose of upgrading and widening of an existing Seoul City road, and

Whereas, USFK has conducted a feasibility investigation relative to the above MND-ROK/Seoul City's requirements and accordingly, has established a US position, that said requirements can be met provided: That all USFK facilities affected by above requirements will be relocated/constructed, at no cost to the US Government, in accordance with the following conditions and provisions:

a. MND-ROK/Seoul City agrees: (1) To temporarily relocate the existing 390 feet of security fence to within 3 feet of Bldg T-1139 and T-1140 with concertina wire next to the buildings.

(2) That upon construction of retaining wall (420 LF in length), the security fence will be relocated to its original position.

(3) That at no time the fence be left open at night during construction.

(4) That relocation/construction of the security fence will be subject to inspection surveillance by the inspection personnel of the Facilities Engineer concerned.

38

64th JC (Incl 17)
29 July 71

149

SUBJECT: Task No. 1031 - - 13 July 1971

(5) That normal ingress/egress by MND-ROK/Seoul City personnel concerned, within USFK controlled areas, for purpose of above relocation/construction activities, will be subject to security control and regulations imposed by the Commanding Officer of the ASP 046 Installation.

b. USFK agrees: That upon completion of retaining wall construction and relocation of the security fence, 0.244 acre of land, a portion of ASP 046, Acquisition No. SAC-715, as shown on inclosed map (Inclosure No. 2), will be released to MND/ROK.

3. The US Government, its officers and assigns, will be held harmless and clear by MND/ROK for any claims for real property and/or personal damages incident to above relocation/construction work.

4. Direct coordination between the responsible Facilities Engineer; Installation Commander and MND-ROK/Seoul City authorized representatives, for purpose of accomplishing provisions of this agreement, is hereby authorized.

LEE YONG SANG, Major
Real Estate Division
Installation Bureau, MND/ROK

STANLEY F. O'HOP, DAC
Real Estate Division
Engineer Section, UNC/USFK

150

64th JC (Incl 17)
29 July 71

REPUBLIC OF KOREA -- UNITED STATES
FACILITIES AND AREAS SUBCOMMITTEE

21 June 1971

MEMORANDUM FOR: THE JOINT COMMITTEE

1. Subcommittee Members:

United States	Republic of Korea
BG Kenneth T. Sawyer, Chairman	BG PAK Woo Bum, Chairman
COL W. D. Lewis, Alt. Chairman	Mr. SONG Yong Tai, Secty
LTC E. W. Lingel, USAF	Mr. KANG Hong Suk, Asst Secty
LTC H. C. Goodson, J4, USFK	LTC SHIN Sang Pil
MAJ M. Jacobs, USAFCS, K	Mr. KIM Hyung Kun
Mr. Francis K. Cook, J5, USFK	Mr. PAK Bung Hun
Mr. S. F. O'Hop, EAEN-RE, Secty	Mr. KIM Moo Young
Mr. E. H. Brummett, EAEN-RE, Alt. Secty	Mr. PARK Byong Yong
	Mr. BAE Myong In
	Mr. KANG Dae Bin
	Mr. LEE Soung Woo
	Mr. PARK Dahl Young
	Mr. KIM Han Mo
	Mr. BAE Jeung Sun

2. Subject of Recommendation: Request for Partial Release of Real Estate, Joint Committee memorandum dated 22 April 1971.

3. Recommendation: <u>Task 997</u> The request for release of 0.12 acre of land, which constitutes a portion of SP-51A held under Acq. No. SAC-103 (partial), and located in Majangdong, Sungbuk-ku, Seoul City, required for upgrading and widening of adjacent Seoul City street, has been accepted by the Ministry of National Defense and the Eighth US Army, subject to the conditions for release as stated in the attached mutual agreement. The Ministry of National Defense

40

64th JC (Incl 18)
29 July 71

151

and the Eighth US Army Engineer will prepare the necessary documents. It is recommended that the Joint Committee, SOFA, approve this release request.

4. Security Classification: Unclassified.

Brigadier General PAK Woo Bum
Chairman, ROK Component
Facilities and Areas Subcommittee

Brigadier General Kenneth T. Sawyer
Chairman, US Component
Facilities and Areas Subcommittee

1 Incl
as

APPROVED BY THE JOINT COMMITTEE ON
29 JULY 1971 AT THE SIXTY-FOURTH MEETING

KOO CHOONG WHAY
Republic of Korea
Representative

for ROBERT N. SMITH
Lieutenant General
United States Air Force
United States Representative

64th JC (Incl 18)
29 July 1971

27 May 1971

SUBJECT: Memorandum of Agreement - Conditional Release of a Portion of Real Estate, SP 51A, Acquisition No. SAC-103, TASK No. 997

US-ROK Chairmen
Facilities and Areas Subcommittee
US-ROK Joint Committee, SOFA

1. Authority: Pursuant to Memorandum for: Chairmen, Facilities and Areas Subcommittee (FASC) from Joint Committee (JC), US-ROK Status of Forces Agreement (SOFA), Subject: Request for Partial Release of Real Estate, dated 22 April 1971 (Inclosure No. 1), the FASC ROK Chairman appointed Major LEE Yong Sang, MND, as the ROK Component Working Group Committee Chairman. The FASC US Chairman appointed Mr. Eugene H. BRUMMETT, DAC, as the US Component Working Group Committee Chairman. The above chairmen were charged with the responsibility for investigating subject matter and to conduct negotiations to reach a mutual agreement as basis for a proposed recommendations to the JC, SOFA in resolution of subject TASK No. 997.

2. Whereas, the Ministry of National Defense, Republic of Korea (MND/ROK) has requested the partial release of Acquisition No. SAC-103, SP 51A, for upgrading and widening of the adjacent Seoul City street as shown on inclosed

64th JC (Incl 18)-
29 July 71

153

SUBJECT: TASK No. 997 — 27 May 1971

map (Inclosure No. 2), and has proposed that their request be processed in accordance with SOFA real estate procedures, and to relocate/construct existing facilities within the area to be released, at no cost to the US Government, and Whereas USFK agrees to the above proposed actions and has conducted a feasibility of release investigation to establish a USFK position contingent upon reaching a mutual agreement as follows: a. The USFK agrees to release the requested real estate consisting of 0.12 acre of land (Partial), Acquisition No. SAC-103 to MND/ROK in accordance with following conditions and provisions:

b. MND-ROK/Seoul City agrees: (1) To relocate/construct existing building, T-29 (1,242 SF), in same configuration, design and condition as the existing structure, to the location determined by the responsible Facilities Engineer, as shown on inclosed map (Inclosure No. 2).

(2) To earthfill the site (approximately 14,000 SF) to four feet in depth, properly compacted for the location of above building T-29.

(3) Construct a 250 LF long, four feet high stone or concrete block rip rap retaining wall around the above filled-in area, as shown on inclosed map (Inclosure No. 2).

64th JC (Incl 18)
29 July 71

154

SUBJECT: TASK No. 997 — 27 May 1971

(4) To relocate/construct 255 LF of security fence line to the same existing design and standard as shown on inclosed map (Inclosure No. 2).

(5) To acquire a satisfactory and acceptable alternate POL pipeline relocation/construction site, consisting of approximately 0.257 acre of land, on a perpetual restrictive easement acquisition basis for an indefinite period of time for USFK, as shown in orange on Inclosure No. 2.

(6) To relocate/construct existing four each steel 6" diameter POL pipelines, shown on Inclosure No. 2, to the above new 0.257 acre USFK acquired site, shown in orange on Inclosure No. 2, connecting SP 51A admin/operational area, Acquisition No. SAC-103 with the existing POL tank farm storage area, Acquisition No. SAC-24, as shown on Inclosure No. 2.

(7) All POL pipeline relocation/construction work will be accomplished by MND-ROK/Seoul City at no cost to the US Government and in close prior coordination between the using activity, responsible area Facilities Engineer and the authorized representatives of MND-ROK/Seoul City. All such work will be accomplished under the technical supervision and in accordance with

44

64th JC (Incl 18)
29 July 71
1181

155

specifications of the using activity and the Facilities Engineer concerned.

(8) That relocation/construction work will be accomplished in accordance with existing applicable US Army standards, quality of existing materials used, and plans and drawings prepared by the responsible Area Command Facilities Engineer.

(9) That all relocation/construction work will be subject to inspection surveillance by the inspection personnel of the Facilities Engineer concerned. All noted inspection deficiencies will be immediately corrected by MND-ROK/ Seoul City.

c. USFK agrees: That upon completion of relocation/construction required and the acceptance thereof by the USFK of the said relocated/constructed facilities, 0.12 acre of land, a portion of SP 51A, held under Acquisition No. SAC-103, as shown on inclosed map in green (Inclosure No. 2), will be released to MND/ROK.

3. Normal ingress/egress by MND-ROK/Seoul City personnel concerned, within USFK controlled areas, for purpose of above relocation/construction activities, will be subject to security control and regulations imposed by the Commanding

SUBJECT: TASK No. 997 -- 27 May 1971

Officer of the SP 51A or his representative.

4. The US Government, its officers and assigns, will be held harmless and clear by MND/ROK for any claims for real property and personal damage incident to above relocation/construction work.

5. Direct coordination between the responsible Facilities Engineer; Installation Commander and the authorized representatives of MND-ROK/Seoul City, for purpose of accomplishing provisions of this agreement, is hereby authorized.

LEE YONG SANG, Major
Real Estate Division
Installation Bureau, MND/ROK

EUGENE H. BRUMMETT, DAC
Real Estate Division
Engineer Section, UNC/USFK

2 Incl
as

64th JC (Incl 18)
29 July 71

22 July 1971

SUBJECT: Amendment No. 1, Memorandum of Agreement, Conditional Release of a Portion of Real Estate, SP 51A, Acquisition No. SAC-103, TASK No. 997

US-ROK Chairmen
Facilities and Areas Subcommittee
US-ROK Joint Committee, SOFA

1. Reference is made to Basic Agreement, Subject: Memorandum of Agreement - Conditional Release of a Portion of Real Estate, SP 51A, Acquisition No. SAC-103, TASK No. 997, dated 27 May 1971.

2. It has been determined that the relocation of existing POL pipeline by the MND-ROK/Seoul City, specified in referenced basic agreement, is to be changed. Paragraph 2b(6) is amended to read: "To construct/install one each steel 8" diameter and one each steel 12" diameter POL pipelines. The new required 8" and 12" diameter POL steel pipelines will be furnished by USFK. Further the US Government reserves the right to remove the now existing pipeline."

3. All other conditions and provisions in referenced basic agreement, except as noted in above paragraph 2 of herein Amendment No. 1, remain the same and unchanged.

1187

64th JC (Incl 18)
29 July 71

LEE YONG SANG, Major
Real Estate Division
Installation Bureau, MND/ROK

EUGENE H. BRUMMETT, DAC
Real Estate Division
Engineer Section, UNC/USFK

158

47

These minutes are considered as official documents pertaining to both Governments and will not be released without mutual agreement.

REPUBLIC OF KOREA -- UNITED STATES
FACILITIES AND AREAS SUBCOMMITTEE

15 July 1971

MEMORANDUM FOR: THE JOINT COMMITTEE

1. Subcommittee Members:

United States	Republic of Korea
BG Kenneth T. Sawyer, Chairman	BG PAK Woo Bum, Chairman
COL W. D. Lewis, Alt. Chairman	Mr. SONG Yong Tai, Secty
LTC E. W. Lingel, USAF	Mr. KANG Hong Suk, Asst Secty
LTC H. C. Goodson, J4, USFK	LTC SHIN Sang Pil
Mr. Francis K. Cook, J5, USFK	Mr. KIM Hyoung Kun
Mr. S. F. O'Hop, EAEN-RE, Secty	Mr. PAK Bung Hun
Mr. E. H. Brummett, EAEN-RE, Alt. Secty	Mr. KIM Moo Young
	Mr. PARK Byong Yong
	Mr. BAE Myong In
	Mr. KANG Dae Bin
	Mr. LEE Soung Woo
	Mr. PARK Dahl Young
	Mr. KIM Han Mo
	Mr. BAE Jeung Sun

2. Subject of Recommendation: Requests for Acquisition of Real Estate, para 2b, Joint Committee memorandum dated 28 January 1971.

3. Recommendation: Task 867 The request for acquisition on a permanent use basis of 4.178 acres of land located in Pyongtaek-gun, Kyonggi-do, adjacent to Camp Humphreys Installation, required for construction of quarters and a mess hall, has been accepted by the Ministry of National Defense. The Ministry of National Defense and the Eighth US Army Engineer will prepare the necessary documents. It is recommended that the Joint Committee, SOFA, approve this acquisition request.

64th JC (Incl 19)
48 29 July 71

159

These minutes are considered as official documents pertaining to both Governments and will not be released without mutual agreement.

Task 867

4. Security Classification: Unclassified.

Brigadier General PAK Woo Bum
Chairman, ROK Component
Facilities and Areas Subcommittee

Brigadier General Kenneth T. Sawyer
Chairman, US Component
Facilities and Areas Subcommittee

APPROVED BY THE JOINT COMMITTEE ON
29 JULY 1971 AT THE SIXTY-FOURTH MEETING

KOO CHOONG WHAN
Republic of Korea
Representative

for ROBERT N. SMITH
Lieutenant General
United States Air Force
United States Representative

49

64th JC (Incl 19)
29 July 71

160

These minutes are considered as official documents pertaining to both Governments and will not be released without mutual agreement.

REPUBLIC OF KOREA -- UNITED STATES
FACILITIES AND AREAS SUBCOMMITTEE

15 July 1971

MEMORANDUM FOR: THE JOINT COMMITTEE

1. Subcommittee Members:

United States	Republic of Korea
BG Kenneth T. Sawyer, Chairman	BG PAK Woo Bum, Chairman
COL W. D. Lewis, Alt. Chairman	Mr. SONG Yong Tai, Secty
LTC E. W. Lingel, USAF	Mr. KANG Hong Suk, Asst Secty
LTC H. C. Goodson, J4, USFK	LTC SHIN Sang Pil
Mr. Francis K. Cook, J5, USFK	Mr. KIM Hyoung Kun
Mr. S. F. O'Hop, EAEN-RE, Secty	Mr. PAK Bung Hun
Mr. E. H. Brummett, EAEN-RE, Alt. Secty	Mr. KIM Moo Young
	Mr. PARK Byong Yong
	Mr. BAE Myong In
	Mr. KANG Dae Bin
	Mr. LEE Soung Woo
	Mr. PARK Dahl Young
	Mr. KIM Han Mo
	Mr. BAE Jeung Sun

2. Subject of Recommendation: Requests for Acquisition of Real Estate, para 2a, Joint Committee memorandum dated 25 February 1971.

3. Recommendation: Task 922 The request for acquisition on a permanent exclusive use basis of 25.6 acres of land located at Pyongtaek, Kyonggi-do, required for the construction of buildings and facilities for Camp Humphreys Installation has been accepted by the Ministry of National Defense. The Ministry of National Defense and the Eighth US Army Engineer will prepare the necessary documents. It is recommended that the Joint Committee, SOFA, approve this acquisition request.

64th JC (Incl 20)
29 July 71

50

161

These minutes are considered as official documents pertaining to both Governments and will not be released without mutual agreement.

Task 922

4. Security Classification: Unclassified.

Brigadier General PAK Woo Bum Chairman, ROK Component Facilities and Areas Subcommittee	Brigadier General Kenneth T. Sawyer Chairman, US Component Facilities and Areas Subcommittee

APPROVED BY THE JOINT COMMITTEE ON
29 JULY 1971 AT THE SIXTY-FOURTH MEETING

KOO CHOONG WHAY Republic of Korea Representative	for ROBERT N. SMITH Lieutenant General United States Air Force United States Representative

These minutes are considered as official documents pertaining to both Governments and will not be released without mutual agreement.

REPUBLIC OF KOREA -- UNITED STATES
FACILITIES AND AREAS SUBCOMMITTEE

15 July 1971

MEMORANDUM FOR: THE JOINT COMMITTEE

1. Subcommittee Members:

United States	Republic of Korea
BG Kenneth T. Sawyer, Chairman	BG PAK Woo Bum, Chairman
COL W. D. Lewis, Alt. Chairman	Mr. SONG Yong Tai, Secty
LTC E. W. Lingel, USAF	Mr. KANG Hong Suk, Asst Secty
Mr. Francis K. Cook, J5, USFK	LTC SHIN Sang Pil
LTC H. C. Goodson, J4, USFK	Mr. KIM Hyung Kun
Mr. S. F. O'Hop, EAEN-RE, Secty	Mr. PAK Bung Hun
Mr. E. H. Brummett, EAEN-RE, Alt. Secty	Mr. KIM Moo Young
	Mr. PARK Byong Yong
	Mr. BAE Myong In
	Mr. KANG Dae Bin
	Mr. LEE Soung Woo
	Mr. PARK Dahl Young
	Mr. KIM Han Mo
	Mr. BAE Jeung Sun

2. Subject of Recommendation: Requests for Extension of Temporary Use Permits, Joint Committee memorandum dated 17 June 1971.

3. Recommendation: Tasks 1034-1035 The following requests for extension of temporary use permits have been accepted by the Ministry of National Defense:

a. Task 1034 Extension of Temporary Use Permit K-H-T-2, involving 9.65 acres of land including 600 linear feet of railroad spur, located in Pusan City, from 16 July 1971 through 15 July 1972. This real estate has been used since 1969 as a temporary property disposal holding area and there is a continuing requirement for its use for that purpose.

64th JC (Incl 21)
29 July 71

163

These minutes are considered as official documents pertaining to both Governments and will not be released without mutual agreement.

Tasks 1034-1035

b. Task 1035 Extension of Temporary Use Permit K-G-T-12, involving 10 acres of riverbed area located in Kwangsan-gun, Chollanam-do, from 10 September 1971 through 9 September 1972. This real estate has been used since 1969 as a source of fill material for land reclamation and there is a continuing need for its use for that purpose.

The Ministry of National Defense and the Eighth US Army Engineer will prepare the necessary documents. It is recommended that the Joint Committee, SOFA, approve these two requests for extensions.

4. Security Classification: Unclassified.

Brigadier General PAK Woo Bum
Chairman, ROK Component
Facilities and Areas Subcommittee

Brigadier General Kenneth T. Sawyer
Chairman, US Component
Facilities and Areas Subcommittee

APPROVED BY THE JOINT COMMITTEE ON
29 JULY 1971 AT THE SIXTY-FOURTH MEETING

KOO CHOONG WHAY
Republic of Korea
Representative

ROBERT N. SMITH
for Lieutenant General
United States Air Force
United States Representative

64th JC (Incl 21)
29 July 71

53

165

945

1193

These minutes are considered as official documents pertaining to both Governments and will not be released without mutual agreement.

REPUBLIC OF KOREA -- UNITED STATES
FACILITIES AND AREAS SUBCOMMITTEE

15 July 1971

MEMORANDUM FOR: THE JOINT COMMITTEE

1. Subcommittee Members:

United States	Republic of Korea
BG Kenneth T. Sawyer, Chairman	BG PAK Woo Bum, Chairman
COL W. D. Lewis, Alt. Chairman	Mr. SONG Yong Tai, Secty
LTC E. W. Lingel, USAF	Mr. KANG Hong Suk, Asst Secty
LTC H. C. Goodson, J4, USFK	LTC SHIN Sang Pil
Mr. Francis K. Cook, J5, USFK	Mr. KIM Hyoung Kun
Mr. S. F. O'Hop, EAEN-RE, Secty	Mr. PAK Bung Hun
Mr. E. H. Brummett, EAEN-RE, Alt. Secty	Mr. KIM Moo Young
	Mr. PARK Byong Yong
	Mr. BAE Myong In
	Mr. KANG Dae Bin
	Mr. LEE Soung Woo
	Mr. PARK Dahl Young
	Mr. KIM Han Mo
	Mr. BAE Jeung Sun

2. Subject of Recommendation: Request for Authorization to Dispose of Facility, Joint Committee memorandum dated 17 June 1971.

3. Recommendation: Task 1032 The request for authorization to dispose of one facility, consisting of one Korean-constructed smoke stack, currently held as a portion of Camp Randall E. Coiner Installation in Seoul City, under Acq. No. SAC-526, has been accepted by the Ministry of National Defense with the request that prior coordination be made with the local MND real estate representative. This facility has become excess to USFK requirements. The Ministry of National Defense and the Eighth US Army Engineer will prepare the necessary documents. It is recommended that the Joint Committee, SOFA, approve this request.

64th JC (Incl 22)
29 July 71

54

165

These minutes are considered as official documents pertaining to both Governments and will not be released without mutual agreement.

Task 1032

4. Security Classification: Unclassified.

Brigadier General PAK Woo Bum
Chairman, ROK Component
Facilities and Areas Subcommittee

Brigadier General Kenneth T. Sawyer
Chairman, US Component
Facilities and Areas Subcommittee

APPROVED BY THE JOINT COMMITTEE ON
29 JULY 1971 AT THE SIXTY-FOURTH MEETING

KOO CHOONG WHAY
Republic of Korea
Representative

for ROBERT N. SMITH
Lieutenant General
United States Air Force
United States Representative

1195

64th JC (Incl 22)
29 July 71

166

These minutes are considered as official documents pertaining to both Governments and will not be released without mutual agreement.

REPUBLIC OF KOREA -- UNITED STATES
FACILITIES AND AREAS SUBCOMMITTEE

15 July 1971

MEMORANDUM FOR: THE JOINT COMMITTEE

1. Subcommittee Members:

United States	Republic of Korea
BG Kenneth T. Sawyer, Chairman	BG PAK Woo Bum, Chairman
COL W. D. Lewis, Alt. Chairman	Mr. SONG Yong Tai, Secty
LTC E. W. Lingel, USAF	Mr. KANG Hong Suk, Asst Secty
LTC H. C. Goodson, J4, USFK	LTC SHIN Sang Pil
Mr. Francis K. Cook, J5, USFK	Mr. KIM Hyoung Kun
Mr. S. F. O'Hop, EAEN-RE, Secty	Mr. PAK Bung Hun
Mr. E. H. Brummett, EAEN-RE, Alt. Secty	Mr. KIM Moo Young
	Mr. PARK Byong Yong
	Mr. BAE Myong In
	Mr. KANG Dae Bin
	Mr. LEE Soung Woo
	Mr. PARK Dahl Young
	Mr. KIM Han Mo
	Mr. BAE Jeung Sun

2. Subject of Recommendation: Request for Authorization to Dispose of Facility, Joint Committee memorandum dated 17 June 1971.

3. Recommendation: Task 1033 The request for authorization to dispose of one facility, consisting of one Korean-constructed building (S-1124), currently held as a portion of Camp Randall E. Coiner Installation in Seoul City, under Acq. No. SAC-526, has been accepted by the Ministry of National Defense with the request that prior coordination be made with the local MND real estate representative. This facility has become excess to USFK requirements. The Ministry of National Defense and the Eighth US Army Engineer will prepare the necessary documents. It is recommended that the Joint Committee, SOFA, approve this request.

64th JC (Incl 23)
29 July 71

56

167

These minutes are considered as official documents pertaining to both Governments and will not be released without mutual agreement.

Task 1033

4. Security Classification: Unclassified.

Brigadier General PAK Woo Bum Chairman, ROK Component Facilities and Areas Subcommittee	Brigadier General Kenneth T. Sawyer Chairman, US Component Facilities and Areas Subcommittee

APPROVED BY THE JOINT COMMITTEE ON
29 JULY 1971 AT THE SIXTY FOURTH MEETING

KOO CHOONG WHAY Republic of Korea Representative	for ROBERT N. SMITH Lieutenant General United States Air Force United States Representative

These minutes are considered as official documents pertaining to both Governments and will not be released without mutual agreement.

REPUBLIC OF KOREA -- UNITED STATES
FACILITIES AND AREAS SUBCOMMITTEE

15 July 1971

MEMORANDUM FOR: THE JOINT COMMITTEE

1. Subcommittee Members:

United States	Republic of Korea
BG Kenneth T. Sawyer, Chairman	BG PAK Woo Bum, Chairman
COL W. D. Lewis, Alt. Chairman	Mr. SONG Yong Tai, Secty
LTC E. W. Lingel, USAF	Mr. KANG Hong Suk, Asst Secty
LTC H. C. Goodson, J4, USFK	LTC SHIN Sang Pil
Mr. Francis K. Cook, J5, USFK	Mr. KIM Hyoung Kun
Mr. S. F. O'Hop, EAEN-RE, Secty	Mr. PAK Bung Hun
Mr. E. H. Brummett, EAEN-RE, Alt. Secty	Mr. KIM Moo Young
	Mr. PARK Byong Yong
	Mr. BAE Myong In
	Mr. KANG Dae Bin
	Mr. LEE Soung Woo
	Mr. PARK Dahl Young
	Mr. KIM Han Mo
	Mr. BAE Jeung Sun

2. Subject of Recommendation: Requests for Acquisition of Real Estate, para 2b, Joint Committee memorandum dated 25 February 1971.

3. Recommendation: Task 923 The request for acquisition of a total of 52.41 acres of land located at Chilgok-gun, Kyongsangbuk-do (19.71 acres on a permanent exclusive use basis and the remaining 32.7 acres on a perpetual restrictive easement basis) required for a permanent rock quarry to provide construction materials for Camp Carroll Depot and ALOC Airfield projects, has been withdrawn by the US requesting agency in lieu of reacquisition of existing old rock quarry (Acq. No. PAC-152). Therefore, it is recommended that no further action be taken on this task.

64th JC (Incl 24)
29 July 71

169
324

These minutes are considered as official documents pertaining to both Governments and will not be released without mutual agreement.

Task 923

The Ministry of National Defense and the Eighth US Army Engineer will prepare the necessary documents. It is recommended that the Joint Committee, SOFA, approve this request.

4. Security Classification: Unclassified.

Brigadier General PAK Woo Bum Chairman, ROK Component Facilities and Areas Subcommittee	Brigadier General Kenneth T. Sawyer Chairman, US Component Facilities and Areas Subcommittee

APPROVED BY THE JOINT COMMITTEE ON
29 JULY 1971 AT THE SIXTY-FOURTH MEETING

KOO CHOONG WHAY Republic of Korea Representative	for ROBERT N. SMITH Lieutenant General United States Air Force United States Representative

59

64th JC (Incl 24)
29 July 71

These minutes are considered as official documents pertaining to both Governments and will not be released without mutual agreement.

REPUBLIC OF KOREA -- UNITED STATES
FACILITIES AND AREAS SUBCOMMITTEE

15 July 1971

MEMORANDUM FOR: THE JOINT COMMITTEE

1. Subcommittee Members:

United States	Republic of Korea
BG Kenneth T. Sawyer, Chairman	BG PAK Woo Bum, Chairman
COL W. D. Lewis, Alt. Chairman	Mr. SONG Yong Tai, Secty
LTC E. W. Lingel, USAF	Mr. KANG Hong Suk, Asst Secty
LTC H. C. Goodson, J4, USFK	LTC SHIN Sang Pil
Mr. Francis K. Cook, J5, USFK	Mr. KIM Hyung Kun
Mr. S. F. O'Hop, EAEN-RE, Secty	Mr. PAK Bung Hun
Mr. E. H. Brummett, EAEN-RE, Alt. Secty	Mr. KIM Moo Young
	Mr. PARK Byong Yong
	Mr. BAE Myong In
	Mr. KANG Dae Bin
	Mr. LEE Soung Woo
	Mr. PARK Dahl Young
	Mr. KIM Han Mo
	Mr. BAE Jeung Sun

2. Subject of Recommendation: Requests for Release of Real Estate, Joint Committee memorandum dated 17 June 1971.

3. Recommendations: Tasks 1020-1030 The following requests for release of real estate have been accepted by the Ministry of National Defense and the Eighth US Army:

a. Task 1020 Release of a total of 0.75 acre of land, comprising 0.043 acre held under Acq. No. I-41, 0.025 acre held under Acq. No. I-42, and 0.682 acre held under Acq. No. AAC-395, and located on Seattle Installation in Inchon City, Kyonggi-do

64th JC (Incl 25)
29 July 71

Tasks 1020-1030 contd

b. Task 1021 Release of 52.47 acres of land, constituting Tac 4, Site 40 Installation, located in Chunsong-gun, Kangwon-do, and currently held under Acq. Nos. SAC-729 and SAC-780, including a total of 53 buildings and facilities existing at the time of release.

c. Task 1022 Release of 23.18 acres of land, constituting Tac 2, Site 31 Installation, located in Pochon-gun, Kyonggi-do, and currently held under Acq. No. 7X-136, including a total of 14 buildings and facilities existing at the time of release.

d. Task 1023 Release of 68.3626 acres of land, constituting Tac 4, Site 35 Installation, located in Kapyong-gun, Kyonggi-do, and currently held under Acq. Nos. SAC-737, SAC-750, SAC-751, and SAC-784. This request for release includes a total of 53 buildings and facilities existing at the time of release.

e. Task 1024 Release of approximately 0.91 acre of land held on an easement basis as a portion of the area held under Acq. No. IC-168 and located in Uijongbu-si, Kyonggi-do, including 3,965 LF of USFK-installed electric power line currently held under Facility No. F-115.

f. Task 1025 Release of 2.17 acres of land, constituting a portion of Camp Albany Installation, located within and in the vicinity of Uijongbu-si, Kyonggi-do, and currently held as a portion of the area under Acq. No. IC-164. This request for release includes a total of 11 buildings and facilities existing at the time of release.

g. Task 1026 Release of 2,722.68 acres of land, constituting the remaining portion of Camp Saint Barbara Installation, located in Pochon-gun, Kyonggi-do, and currently held under Acq. Nos. 7X-100, 7X-101, and K-C-201, including a total of 247 buildings and facilities existing at the time of release.

h. Task 1027 Release of 22.208 acres of land held on an easement basis under Acq. No. K-B-319 and used in support of an overhead electric power line, located in Paju-gun, Kyonggi-do.

i. Task 1028 Release of 0.80 acre of land held on an easement basis under Acq. No. CAV-269 and used in support of an overhead electric power line, located in Paju-gun, Kyonggi-do.

These minutes are considered as official documents pertaining to both Governments and will not be released without mutual agreement.

Tasks 1020-1030 contd

j. Task 1029 Release of 0.60 acre of land held on an easement basis under Acq. No. CAV-268 and used in support of an overhead electric power line, located in Paju-gun, Kyonggi-do.

k. Task 1030 Release of 14.61 acres of land, constituting the remaining portion of Love Installation, located in Paju-gun, Kyonggi-do, and currently held under Acq. No. CAV-208, including a total of 27 buildings and facilities existing at the time of release.

The Ministry of National Defense and the Eighth US Army Engineer will prepare the necessary documents. It is recommended that the Joint Committee, SOFA, approve these 11 requests for release of real estate.

4. Security Classification: Unclassified.

Pak Woo Bum
Brigadier General PAK Woo Bum
Chairman, ROK Component
Facilities and Areas Subcommittee

K T Sawyer
Brigadier General Kenneth T. Sawyer
Chairman, US Component
Facilities and Areas Subcommittee

APPROVED BY THE JOINT COMMITTEE ON
29 JULY 1971 AT THE SIXTY-FOURTH MEETING

Choong Whay Koo
KOO CHOONG WHAY
Republic of Korea
Representative

for
ROBERT N. SMITH
Lieutenant General
United States Air Force
United States Representative

64th JC (Incl 25)
29 July 71

62

173

These minutes are considered as official documents pertaining to both Governments and will not be released without mutual agreement.

REPUBLIC OF KOREA -- UNITED STATES
FACILITIES AND AREAS SUBCOMMITTEE

15 July 1971

MEMORANDUM FOR: THE JOINT COMMITTEE

1. Subcommittee Members:

United States	Republic of Korea
BG Kenneth T. Sawyer, Chairman	BG PAK Woo Bum, Chairman
COL W. D. Lewis, Alt. Chairman	Mr. SONG Yong Tai, Secty
LTC E. W. Lingel, USAF	Mr. KANG Hong Suk, Asst Secty
LTC H. C. Goodson, J4, USFK	LTC SHIN Sang Pil
Mr. Francis K. Cook, J5, USFK	Mr. KIM Hyung Kun
Mr. S. F. O'Hop, EAEN-RE, Secty	Mr. PAK Bung Hun
Mr. E. H. Brummett, EAEN-RE, Alt. Secty	Mr. KIM Moo Young
	Mr. PARK Byong Yong
	Mr. BAE Myong In
	Mr. KANG Dae Bin
	Mr. LEE Soung Woo
	Mr. PARK Dahl Young
	Mr. KIM Han Mo
	Mr. BAE Jeung Sun

2. Subject of Recommendation: Requests for Release of Real Estate.

3. Recommendations: Tasks 1039-1043 The following requests for release of real estate have been accepted by the Ministry of National Defense and the Eighth US Army:

a. Task 1039 Release of 209.50 acres of land with two Korean-constructed facilities, constituting Wolmido Installation, held under Acq. Nos. ASCOM-363, ASCOM-375, AAC-381 and AAC-383, and located in Inchon City, Kyonggi-do. This release includes all USFK-constructed facilities located on the Installation

64th JC (Incl 26)
29 July 71

174

3. Tasks 1039-1043

a. Task 1039 contd

to be released, with the exception of two water tank facilities (Nos T-3421 and T-3422) and Building No. T-3343 with ingress and egress rights thereto, which will be retained under USFK control until 30 October 1971.

b. Task 1040 Release of 7.8 acres of land, constituting Area #3 portion of Camp Pililaau Installation, held under Acq. No. IC-264 and located in Uijongbu-si, Kyonggi-do, including a total of 50 USFK-constructed buildings and facilities located on the Installation.

c. Task 1041 Release of 20.942 acres of land, constituting Camp Nabors Installation, held under Acq. Nos. SAC-705 and SAC-766, and located in Seoul City, including a total of 108 USFK-constructed buildings and facilities located on the Installation.

d. Task 1042 Release of 23.86 acres of land, constituting the remaining portion of Camp Pililaau Installation, held under Acq. No. IC-264 and located in Uijongbu-si, Kyonggi-do. This request for release includes a total of 78 USFK-constructed buildings and facilities located on the Installation.

e. Task 1043 Release of 21.27 acres of land containing two Korean-constructed buildings, constituting a portion of Market Installation held under Acq. No. ACS-193, and located in Inchon City, Kyonggi-do. This request for release includes a total of 66 USFK-constructed buildings and facilities located on the Installation. Exempted from this release request are 0.659 acre of land containing an underground sanitary sewer line and an overhead electric power line, which will be retained together with unrestricted rights-of-entry for ingress and egress thereto. (Tyler)

The Ministry of National Defense and the Eighth US Army Engineer will prepare the necessary documents. It is recommended that the Joint Committee, SOFA, approve these five release requests.

64th JC (Incl 26)
29 July 71

175

These minutes are considered as official documents pertaining to both Governments and will not be released without mutual agreement.

Tasks 1039-1043

4. Security Classification: Unclassified.

Brigadier General PAK Woo Bum Chairman, ROK Component Facilities and Areas Subcommittee	Brigadier General Kenneth T. Sawyer Chairman, US Component Facilities and Areas Subcommittee

APPROVED BY THE JOINT COMMITTEE ON
29 JULY 1971 AT THE SIXTY-FOURTH MEETING

KOO CHOONG WHAY Republic of Korea Representative	ROBERT N. SMITH Lieutenant General United States Air Force United States Representative

64th JC (Incl 26)
29 July 71

REPUBLIC OF KOREA - UNITED STATES
FINANCE (PERSONNEL AFFAIRS) SUBCOMMITTEE

20 July 1971

MEMORANDUM FOR: THE JOINT COMMITTEE

1. Subcommittee Members:

United States	Republic of Korea
COL Dana F. McFall, Chairman	Mr. PARK Dong Hee, Chairman
COL Thomas F. Henderson, USAF	Mr. KWON Tai Won
COL D. J. Helterbran, USA	Mr. SHIN Myoung Ho
COL Robert J. Kriwanek, USA	Mr. LEE Jin Moo
CDR George E. Thibault, USN	Mr. KANG Yung Joo
LTC Ronald S. McCaul, USA	Mr. LEE Chul Hee
LTC William T. Tinsley, USA	Mr. CHOO Byung Guk
LTC Fred L. Bowden, USAF	Mr. KIM Kyung Tai
MAJ Allen D. Adams, USA	Mr. SHIN Yung Su
Mr. Francis K. Cook	Mr. KIM Kee Joe

2. Subject to Recommendation: Review of procedures established by the Joint Committee at its ninth meeting on 5 June 1967, relating to the examination by Republic of Korea Customs Inspectors of parcel post packages delivered through United States military post office channels, contained as Inclosure (6) to the minutes of the ninth Joint Committee meeting.

3. Recommendation: Paragraph 3c and d of the above referenced Inclosures be revised to read:

a. "3c. It is mutually agreed that, in the interest of full compliance with the Agreed Understandings of Article IX, Republic of Korea-United States Status of Forces Agreement, whereby delay of mail and increased administrative burden on postal authorities will be held to a minimum, sufficient Republic of Korea customs inspectors and repackers will be present to conduct inspections.

64th JC (Incl 27)
29 July 71

66

(1) The "sample" inspection will consist of no more than 10% of the incoming bags/containers of nonofficial parcel mail. The sample will be selected jointly by United States postal personnel and Republic of Korea customs inspectors.

(2) At Inchon inspections will be completed sufficiently before the scheduled loading time to permit onward transportation to depart on schedule. At Kimpo Air Base the inspection will be completed within six hours after the arrival of the airline flight. When customs officials are not present to designate mail for examination, it will be forwarded to its final destination without delay.

d. A "customs inspection area" will be designated by the respective commander in charge and all examinations will be conducted in this designated area. United States military postal personnel will be present in the inspection area during the conduct of all such customs inspections."

b. It is further recommended that paragraph 5c of the above-referenced Inclosure be revised to read:

"5c. Parcels containing items which, per se, appear to be unreasonable in quantity will be retained under the control of the United States military postal authorities until their disposition is mutually determined by appropriate Republic of Korea and United States authorities. It is mutually agreed that the determination as to what constitutes a reasonable/unreasonable quantity of any given item rests with United States officials based upon the addressee's mission, family requirements, stated purpose for importation, and any other considerations deemed appropriate by the United States. A guide as to what represents reasonable quantities of specified items is attached as Inclosure 2."

c. Questions concerning increased personnel and space for the conduct of customs examination continue under review by the Finance/ Personnel Affairs Subcommittee.

d. It is further recommended that the effective date of this recommendation be the date upon which it is approved by the Joint Committee.

4. Security Classification: Unclassified.

Mr. PARK Dong Hee Chairman, ROK Component Finance (Personnel Affairs)Subcommittee	COL Dana F. McFall, USAF Chairman, US Component Finance (Personnel Affairs) Subcommittee

APPROVED BY THE JOINT COMMITTEE ON
29 JULY 1971 AT THE SIXTY-FOURTH MEETING

ROBERT N. SMITH Lieutenant General United States Air Force United States Representative	KOO CHOONG WHAY Republic of Korea Representative

64th JC (Incl 27)
29 July 71

179

Reasonable Quantities of Specified Items Delivered through US Military Post Office During an Individual's tour of duty in Korea.

No.	Item	Quantity
1.	Air Conditioner	1 per individual (See Note 1) 2 per family
2.	Dryer	1 per family
3.	Electric Fan	1 per individual
4.	Freezer	1 per family
5.	Water Heater	1 per family
6.	Movie Camera	1 per individual
7.	Gramophone	1 per individual
8.	Turntable	1 per individual
9.	Radio	1 per individual
10.	Gas Range	1 per family
11.	Refrigerator	1 per family
12.	Speaker System	1 per individual
13.	Camera (still)	1 per individual
14.	Tape Deck	1 per individual
15.	Tape Recorder	1 per individual
16.	Television	1 per individual
17.	Amplifier Tuner	1 per individual
18.	Typewriter	1 per individual
19.	Washing Machine	1 per family
20.	Binoculars	1 per individual
21.	Stereo Music System	1 per individual
22.	Mixer	1 per family
23.	Rice Cooker	1 per family
24.	Toaster	1 per family
25.	Coffee Maker	1 per individual
26.	Cleaner (Vacuum)	1 per family
27.	Golf Set	1 per individual
28.	Car Cooler	1 per car
29.	Car Radio	1 per car
30.	Receiver	1 per individual
31.	Mink (coat, shawl, collar)	1 each per individual
32.	Handbag (alligator)	not authorized
33.	Ring (US value over $100 US)	1 per individual
34.	Watch (US value over $100 US)	1 per individual
35.	Textiles	Maximum of 25 yds per shipment, to include no more than 5 yds same color/design.

Note 1: If an individual is authorized to live off-post he will be considered as a "family" for the purposes of this list.

Mr. PARK Dong Hee COL Dana F. McFall, USAF

64th JC (Incl 27)
29 July 71

69

JOINT COMMITTEE
UNDER
THE REPUBLIC OF KOREA AND THE UNITED STATES
STATUS OF FORCES AGREEMENT

22 JUL 1971

MEMORANDUM FOR: The Joint Committee

SUBJECT: Designation of US Invited Contractor Under Article XV, Status of Forces Agreement

1. References:

a. Paragraph 2, Article XV, Status of Forces Agreement.

b. US Chairman, Commerce Subcommittee letter, dated 28 April 1971, subject as above (Inclosure 1).

c. ROK Chairman, Commerce Subcommittee letter, dated 15 May 1971, subject as above (Inclosure 2).

2. The United States, after consultation with the ROK Commerce Subcommittee and having duly considered their views, has designated Campbell Construction and Equipment Company, Inc., as a US invited contractor, in joint venture with a Korean firm, for execution of contract DACA79-72-C-0006 for upgrading of utilities, Yongsan.

3. Pertinent data concerning US citizen employees will be provided to the Joint Secretariat in the established format.

2 Incl
as

ROBERT N. SMITH
Lieutenant General, USAF
United States Representative
Joint Committee

64th JC (Incl 28)
29 July 71

70

181

REPUBLIC OF KOREA - UNITED STATES
COMMERCE SUBCOMMITTEE

28 April 1971

SUBJECT: Designation of US Invited Contractor Under Article XV, Status of Forces Agreement

ROK Chairman, Commerce Subcommittee

1. Reference: Paragraph 2, Article XV, of the Status of Forces Agreement.

2. The Government of the Republic of Korea is informed through this written consultative process that the United States Forces, Korea, proposes to extend invited contractor status to the US member firm of the US-ROK joint venture contractor awarded the contract for the Upgrading of Utilities Yongsan, Korea, construction project.

3. The following data are provided:

a. Company Name:

A list of qualified US Firms is attached as Inclosure 1.

b. Local Address: To be supplied when designation is made.

c. Identification of US Citizen Employees: To be supplied on on conclusion of negotiations.

d. Number of US and ROK Employees: Number of US Citizen and Koreans is not known at this time and will be supplied upon conclusion of negotiations.

e. Reasons for Designation of an Invited Contractor: Open competitive bidding among local contractors is not practical due to the following.

(1) Limited technical qualifications of the contractors involved.

(2) Unavailability of services required by US Standards.

f. Location of contracts: Yongsan, Seoul, Korea.

71

64th JC (Incl 1 to Incl 28)
29 July 71

182

SUBJECT: Designation of US Invited Contractor Under Article XV, Status of Forces Agreement

g. Type of Contracts: Fixed Price

h. Length of Contracts: To be supplied on conclusion of negotiations.

i. Sponsoring Component Commander: USAEDFE.

1 Incl
as

RICHARD T. CANN
Colonel, U.S. Army
United States Chairman
Commerce Subcommittee

72

64th JC (Incl 1 to Incl 28)
29 July 71

MINISTRY OF COMMERCE AND INDUSTRY
REPUBLIC OF KOREA
SEOUL, KOREA

15 May 1971

Subject: Designation of US Invited Contractor under Article XV Status of Forces Agreement

US Chairman, Commerce Subcommittee

1. Reference:

a. Paragraph 2, Article XV, Status of Forces Agreement

b. US Commerce Subcommittee Memorandum of Consultation, dated 28 April 1971, subject as above, pertaining to contract for the Upgrading of Utilities at Yongsan, Korea, construction project.

2. The US memorandum reference 1b above, has been reviewed and the Government of the Republic of Korea understands the requirement for an invited contractor status to the US member firm of the ROK-US joint venture contract in this instance.

Chung Min Kil
Chairman
Commerce Subcommittee, ROK

73

64th JC (Incl 2 to Incl 28)
29 July 71

184

JOINT COMMITTEE
UNDER
THE REPUBLIC OF KOREA AND THE UNITED STATES
STATUS OF FORCES AGREEMENT

22 JUL 1971

MEMORANDUM FOR: The Joint Committee

SUBJECT: Designation of US Invited Contractor Under Article XV, Status of Forces Agreement

1. References:

a. Paragraph 2, Article XV, Status of Forces Agreement.

b. US Chairman, Commerce Subcommittee, letter dated 1 February 1971, subject as above (Inclosure 1).

c. ROK Chairman, Commerce Subcommittee, letter dated 24 February 1971, subject as above (Inclosure 2).

2. The United States, after consultation with the ROK Commerce Subcommittee and having duly considered their views, has designated International Electronics Corporation as an invited contractor to install microwave equipment at 21 sites throughout the Republic of Korea, contract DAJB03-71-C-6385.

3. Pertinent data concerning US citizen employees will be provided to the Joint Secretariat in the established format.

2 Incl
as

ROBERT N. SMITH
Lieutenant General, USAF
United States Representative
Joint Committee

64th JC (Incl 29)
29 July 71

74

185

REPUBLIC OF KOREA - UNITED STATES
COMMERCE SUBCOMMITTEE

1 February 1971

SUBJECT: Designation of US Invited Contractor Under Article XV, Status of Forces Agreement

ROK Chairman, Commerce Subcommittee

1. References: Paragraph 2, Article XV of the Status of Forces Agreement.

2. The Government of the Republic of Korea is informed through this written consultative process that the United States Forces, Korea, proposes to extend invited contractor status to the qualified US firm on the contract described in paragraph 3 below for the installation of US Government furnished microwave and ancilliary equipment at 21 sites throughout the Republic of Korea.

3. The following data are provided:

a. Company Name: The list of contractors being considered is attached at inclosure 1.

b. Local Address: To be supplied upon designation.

c. Identification of US Citizen Employees: To be supplied upon designation.

d. Number of US and ROK Employees: To be supplied upon designation.

e. Reason for Designation of an Invited Contractor: Open competitive bidding is not practicable due to the following:

(1) Limited "State of the Art" qualifications of local contractors.

(2) Unavailability of services required by US standards.

f. Location of Contract: Various locations throughout the Republic of Korea.

g. Type of Contract: Fixed price contract.

1 February 1971

SUBJECT: Designation of US Invited Contractor Under Article XV, Status of Forces Agreement

h. Length of Contract: To be supplied upon conclusion of negotiations.

i. Sponsoring Component Command: Assistant Chief of Staff, Communications-Electronics, Eighth United States Army, APO San Francisco 96301.

1 Incl
Contractor list

RICHARD T. CANN
Colonel, U.S. Army
ACofS, J4

64th JC (Incl 1 to Incl 29)
29 July 71

76

MINISTRY OF COMMERCE AND INDUSTRY
REPUBLIC OF KOREA
SEOUL, KOREA

24 February 1971

Subject: Designation of US Invited Contractor under Article XV Status of Forces Agreement

US Chairman, Commerce Subcommittee

1. Reference:

a. Paragraph 2, Article XV, Status of Forces Agreement.

b. US Commerce Subcommittee Memorandum of Consultation, dated 1 February 1971, subject as above, pertaining to contract for the installation of US Government furnished microwave and ancilliary equipment at 21 sites throughout Korea.

2. The US memorandum reference 1b above, has been reviewed and the Government of the Republic of Korea understands the requirement for an invited contractor in this instance.

Chung Min Kil
Chairman
Commerce Subcommittee, ROK

64th JC (Incl 2. to Incl 29)
29 July 71

LIST OF US FIRMS TO BE CONSIDERED FOR INSTALLATION OF MICROWAVE AND ANCILLIARY EQUIPMENT

1. Collins Radio Corporation

2. International Electronics Corporation

3. Kentron Hawaii Ltd.

4. Lenkurt Electric Company

5. Nippon Electric Company, New York

6. Page Communications Engineers, Inc.

7. Philco-Ford Coproration

8. Raytheon Service Corporation

9. Tectonics, Inc.

78

64th JC (Incl 29)
29 July 71

JOINT COMMITTEE
UNDER
THE REPUBLIC OF KOREA AND THE UNITED STATES
STATUS OF FORCES AGREEMENT

2 ? JUL 1971

MEMORANDUM FOR: The Joint Committee

SUBJECT: Designation of US Invited Contractor Under Article XV, Status of Forces Agreement

1. References:

a. Paragraph 2, Article XV, Status of Forces Agreement.

b. US Chairman, Commerce Subcommittee, letter dated 14 May 1971, subject as above (Inclosure 1).

c. ROK Chairman, Commerce Subcommittee, letter dated 24 May 1971, subject as above (Inclosure 2).

2. The United States, after consultation with the ROK Commerce Subcommittee and having duly considered their views, has designated the Fischer Engineering and Maintenance Company, Inc., as a US invited contractor, in joint venture with a Korean firm, for execution of contract DACA79-71-C-0070 for construction of troop housing, KORSCOM, Camp Walker, Taegu, Korea.

3. Pertinent data concerning US citizen employees will be provided to the Joint Secretariat in the established format.

2 Incls
as

ROBERT N. SMITH
Lieutenant General, USAF
United States Representative
Joint Committee

64th JC (Incl 30)
29 July 71

160

REPUBLIC OF KOREA - UNITED STATES
COMMERCE SUBCOMMITTEE

14 May 1971

SUBJECT: Designation of US Invited Contractor Under Article XV, Status of Forces Agreement

ROK Chairman, Commerce Subcommittee

1. Reference: Paragraph 2, Article XV, of the Status of Forces Agreement.

2. The Government of the Republic of Korea is informed through this written consultative process that the United States Forces, Korea, proposes to extend invited contractor status to the US member firm of the US-ROK joint venture contractor awarded the contract for the FY-70 MCA, Troop Housing, KORSCOM, Camp Walker, Taegu, Korea.

3. The following data are provided:

a. Company Name: A list of qualified US Firms is attached as Inclosure 1.

b. Local Address: To be supplied when designation is made.

c. Identification of US Citizen Employees: To be supplied on conclusion of negotiations.

d. Number of US and ROK Employees: Number of US Citizen and Koreans is not known at this time and will be supplied upon conclusion of negotiations.

e. Reasons for Designation of an Invited Contractor: Open competitive bidding among local contractors is not practical due to the following:

(1) Limited technical qualifications of the contractors involved.

(2) Unavailability of services required by US standards.

f. Location of Contract: Taegu, Korea.

g. Type of Contract: Fixed price.

64th JC (Incl 1 to Incl 30)
80 29 July 71

191

SUBJECT: Designation of US Invited Contractor Under Article XV,
Status of Forces Agreement

h. Length of Contract: To be supplied upon award of contract.

i. Sponsoring Component Commander: USAEDFE.

1 Incl
as

RICHARD T. CANN
Colonel, U.S. Army
United States Chairman
Commerce Subcommittee

81

64th JC (Incl 1 to Incl 30)
29 July 71

MINISTRY OF COMMERCE AND INDUSTRY
REPUBLIC OF KOREA
SEOUL, KOREA

24 May 1971

Subject: Designation of US Invited Contractor under Article XV Status of Forces Agreement

US Chairman, Commerce Subcommittee

1. Reference:

a. Paragraph 2, Article XV, Status of Forces Agreement

b. US Commerce Subcommittee Memorandum of Consultation, dated 14 May 1971, subject as above, pertaining to contract for the construction of FY-70 MCA, Troop Housing, KORSCOM, Camp Walker, Taegu, Korea.

2. The US memorandum reference 1b above, has been reviewed and the Government of the Republic of Korea understands the requirement for an invited contractor status to the US member firm of the ROK-US joint venture contract in this instance.

Chung Min Kil
Chairman
Commerce Subcommittee, ROK

82

64th JC (Incl 2 to Incl 30)
29 July 71

JOINT COMMITTEE
UNDER
THE REPUBLIC OF KOREA AND THE UNITED STATES
STATUS OF FORCES AGREEMENT

22 JUL 1971

MEMORANDUM FOR: The Joint Committee

SUBJECT: Designation of US Invited Contractor Under Article XV, Status of Forces Agreement

1. References:

a. Paragraph 2, Article XV, Status of Forces Agreement.

b. US Chairman, Commerce Subcommittee, letter dated 30 March 1971, subject as above (Inclosure 1).

c. US Chairman, Commerce Subcommittee, letter dated 6 April 1971, subject as above (Inclosure 2).

d. ROK Chairman, Commerce Subcommittee, letter dated 8 April 1971, subject as above (Inclosure 3).

2. The United States, after consultation with the ROK Commerce Subcommittee and having duly considered their views, has designated the Fischer Engineering and Maintenance Company, Inc., as a US invited contractor, in joint venture with a Korean firm, for execution of contract DAJB03-72-6001 for facilities engineering services for the Northern Sector Comprehensive Facilities Engineering area.

3. Pertinent data concerning US citizen employees will be provided to the Joint Secretariat in the established format.

3 Incl
as

ROBERT N. SMITH
Lieutenant General, USAF
United States Representative
Joint Committee

83

64th JC (Incl 31)
29 July 71

194

REPUBLIC OF KOREA - UNITED STATES
COMMERCE SUBCOMMITTEE

30 March 1971

SUBJECT: Designation of US Invited Contractor Under Article XV, Status of Forces Agreement

ROK Chairman, Commerce Subcommittee

1. Reference: Paragraph 2, Article XV of the Status of Forces Agreement.

2. The Government of the Republic of Korea is informed through this written consultative process that the United States Forces, Korea, proposes to extend invited contractor status to the US firm awarded the contract for the Northern Sector Comprehensive Facilities Engineering Area or to the US member firm of the US-ROK Joint Venture contractor awarded this contract. This new contract will encompass the existing Forward Area facilities engineering contract and the Camp Page portion of the present Camp Page-Sihung facilities engineering contract.

3. The following data are provided:

a. Company Name: The names of the US firms to be considered are attached as Inclosure 1.

b. Local Address: As shown in Inclosure 1.

c. Identification of US Citizen Employees: To be supplied after the contract has been awarded.

d. Number of US and ROK Employees: To be supplied after the contract has been awarded.

e. Reasons for Designation of an Invited Contractor:

(1) Security considerations. A contract utilizing a Korean contract only is not feasible due to the extensive security requirements demanded by the US Army. The contractor will be involved in the operations and maintenance of critical support facilities which directly affect the mission capabilities of the US Army. He will also be involved in programming actions which may be classified and releasable only to US personnel holding valid security clearances.

30 March 1971

SUBJECT: Designation of US Invited Contractor Under Article XV, Status of Forces Agreement

(2) Technical qualifications of the contractor personnel. Fully qualified and trained managers and supervisors are essential to meet facility engineering requirements.

(3) Materials and services required by US standards. The management of government resources such as supplies, equipment, tools and vehicles require the contractor to be responsible for and responsive to US Army policies and requirements. The contractor is required to comply with various Army manuals and regulations and other applicable publications which are technical in nature. The facilities and technical equipment are US design and manufacture and must be maintained to US standards.

f. Location of Contract: Northern Sector Comprehensive Facilities Engineering area.

g. Type of Contract: A cost-plus-fixed-fee type contract for the management, operations, maintenance and repair of real property facilities.

h. Length of Contract: 1 July 1971 thru 30 June 1972. Additionally, the contract would have a 30-day transition period at the end of the contract as determined above.

i. Sponsoring Component Commander: Commanding General, Eighth United States Army.

1 Incl
as

Richard T. Cann
RICHARD T. CANN
Colonel, US Army
United States Chairman
Commerce Subcommittee

REPUBLIC OF KOREA - UNITED STATES
COMMERCE SUBCOMMITTEE

6 April 1971

SUBJECT: Designation of US Invited Contractor Under Article XV, Status of Forces Agreement

ROK Chairman, Commerce Subcommittee

1. Reference: a. Paragraph 2, Article XV, Status of Forces Agreement.

b. US Chairman, Commerce Subcommittee, letter of consultation, dated 30 March 1971, subject as above.

c. Verbal discussion on 2 April 1971 between members of the US and ROK Commerce Subcommittees.

2. Based on the verbal request of the ROK Commerce Subcommittee, paragraph 2 of reference 1b above is amended to read as follows: The Government of the Republic of Korea is informed through this written consultative process that the United States Forces, Korea, proposes to extend invited contractor status to the US member firm of the US-ROK joint venture contractor awarded the contract for the Northern Sector Comprehensive Facilities Engineering area. This new contract will encompass the existing forward area facilities engineering contract and the Camp Page portion of the present Camp Page-Sihung facilities engineering contract.

Richard T. Cann
RICHARD T. CANN
Colonel, US Army
United States Chairman
Commerce Subcommittee

64th JC (Incl 2 to Incl 31)
29 July 71

86

197

MINISTRY OF COMMERCE AND INDUSTRY
REPUBLIC OF KOREA
SEOUL, KOREA

8 April 1971

Subject: Designation of US Invited Contractor under Article XV Status of Forces Agreement

US Chairman, Commerce Subcommittee

1. Reference:

a. Paragraph 2, Article XV, Status of Forces Agreement

b. US Commerce Subcommittee Memorandum of Consultation, dated 30 March 1971, subject as above, pertaining to joint venture contract for Facilities Engineering Services for the Forward Area and Camp Page-Sihung-ri, Korea.

2. The US memorandum reference 1b above, has been reviewed and the Government of the Republic of Korea understands the requirement for invited contractor status to the US member firm of the ROK/US joint venture contract in this instance.

3. The list of qualified Korean contractors to be considered for joint venture with US firms for the above contract is attached herewith.

Chung Min Kil
Chairman
Commerce Subcommittee, ROK

JOINT COMMITTEE
UNDER
THE REPUBLIC OF KOREA AND THE UNITED STATES
STATUS OF FORCES AGREEMENT

MEMORANDUM FOR: The Joint Committee 10 JUL 1971

SUBJECT: Designation of U.S. Invited Contractor Under Article XV, Status of Forces Agreement

1. References:

a. Paragraph 2, Article XV, Status of Forces Agreement.

b. U.S. Chairman, Commerce Subcommittee, letter dated 11 May 1971, subject as above (Inclosure 1).

c. ROK Chairman, Commerce Subcommittee, letter dated 15 May 1971, subject as above (Inclosure 2).

2. The United States, after consultation with the ROK Commerce Subcommittee and having duly considered their views, has designated Zurn Engineers and Huwin Corporation U.S. invited contractors, in joint venture with a Korean firm, for the FY-70 MCA Project, construction of troop housing, Yongsan, Korea, contract #DACA79-71-C-0075.

3. Pertinent data concerning U.S. citizen employees will be provided to the Joint Secretariat in the established format.

2 Incls
as

ROBERT N. SMITH
Lieutenant General, USAF
United States Representative
Joint Committee

64th JC (Incl 32)
29 July 71

88

ICP

These minutes are considered as official documents pertaining to both Governments and will not be released without mutual agreement.

REPUBLIC OF KOREA - UNITED STATES
COMMERCE SUBCOMMITTEE

11 May 1971

SUBJECT: Designation of US Invited Contractor Under Article XV, Status of Forces Agreement

ROK Chairman, Commerce Subcommittee

1. Reference: Paragraph 2, Article XV, Status of Forces Agreement.

2. The Government of the Republic of Korea is informed through this written consultative process that the United States Forces, Korea, proposes to extend invited contractor status to the qualified US/ROK Joint Venture firm on the contract described in paragraph 3 below for the construction of Troop Housing, Yongsan.

3. The following data are provided:

a. Company Name: A list of qualified US firms has been previously provided.

b. Local Address: To be supplied when designation is made.

c. Identification of US Citizen Employees: To be supplied upon conclusion of negotiations.

d. Number of US and ROK Employees: To be supplied upon conclusion of negotiations.

e. Reason for Designation of an Invited Contractor: Open competitive bidding is not practicable due to the following:

(1) Limited technical qualifications of the contractor involved.

(2) Unavailability of services required by US standards.

f. Location of Contract: Yongsan Garrison, Korea.

g. Type of Contract: Fixed Price.

64th JC (Incl 1 to Incl 32)
29 July 71

These minutes are considered as official documents pertaining to both Governments and will not be released without mutual agreement.

11 May 1971

SUBJECT: Designation of US Invited Contractor Under Article XV, Status of Forces Agreement

h. Length of Contract: To be supplied upon conclusion of negotiations.

i. Sponsoring Component Commander: Commanding General, Eighth United States Army.

RICHARD T. CANN
Colonel, U.S. Army
United States Chairman
Commerce Subcommittee

90

64th JC (Incl 1 to Incl 32)
29 July 71

201

MINISTRY OF COMMERCE AND INDUSTRY
REPUBLIC OF KOREA
SEOUL, KOREA

15 May 1971

Subject: Designation of US Invited Contractor under Article XV Status of Forces Agreement

US Chairman, Commerce Subcommittee

1. Reference:

a. Paragraph 2, Article XV, Status of Forces Agreement

b. US Commerce Subcommittee Memorandum of Consultation, dated 11 May 1971, subject as above, pertaining to contract for the construction of Troop Housing, Yongsan, Korea.

2. The US memorandum reference 1b above, has been reviewed and the Government of the Republic of Korea understands the requirement for an invited contractor status to the US member firm of the ROK-US joint venture contract in this instance.

Chung Min Kil
Chairman
Commerce Subcommittee/ROK

64th JC (Incl 2 to Incl 32)
29 July 71

202

These minutes are considered as official documents pertaining to both Governments and will not be released without mutual agreement.

JOINT COMMITTEE
UNDER
THE REPUBLIC OF KOREA AND THE UNITED STATES
STATUS OF FORCES AGREEMENT

3 0 JUN 1971

MEMORANDUM FOR: The Joint Committee

SUBJECT: Designation of U.S. Invited Contractor Under Article XV, Status of Forces Agreement

1. References:

a. Paragraph 2, Article XV, Status of Forces Agreement.

b. U.S. Chairman, Commerce Subcommittee, letter dated 11 September 1970, subject as above (Inclosure 1).

c. ROK Chairman, Commerce Subcommittee, letter dated 29 September 1970, subject as above (Inclosure 2).

2. The United States, after consultation with the ROK Commerce Subcommittee and having duly considered their views, has designated Associated American Engineers Overseas, Incorporated as a U.S. Invited Contractor for Repair of Intrusion Detection Alarm System and Installation of Intrusion Detection Alarm System, Kunsan AB, Korea, contract #F62087-71-C-0046.

3. Pertinent data concerning U.S. citizen employees will be provided to the Joint Secretariat in the established format.

2 Incl
as

ROBERT N. SMITH
Lieutenant General, USAF
United States Representative
Joint Committee

92

64th JC (Incl 33)
29 July 71

203

These minutes are considered as official documents pertaining to both Governments and will not be released without mutual agreement.

REPUBLIC OF KOREA - UNITED STATES
COMMERCE SUBCOMMITTEE

11 September 1970

SUBJECT: Designation of US Invited Contractor under Article XV, Status of Forces Agreement

ROK Chairman, Commerce Subcommittee

1. Reference: Paragraph 2, Article XV, Status of Forces Agreement.

2. The Government of the Republic of Korea is informed through this written consultative process that the United States Forces, Korea, proposes to extend invited contractor status to the qualified US firm on the contract described in paragraph 3 below for installation, inspection, maintenance and repair of an Intrusion Detection System at Kunsan Air Base, Korea.

3. The following data are provided:

a. Company Name: The following qualified US firms are to be considered for performance of this contract.

(1) Associated American Engineers Overseas, Inc., APO 96301

(2) International Electronics Corp., APO 96301

(3) Tectonics Inc., APO 96301

b. Local Address: To be supplied upon designation.

c. Identification of US Citizen Employees: To be supplied upon designation.

d. Number of US and ROK Employees: To be supplied upon designation.

e. Reasons for Designation of an Invited Contractor: Open competitive bidding is not practicable due to the following:

(1) Unavailability of materials and services required from local sources.

(2) The work includes classified items and requires utilization of a contractor who has a Security Clearance. All operation, maintenance and spare parts manuals required in this procurement are marked SECRET

64th JC (Incl 1 to Incl 33)
29 July 71

204

11 September 1970

SUBJECT: Designation of US Invited Contractor under Article XV, Status of Forces Agreement

in accordance with AFR 205-1.

(3) Local contractors do not possess the required technical qualifications or security clearances.

f. Location of Contract: Kunsan Air Base, Korea.

g. Type of Contract: Firm Fixed Price.

h. Length of Contract: Thru January 30, 1971.

i. Sponsoring Component Command: Commander, Air Forces, Korea.

GERALD L. HAYMAKER
Colonel, U.S. Army
United States Chairman
Commerce Subcommittee

64th JC (Incl 1 to Incl 33)
29 July 71

205

These minutes are considered as official documents pertaining to both Governments and will not be released without mutual agreement.

MINISTRY OF COMMERCE AND INDUSTRY
REPUBLIC OF KOREA
SEOUL, KOREA

29 September 1970

SUBJECT: Designation of US Invited Contractor under Article XV Status of Forces Agreement.

US Chairman, Commerce Subcommittee.

1. Reference:

a. Paragraph 2, Article XV, Status of Forces Agreement.

b. US Commerce Subcommittee Memorandum of Consultation, dated 11 September 1970, subject as above, pertaining to fixed price contract for installation, inspection, maintenance and repair of an Intrusion Detection System at Kunsan Air Base, Korea.

2. The US memorandum, reference 1b above, has been reviewed and the Government of the Republic of Korea understand the requirement for an invited contractor in this instance.

Chung Min Kil
Chairman
Commerce Subcommittee, ROK

64th JC (Incl 2 to Incl 33)
29 July 71

206

JOINT COMMITTEE
UNDER
THE REPUBLIC OF KOREA AND THE UNITED STATES
STATUS OF FORCES AGREEMENT

15 JUL 1971

MEMORANDUM FOR: The Joint Committee

SUBJECT: Designation of U.S. Invited Contractor Under Article XV, Status of Forces Agreement

1. References:

a. Paragraph 2, Article XV, Status of Forces Agreement.

b. U.S. Chairman, Commerce Subcommittee, letter dated 27 April 1971, subject as above (Inclosure 1).

c. ROK Chairman, Commerce Subcommittee, letter dated 4 May 1971, subject as above (Inclosure 2).

2. The United States, after consultation with the ROK Commerce Subcommittee and having duly considered their views, has designated Daniel, Mann, Johnson, and Mendenhall as a US Invited Contractor for design of integrated communications system for USFK/EUSA - Underground Command Post, Seoul, Korea, contract #DACA79-71-C-0082.

3. Pertinent data concerning U.S. citizen employees will be provided to the Joint Secretariat in the established format.

2 Incl
as

ROBERT N. SMITH
Lieutenant General, USAF
United States Representative
Joint Committee

64th JC (Incl 34)
29 July 71

96

207

REPUBLIC OF KOREA - UNITED STATES
COMMERCE SUBCOMMITTEE

27 April 1971

SUBJECT: Designation of US Invited Contractor Under Article XV, Status of Forces Agreement

ROK Chairman, Commerce Subcommittee

1. Reference: Paragraph 2, Article XV, Status of Forces Agreement.

2. The Government of the Republic of Korea is informed through this written consultative process that the United States Forces, Korea, proposes to extend invited contractor status to the US firm awarded the contract for design of Integrated Communications System for USFK/EUSA Underground Command Post, Korea.

3. The following data are provided:

a. Company Name:

(1) Lyon Associates

(2) Daniel, Mann, Johnson and Mendenhall

(3) Adrian Wilson Associates

b. Local Address: APO 96301

c. Identification of US Citizen Employees: Information will be provided as soon as received from the contractor.

d. Number of US and ROK Employees: Information will be provided as soon as received from the contractor.

e. Reason for Designation of an Invited Contractor:

(1) Security Considerations.

(2) Technical Qualifications of the contractors involved.

f. Location of Contract: Underground Command Post, Korea.

64th JC (Incl 1 to Incl 34)
29 July 71

208

27 April 1971

SUBJECT: Designation of US Invited Contractor Under Article XV, Status of Forces Agreement

g. Type of Contract: Fixed Price, Type B.

h. Length of Contract: To be supplied upon award award of contract.

i. Sponsoring Component Commander: USAEDFE

RICHARD T. CANN
Colonel, U.S. Army
United States Chairman
Commerce Subcommittee

64th JC (Incl 1 to Incl 34)
29 July 71

209

These minutes are considered as official documents pertaining to both Governments and will not be released without mutual agreement.

MINISTRY OF COMMERCE AND INDUSTRY
REPUBLIC OF KOREA
SEOUL, KOREA

4 May 1971

Subject: Designation of US Invited Contractor under Article XV Status of Forces Agreement

US Chairman, Commerce Subcommittee

1. Reference:

a. Paragraph 2, Article XV, Status of Forces Agreement

b. US Commerce Subcommittee Memorandum of Consultation, dated 27 April 1971, subject as above, pertaining to contract for design of Integrated Communications System for USFK/EUSA Underground Command Post, Korea.

2. The US memorandum reference 1b above, has been reviewed and the Government of the Republic of Korea understands the requirement for an invited contractor in this instance.

Chung Min Kil
Chairman
Commerce Subcommittee, ROK

64th JC (Incl 2 to Incl 34)
29 July 71

These minutes are considered as official documents pertaining to both Governments and will not be released without mutual agreement.

JOINT COMMITTEE
UNDER
THE REPUBLIC OF KOREA AND THE UNITED STATES
STATUS OF FORCES AGREEMENT

15 JUL 1971

MEMORANDUM FOR: The Joint Committee

SUBJECT: Designation of U.S. Invited Contractor Under Article XV, Status of Forces Agreement

1. References:

a. Paragraph 2, Article XV, Status of Forces Agreement.

b. U.S. Chairman, Commerce Subcommittee, letter dated 2 June 1971, subject as above (Inclosure 1).

c. ROK Chairman, Commerce Subcommittee, letter dated 25 June 1971, subject as above (Inclosure 2).

2. The United States, after consultation with the ROK Commerce Subcommittee and having duly considered their views, has designated Adrian Wilson Associates, Incorporated as a US Invited Contractor for design of ordnance storage facilities, Taegu and Kwang-Ju Air Bases, Korea, contract #DACA79-71-C-0076.

3. Pertinent data concerning U.S. citizen employees will be provided to the Joint Secretariat in the established format.

2 Incl
as

ROBERT N. SMITH
Lieutenant General, USAF
United States Representative
Joint Committee

64th JC (Incl 35)
29 July 71

100

211

These minutes are considered as official documents pertaining to both Governments and will not be released without mutual agreement.

REPUBLIC OF KOREA - UNITED STATES
COMMERCE SUBCOMMITTEE

2 June 1971

SUBJECT: Designation of US Invited Contractor Under Article XV, Status of Forces Agreement

ROK Chairman, Commerce Subcommittee

1. Reference: Paragraph 2, Article XV, of the Status of Forces Agreement.

2. The Government of the Republic of Korea is informed through this written consultative process that the United States Forces, Korea, proposes to extend invited contractor status to the US firm awarded the contract for the Design of Ordance Storage Facility, Taegu and Kwang-Ju Air Bases, Korea.

3. The following data are provided:

a. Company Name:

(1) Adrian Wilson Associates

(2) Daniel, Mann, Johnson & Mendenhall

(3) Pacific Architects and Engineers, Inc.

b. Local Address: APO 96301

c. Identification of US Citizen Employees: Information will be provided as soon as received from the contractor.

d. Number of US and ROK Employees: Information will be provided as soon as received from the contractor.

e. Reason for Designation of an Invited Contractor: Open competitive bidding among local contractors is not practicable due to technical qualifications of the contractors involved.

f. Location of Contract: Taegu and Kwang-Ju, Korea.

64th JC (Incl 1 to Incl 35)
29 July 71

These minutes are considered as official documents pertaining to both Governments and will not be released without mutual agreement.

2 June 1971

SUBJECT: Designation of US Invited Contractor Under Article XV, Status of Forces Agreement

g. Type of Contract: Fixed Price, Type B.

h. Length of Contract: To be supplied upon conclusion of negotiations.

i. Sponsoring Component Commander: USAEDFE

Herman W. Hommes, COL
for
RICHARD T. CANN
Colonel, U.S. Army
United States Chairman
Commerce Subcommittee

64th JC (Incl 1 to Incl 35)
29 July 71

102

MINISTRY OF COMMERCE AND INDUSTRY
REPUBLIC OF KOREA
SEOUL, KOREA

25 June 1971

Subject : Designation of US Invited Contractor under Article XV, Status of Forces Agreement

US Chairman, Commerce Subcommittee

1. Reference :

a. Paragraph 2, Article XV, Status of Forces Agreement

b. US Commerce Subcommittee Memorandum of Consultation, dated 2 June 1971 subject as above, pertaining to contract for Design of Ordnance Storage Facility, Taegu and Kwang-Ju, Air Bases, Korea.

2. The US memorandum, reference lb above, has been reviewed and the government of the Republic of Korea understands the requirement for an invited contractor in this instance.

Chung Min Kil
Chairman
Commerce Subcommittee, ROK

64th JC (Incl 2 to Incl 35)
29 July 71

214

These minutes are considered as official documents pertaining to both Governments and will not be released without mutual agreement.

JOINT ROK-US PRESS RELEASE
SIXTY-FOURTH ROK-US JOINT COMMITTEE MEETING
29 JULY 1971

The ROK-US Joint Committee approved 27 recommendations of its Facilities and Areas Subcommittee and assigned 28 new tasks to the same Subcommittee at its sixty-fourth meeting, held on 29 July 1971 in the US SOFA Conference Room.

The Joint Committee approved the recommendation of its Finance (Personnel Affairs) Subcommittee, concerning revised procedures for examination of incoming APO parcel post packages by ROK customs inspectors. The Joint Committee also discussed the recent incidents involving US military personnel and Korean nationals which have taken place in the vicinity of some US military installations, with a view to forestalling recurrence of such incidents.

The next meeting of the ROK-US Joint Committee is scheduled to be held on Thursday, 26 August 1971.

64th JC (Incl 36)
29 July 1971

대한민국 외무부
공보관실
전화 74-3576

보 도 자 료

이 기사는 제공처인 외무부를
밝히고 보도할수 있음

외무보도 호

년 월 일 시 분 발표

한.미 합동 위원회 제64차 회의 공 동 발 표 문

1971. 7. 29.

한.미 합동 위원회는 1971. 7. 29. 미측 회의실에서 제64차 회의를 개최하고 27건의 시설구역 분과위원회 건의를 승인하였으며, 28건의 과제를 동 분과위원회에 부여 하였다.

합동 위원회는 군사우편(APO)소포 화물에 대한 한국 세관원의 검사 절차를 개정하는데 관한 재무 분과위원회 건의를 승인하였다.

합동위원회는 또한 최근 일부 미군 시설 근처에서 한국인과 미군인간에 발생한 일련의 사건의 재발을 방지하는 방안을 토의하였다.

다음 한.미 합동 위원회 회의는 1971. 8. 26. 목요일에 개최될 예정이다.

216

외교문서 비밀해제: 주한미군지위협정(SOFA) 25
주한미군지위협정(SOFA) 한 · 미 합동위원회 2

초판인쇄 2024년 03월 15일
초판발행 2024년 03월 15일

지은이 한국학술정보(주)
펴낸이 채종준
펴낸곳 한국학술정보(주)
주 소 경기도 파주시 회동길 230(문발동)
전 화 031-908-3181(대표)
팩 스 031-908-3189
홈페이지 http://ebook.kstudy.com
E-mail 출판사업부 publish@kstudy.com
등 록 제일산-115호(2000. 6. 19)

ISBN 979-11-7217-036-3 94340
979-11-7217-011-0 94340 (set)

책에 대한 더 나은 생각, 끊임없는 고민, 독자를 생각하는 마음으로 보다 좋은 책을 만들어갑니다.